The Spirit has come

1 Cor 2:11-12
- integral + inseparable
- imparted by God
- reveals things previously unknown

Creation : Gen 1
         Job 26:13

THE
SPIRIT
HAS
COME

E.H. Andrews

EVANGELICAL PRESS

EVANGELICAL PRESS
12 Wooler Street, Darlington, Co. Durham DL1 1RQ, England

First published 1982 under the title The Promise of the Spirit
First published under this title 1991

ISBN 0 85234 162 8

Unless otherwise stated, Bible quotations are from the New American
Standard Bible

Other books by the same author:
Christ and the Cosmos
From Nothing to Nature
God, Science and Evolution

Typeset in Great Britain by Inset Ltd., Hertford Heath, Hertfordshire.

Contents

— convince of sin — pg 17
— reveal Christ died to reconcile
— applies work of Christ to soul — raising from death to life & filling with God's love

— indwelling fills with fruit
— strengthens against power of sin

Part One

1. Introduction

Nothing is of greater importance to the Christian than the Holy Spirit's work in his heart and life. The Bible makes it clear that no person even becomes a Christian until the Spirit of God convinces him of his sin and reveals that Christ died to secure his reconciliation to a holy God. But more than this, the Spirit powerfully applies the work of Christ to the individual soul, raising it from spiritual death to spiritual life and shedding abroad the love of God in the believing heart. All Christian love, joy, peace, patience, hope and a host of other 'fruit' are the result of the indwelling Holy Spirit. Without His presence the quality of life and level of faith enjoyed by the Christian would be derisory. Indeed, Christianity, as defined in Scripture, would not exist.

Another vital role of the Spirit of God is to strengthen believers against the power of sin and empower them to serve God. Any attempt to quench the sinful tendencies of the human heart, or any desire to serve the Lord, which is not executed by the enabling grace of the Holy Spirit, is not only doomed to failure but is actually offensive to God.

This is the point at which the Christian feels the greatest need for the work of the Spirit within him. Most believers feel acutely their need for this inward power, this enabling strength. Too many struggle ineffectively against sin in their lives; too many experience depression rather than joy, turmoil instead of peace; too few know power in their witness or fruit in their labour for the Lord. Prayer is a burden, the Bible fails to refresh the soul, and worship is a dull and dutiful routine. And this is not only true of the individual believer, but also of the church, for all the spiritual distempers that affect the one affect the other

1

also. Indeed, the spiritual deadness that can afflict a church may actually magnify and intensify the moribund condition of its members.

It is clear enough from Scripture that the answer to these and many related problems lies in the work of the Holy Spirit. God has not left His people without an answer to these difficulties, nor has He sent us on the warfare of faith without provisions of power and grace beyond our comprehension. But how are we to lay hold upon these supplies, or how avail ourselves of that abundant grace that, we are assured by Scripture, lies ready to hand? It is at this point that much controversy arises.

When and how do believers receive the Holy Spirit? What do the Scriptures mean by the 'baptism' of the Spirit? Have some Christians received it, while others languish without such blessedness? What does it mean to be 'sealed with the Spirit', and does this betoken some additional resource unknown to the average believer? How intensely should Christians experience the presence of the indwelling Holy Spirit, and should this experience involve miraculous or ecstatic abilities like prophecy and speaking in unknown tongues? Has the modern church neglected the 'charismata' or gifts of the Spirit, and do its ailments and its lifelessness stem from this cause? How may believers obey the Pauline injunction to 'be filled with the Spirit'?

Not only do Christians differ over their answers to these questions, but the subject becomes so contentious that it blinds us to the deep spiritual needs and yearnings of God's people. While we pursue our arguments, there is great danger that the flock of God will languish. Fearing the contention, Christians shy away from the whole subject of the Holy Spirit's work in the believer and the church, preferring deadness to debate – and who can blame them?

The answer to this dilemma cannot, of course, be found by turning our backs upon the whole subject. Nor can the contentious issues be bypassed as peripheral questions, for they lie at the very heart of the matter. What, then, are we to do? The answer presented in this book is as follows. We must, as individuals and in our churches, return to a thorough examination of the teaching of Scripture on the work of the Spirit. Rather than allow ourselves to be torn this way and that by conflicting teachings, rather than allow our churches to become battlefields of dissension, rather than become confused and depressed about the whole matter, rather than allow ourselves to be deprived of the Holy Spirit's gracious provisions for our lives in Christ — we must patiently seek out the truth as taught in Scripture. And this is no simple task. After all, the protagonists in this argument all claim the support of Holy Writ for their particular standpoint! Is it possible, then, to arrive at any clear conclusions by studying the Bible? My belief is that it is indeed possible to do so. Although all parties use Scripture to support their interpretations of the Spirit's work, that use is often selective and sometimes even superficial. It will be our purpose in this book to examine each issue in depth, seeking a scriptural consensus and making consistency of interpretation our touchstone, for God's Word cannot contradict itself. This process will make demands upon the reader, but I believe it will yield its rewards to all, whatever our opinions at the outset on the matters under debate. Indeed, it is the chief aim of this book, not only to clear away confusion, but also to enable the reader, whatever his or her initial persuasions, to re-evaluate them in the light of Scripture.

Naturally, it would be excellent if the result of this process were to be the reconciliation of those Bible-believing Christians who find themselves at variance over these issues. One way to seek such a reconciliation would be to define some compromise position, some half-way house, in which both parties could rest at ease. Such an approach, however, would be self-defeating, pleasing none and offending all. The only legitimate method is to return to the Bible and seek afresh its definitive teaching on these disputed questions. 'But has this not been attempted many times before?' you will ask. Surprisingly, the answer appears to be negative. There are innumerable books bearing on the subject, all of which seek, in greater or lesser measure, to justify one stance or another by scriptural argument. Invariably, however, the author sets out to justify his own position, quoting only those arguments that seem to support his case and turning a Nelsonian blind eye to texts and passages which tend to undermine it! The result is usually a convincing case for the particular opinions set forth and is then contradicted by the

next book written from the contrary viewpoint. No wonder
so many are confused.

The fact is, as I hope this present work will demonstrate,
that authors usually employ only a fraction of the biblical
evidence bearing on the subject. Either they are content to
expound a few 'proof texts' or else they do not explore the
full significance of the verses they quote, either neglecting
the context or failing to compare Scripture with Scripture.
I realize, of course, that this is often done to assist the reader.
A simple uncomplicated argument is always easier to follow,
and to present one's case with a few well-chosen texts in
support is a crisp and efficient method. If this theoretical
'case' can then be augmented with a variety of testimonies,
which validate experimentally the claims advanced, so much
the better. But such an approach is unlikely to lead us to the
truth in a complex and controversial subject such as this.
The only safe method lies in a painstaking examination of
the whole counsel of God upon the matter, and that will be
our method in this book. This does not mean, however,
that the reader will find these pages difficult to digest.
Rather, it is my hope that the lavish use of Scripture, and
the attempt to draw from it a biblical consensus, will prove
a means of spiritual refreshment and illumination. It has
certainly done so for the author.

The chapters that follow are based upon a series of Bible
studies in which no prior commitment was made to one
particular viewpoint on such subjects as the baptism of the
Spirit and the charismatic gifts. Naturally, the author had his
own ideas (or prejudices?) on these matters at the outset,
but an attempt was made to set aside all preconceptions and
allow the Scriptures to speak for themselves. This approach
has been retained in this book, and commitments to one
interpretation or another only emerge as required by the
accumulated force of biblical evidence. This means, of
course, that both sides in the debate come in for criticism
at various junctures, and we run the risk of offending everyone and pleasing none. Nevertheless, it is ultimately to
Scripture that we must all defer, and if the reader adopts
this attitude from the outset he will find himself in sym-
pathy with much of what is written here.

Our method of addressing the problem could be described

as 'scientific' rather than theological, and this is appropriate since the author's qualifications lie in the former field rather than the latter. By 'scientific' we mean that the relevant scriptural evidence will first be assembled and then evaluated. Each text will be examined for its own testimony, but we shall also seek to draw out the consensus of the biblical writers on each issue that confronts us. This means that much time will be spent reviewing evidence before conclusions are drawn and 'sides' are taken. Because of this even those who, finally, cannot accept the author's conclusions may find they benefit from reading what he has written.

The book is organized in four parts. The first is introductory and here we are concerned to put the debate in its larger context. We begin by emphasizing the common ground between conflicting points of view, remembering, for example, that a common acceptance of the Bible as the inspired Word of God is necessary before one can dispute over its precise teaching on any matter. There is little sense in arguing about the interpretation of a text of Scripture unless one is first convinced that the statements therein are true and authoritative! An appreciation of this common ground will remind us at the outset that we may disagree with our brethren over certain matters, but that we still have much in common. We shall then be better able to conduct our argument in charity and be careful not to exaggerate our differences.

We next proceed to define the problem before us by setting out the major viewpoints to which Bible-believing Christians subscribe. These viewpoints are given names or labels for convenience and are four in number. We shall call them the 'Old Pentecostal', 'Charismatic', 'Reformed Sealer' and 'Traditional Reformed' positions respectively, and these titles will be explained in due course. Having set out the beliefs represented by these four major viewpoints, we shall then ask three key questions that must be answered in the remainder of the book.

Part 2, embracing a further three chapters, is concerned entirely with the subject of relationships. That is, we shall consider there the relationship that existed between the Holy Spirit and the believer before Pentecost (including the entire

Old Testament era) and how this relationship was changed as a result of the Spirit's Pentecostal advent. This in turn will lead us to consider the relationship that subsists between the Spirit and the believer today, and whether this relation is identical in all believers or 'two-level' in character.

The whole question of 'two-level' experience in the Christian life is the subject of Part 3 of this book. Scripture speaks of two events in the spiritual realm, namely sealing with the Spirit and baptism in the Spirit, which some interpret as post-conversion experiences. These events, they claim, have the power to transform the believer and raise him to a higher level of spiritual life and service. Is this true? What exactly does the Bible teach about these events? Where does the fulness of the Holy Spirit come into the picture and how may it be obtained? These and many other similar questions will occupy us in these important chapters. There can be no argument that many, if not most, Christians exist on a low level of spiritual experience, knowing too little of the power and joy of the Holy Spirit in their lives and too much of the strength of sin. In these chapters, therefore, we shall not only attempt to clarify these matters, but also help ourselves to discover something more of the provision that God has made for us to live spiritually fruitful and victorious lives.

In the fourth and final part of the book we tackle the vexed question of the 'charismata' or spiritual gifts. Some believe that these powers and phenomena, including prophecy, healing and speaking in tongues, are to be practised today. Others insist that they were temporary abilities given to assist the early church until the New Testament Scriptures were complete. This is probably the most difficult of our topics, for it is not easy to find clear teaching in the Bible itself concerning the continuance or cessation of such powers in subsequent eras of the Christian church. In spite of this difficulty we shall avoid the temptation to seek proof of the matter in either history or personal experience, since our purpose in this study is to appeal only to Scripture. We must therefore rest content with what we can learn from the Bible and leave open any questions that do not yield to this approach. Our attitude here is perfectly straightforward. Where God has chosen not to resolve such matters in His revealed testimony, we should be content to allow our fellow Christians liberty in their belief and practice. Having said this, however, we shall find that much more can be deduced from Scripture than is frequently admitted by either side in the debate.

So much for the plan and contents of the book. Let me mention now a few details that may help the reader. We have taken all Bible references from the New American Standard Bible unless a statement is made to the contrary. Occasionally the Authorized Version provides a more helpful or pithy rendering of the text in view, and in this case the initials 'A.V.' have been appended to the reference. Sometimes also the rendering given in the margin of the NASB throws more light on the point under discussion and then we quote this alternative and indicate the fact by adding 'mg.' after the reference. Finally, whenever words quoted from the Bible appear in italics in this book, they have been emphasized by the author to bring out a particular point and do not represent any emphasis or absence of words in the original Scriptures.

One thing that will strike many readers is the complete absence of references to literature other than the Bible itself, and no doubt some will criticize this omission. It is, however, quite deliberate. It is always easy to punctuate a piece of writing with references, to give the appearance of scholarship, but the real purpose of such citations must be kept in mind. This purpose is twofold, namely to acknowledge the source of ideas or quotations and to allow the reader to explore the background of some topic in greater depth. The first of these functions has been intentionally avoided because it has been our object in this book to appeal only to Scripture and to resist the temptation to quote 'authorities', however distinguished they may be, in support of the arguments presented. It is always possible to find some theological authority for a statement or opinion advanced, especially in a controversial area such as this. But unless the reader is convinced of an argument on the basis of the scriptural evidence alone, our purpose will have been defeated. We have therefore turned our back on the many excellent sources and authorities that might have been enlisted to convince the reader of the views put forward in

this book. Our approach requires that the arguments must
stand or fall in the light of Scripture itself. This does not
mean, of course, that we despise the contribution of those
who have already written extensively on the subjects before
us. Indeed, their work must, in many cases, rank superior to
the present offering. It is simply that appeal to human
authority is incompatible with the approach adopted in this
particular book, namely that the reader should be led to consider what the Bible says on these matters and should not be
distracted by frequent appeals to the opinions expressed by
other sources, however erudite and respected. This approach
has its deficiencies, but also its advantages.

The provision of references to allow the reader to explore
the subject in greater depth has also presented certain problems. Not that there is any shortage of books and articles
dealing with these issues. The problem lies in the methods
adopted by most writers, to which we have already made
reference. That is, almost everyone adopts a particular
stance at the outset and proceeds to attempt to prove its
correctness and discredit the opposite view. This means that
the reader will be hard put to locate any literature that
develops in greater detail the kind of approach employed
here. The best we can do is to offer a selection of references
in which the case for one viewpoint or another is set out,
and this is most readily done, not in the text itself, but by
means of a selected bibliography. Such will be found at the
conclusion of the book, but should not be regarded as an
exhaustive catalogue of available literature.

2. Common ground

Like many before it, this book has been written because Christians disagree. The particular disagreement concerns the work of the Holy Spirit in the Christian believer and in the church of Jesus Christ. Our task will be to examine just what the Bible does teach concerning this matter and, as far as possible, to arrive at balanced conclusions about the various aspects of the problem.

It is possible, however, to become so immersed in the debate, and so taken up with issues that divide Christians, that we overlook the extensive common ground to which all subscribe. This is unfortunate, to say the least, since it gives the impression that Christians are for ever squabbling among themselves and are so preoccupied with their petty differences and party lines that their essential mission to make Christ known is all but forgotten.

Of course, true Christian unity must be doctrinal, whatever else it may require. It is useless to proclaim a message to the world, if there is no agreement as to what that message is! Thus there are inevitable conflicts between those who are at odds concerning the nature of the gospel itself. The apostle Paul is very severe at this point, declaring, 'There are some who . . . distort the gospel of Christ. But even though we, or an angel from heaven, should preach to you a gospel contrary to that which we have preached to you, let him be accursed' (Gal. 1:7, 8).

The Bible makes it plain that there will be false gospels, perverted gospels, distorted gospels and 'gospels' which are not gospels at all. These must be opposed, no matter how sincerely their proponents may believe them.

Among those, however, who accept and promote the gospel of Jesus Christ as declared in *all* the Scriptures, both

9

Old and New Testaments, differences remain, and such are
the differences that will occupy us throughout this book.
But before we define and examine these differences it will
be beneficial to set them in the context of the substantial
areas of agreement, the 'common ground' on which all true
believers stand together. The benefit of this will be twofold.
Firstly, of course, the context of agreed doctrine will demonstrate to any non-Christian or nominal Christian reader that
the Bible is perfectly clear about his spiritual condition and
about its remedy. The debate on finer points must never be
allowed to deflect the earnest enquirer from the clear-cut
path of repentance for sin and faith in Jesus Christ, crucified,
risen and ascended, for the forgiveness of sin and reconciliation with God. No disagreements concerning the precise
manner of the Spirit's operation must be allowed to hinder
the accomplishment of His saving work in the sinner's heart.
The common ground needs, therefore, to be emphasized.

Secondly, the Christian reader must be assured that the
major aspects of the Holy Spirit's person and work *are*
clearly delineated in Scripture, lest he become discouraged
by the arguments and lose interest in this most vital of
subjects. The work of the Spirit of God in the sinner and in
the believer is a profound and glorious work, and we neglect
the Bible's teaching on this matter at our peril. All that we
have and are as Christian believers is mediated to us through
the Spirit's work. All that we hope for eternally is secured
for us and confirmed within us by the same gracious Holy
Spirit. Let us not allow the differences that separate
believers on these matters to frustrate our experience and
enjoyment of what God has provided for all His children.
The common ground needs, therefore, to be perceived
and any conflict viewed in its perspective.

The grace of God

The most fundamental 'common ground' shared by all
Christians is their direct experience of the saving grace of
the Lord Jesus Christ. All true believers have been
awakened from their carelessness concerning spiritual
realities and have recognized that human sinfulness separ-
ates men from a holy God. The impossibility of being

reconciled to that God by dint of human effort has also been borne in upon them, so that their lost condition is intensified by their total inability to help themselves in the matter of salvation. This depressing state of affairs is magnified by the discovery that they have no power to control the sin that defiles even the best of their motives and acts, and the further realization that God will punish sin by eternal banishment.

It is into this grim scenario that the gospel of Jesus Christ comes with glorious radiance. For some, that radiance emerges gradually, like a gentle dawn which warms the soul almost imperceptibly. For others, like Saul of Tarsus on the Damascus Road, it comes as a lightning bolt, leaving them prostrate before the risen Christ. But however it comes, the subjects of God's saving power know that He 'has shone in [their] hearts to give the light of the knowledge of the glory of God in the face of Christ' (2 Cor. 4:6). This shining not only reveals the facts of the gospel, that Christ died to liberate His people from the power and penalty of their sins, but also imparts forgiveness and the love of God to the now believing heart. It brings assurance, too, for as we read the Scriptures with new eyes, we learn that none can pluck the believer from his Saviour's hand (John 10:28, 29). We also learn that God has prepared for those He has redeemed in Christ 'an inheritance which is imperishable and undefiled and will not fade away' (1 Peter 1:4). And all this through no merit of our own!

This is what we mean by 'grace', namely the free unmerited giving of God to undeserving sinners. Even the very seeking after God that we may experience, as He prepares our hearts to receive the gift of eternal life, is itself His gracious initiative and not a movement of our sinful souls. Christ came and died and rose again as an expression of pure love from God, and it is pure love, unprompted by ourselves, that effectually applies the work of Christ to our actual salvation as individuals.

Here, then, lie the origin and basis of what Christians have in common − in the grace of God applied to all, and experienced by all who trust in Christ, without distinction or respect of persons. It is well to bear this cardinal point in mind as we pursue our enquiries, especially since some of the disputed questions concern the nature of Christian experience.

The authority of Scripture

The next common ground is to be found in a belief that both Old and New Testaments are the authentic and authoritative revelation of God to man. As Paul expresses it, 'All Scripture is inspired by God and profitable for teaching, for reproof, for correction, for training in righteousness; that the man of God may be adequate, equipped for every good work' (2 Tim. 3:16, 17). Paul uses the word *theopneusta*, that is, God-breathed, emphasizing that divine authorship stands behind the human writers who actually penned the books of the Bible. Peter adds his testimony: 'No prophecy was ever made by an act of human will, but men moved by the Holy Spirit spoke from God' (2 Peter 1:21). What was true of Old Testament Scripture is, by extension, true of the New Testament writings, for Jesus promised His disciples that the Holy Spirit would teach them 'all things' and bring to their remembrance all that He had taught them (John 14:26).

There are, of course, those who call themselves Christians and yet deny the divine inspiration of the Scriptures, reckoning them to be no more than the gropings of fallible men after an understanding of God. True believers must reject this thesis, for it deprives us of revelation and robs the gospel of all authority. No one can logically claim to follow Christ and at the same time deny His teaching that the Scriptures are God's message to mankind. 'If they do not listen to Moses and the Prophets, neither will they be persuaded if someone rises from the dead' (Luke 16:31).

The particular application of this point is that the truth concerning the Spirit of God, and His work in the believer and the church, is to be found in Scripture. This is important. The truth does not reside in my religious experiences or mystical apprehensions. It is not to be found in 'signs and wonders', even though God used such means to attest the message preached by the apostles. It is, insists Peter, to be found in that 'more sure word of prophecy', namely the prophecy of Scripture (2 Peter 1:19, A.V.). All experience must be brought to the touchstone of Scripture. All doctrine must be tested by its criteria, all religious phenomena by its yardstick. All spirits must be tried before its bar, all human testimony tested according to its standards. Once this is agreed, many problems are resolved at once, and a firm foundation is established for the discussion of those that remain.

We need to add a word of caution here. It is not sufficient to base a practice or belief upon a single text or incident recorded in Scripture. We must bring to bear upon any problem *all* Scripture that relates to it. It is all too easy to take a text and build upon it an edifice of doctrine that it simply will not support. This is the *modus operandi* of heresy. It is necessary rather to seek the balance of Scripture teaching on any disputed point, to reject views which contradict any portion of God's Word and adopt only those which harmonize with the whole. This is why, in this book, we shall spend page after page reviewing the teachings of both Old and New Testaments, Gospels and Epistles, prophets and apostles, before coming to conclusions. It is a painstaking method, but it is the only safe one.

The Trinity

It is this very methodology just described that has given us the doctrine of the Trinity. There is no single Bible text that states, 'God is one God in three Persons, Father, Son and Holy Spirit.' Unitarians often mock the historic trinitarian position on this count. But when we search the Scriptures we find that there is one God; that Jesus Christ and the Yahweh of the Old Testament are one and the same (Isa. 6:1–10; cf. John 12:37–41); that Jesus, again, is the coeternal and coexistent Creator of all things (John 1:1–4); that the Spirit of God is not only divine, as must be the case, but is also a Person in His own right (John 14: 15–18). It is these, and many similar allusions, that we are compelled to summarize in the doctrine of the Trinity, difficult as it is for our finite minds to grasp. Yet is that so surprising?

It would surely be even stranger if we *could* comprehend the nature of God, for that would suggest that He was finite and definable in merely human terms. Even in the description of matter and energy, human science must resort to a contradiction, the classic wave-particle duality. Why should we expect to find it easier to describe the anatomy of God, by whom all matter and energy were made? Indeed the incomprehensible Trinity is our assurance that we are on the right lines, that we are looking at the true transcendent God and not at some comfortable, man-sized projection of our own imagination. Again, our little minds can grasp the massive logic of the 'illogical' Trinity when we ask how God, who is love, could have exercised that aspect of His nature before creation, if there were not a plurality of Persons in the Godhead. For, without question, love is a reciprocal activity and requires both subject and object in its glorious syntax.

The Trinity, therefore, is not the stumbling-block that it appears to some to be. It rather represents the best portrayal human minds can contemplate of the ineffable nature of God. Its importance for our subject is immense. It is not just that we need to know at the outset that the Holy Spirit is God, nor even that He is a Person, rather than a thing or force or influence, important though that is. The key issue to grasp is that as the Spirit of God comes to the believer, He brings with Him the divine nature, the triune God, Father and Son, to dwell within the soul. This amazing fact we must investigate at length in what will follow. Suffice it here to say that the concept of the Trinity is essential to our understanding of the Spirit's work within.

The personality of the Holy Spirit

Christians agree that the Spirit of God is a Person, not a mere force or influence. We have already alluded to this fact in our brief statement on the Trinity, but because it is so important to our whole discussion it bears further consideration.

The Spirit of God is just what His title suggests. Paul argues this in 1 Corinthians 2:11, 12: 'Who among men knows the thoughts of a man except the spirit of the man, which is in him? Even so the thoughts of God no one knows except the Spirit of God.' Thus God's Spirit is to God what man's spirit is to man — namely, an integral and inseparable part of His nature. But, Paul continues, 'We have received . . . the Spirit who is from God, that we might know the things freely given to us by God.' Here lies the difference between a human spirit and God's Spirit: the latter is capable of being imparted to others, that is, to men. This could never be true of a human spirit, for the human spirit has no existence independent of the human being to whom it belongs. God's Spirit is not so limited. He may move and enter where He wills, not independently of the Godhead, but in a manner distinct from the other Persons.

The concept of a spirit distinct from its owner is, of course, a difficult one to grasp, simply because it has no parallel in human experience. But that is to say no more than that God *is* unique, which is self-evident. But being distinct in this manner, the Spirit of God cannot thereby be stripped of the attribute of personality; for this would make Him inferior to the human spirit, which always retains this quality. It follows, then, that the Holy Spirit is both a Person and distinct from the other Persons of the triune God.

But we do not need to rely on such reasoning to make our point, for the Spirit is continually referred to in Scripture unmistakably as a Person. He is the 'other helper' who would take Christ's place when He had gone (John 14:16). How could any but a Person be so described? In any case John retains the masculine pronoun 'He', even when referring to the neuter noun 'spirit', as if to emphasize the personality of the *Paracletos* (John 15:26). It is true that in Romans Paul uses the construction 'the Spirit itself' (Rom. 8:16, 26. Gk) but in this case the noun and pronoun are so tightly conjugated that it would be too great an offence against grammar to use a masculine pronoun with a neuter noun. This chapter of Romans leaves us in no doubt that Paul attributes personality to the Spirit of God. The Spirit we are told 'leads' believers, indwells them, bears witness with them; He helps their infirmities, makes intercession for them with unutterable groanings and has a 'mind'. Can these things be true of a force or influence, or must they attach to a person? Surely, only the latter can be admitted. Writing to the Corinthians, Paul again makes his position clear. The Spirit 'searches . . . the depths of God' and teaches men

(1 Cor. 2:10, 13); He distributes spiritual gifts 'as He wills'
(1 Cor. 12:11) and so we could continue. The Spirit can
forbid (Acts 16:6), be grieved (Eph. 4:30), be lied to (Acts
5:3) and obeyed (Acts 13:2, 3).

How important is it that the Spirit of God is a Person
rather than a force or influence? It is profoundly important, for only with a person can we have a personal *relationship*, and in one sense the whole purpose of this book is to
explore and establish the relationship that exists between
true Christians and the Holy Spirit. We may be wrought
upon by forces and directed by influences, but only with a
person may we walk in fellowship. And the fellowship of
the Spirit of God ranks with the love of God and the grace
of Christ as the highest privilege a Christian may know in
this life (2 Cor. 13:14).

The work of the Holy Spirit

Although the work of the Spirit in the believer is the area
of contention at which we must look in the chapters that
follow, there is common ground among Bible-believers even
here. The Spirit of God was at work in creation itself, as
Genesis 1:2 testifies. 'The earth was formless and void . . .
and the Spirit of God was moving over the surface of the
waters.' Although the Hebrew word for Spirit can also be
translated 'breath' or 'wind', this does not permit us to
dismiss this statement as a mere poetical gloss, for it would
still read 'the wind (or breath) of *God*'. In other words, no
natural phenomenon is being described here, but rather the
divine presence brooding over an earth pregnant with all
the potential of creation. 'By His Spirit', testifies Job, 'He
garnished the heavens' (Job 26:13, A.V.).

The Scriptures suggest that the Spirit, like the Son, is ever
present in God's providential upholding of the universe. 'The
Spirit of God has made me', states Elihu, 'and the breath of
the Almighty gives me life' (Job 33:4). The rise of each new
generation of living things is attributed to the Spirit of God
in Psalm 104:30: 'Thou dost send forth Thy Spirit, they are
created; and Thou dost renew the face of the ground.'

Significant as the Spirit's work in creation may be, His
work in the 'new creation' is greater still. Paul uses the

creation of the world to illustrate the creation of spiritual life in the soul of man. 'For God, who said, "Light shall shine out of darkness", is the One who has shone in our hearts to give the light of the knowledge of the glory of God in the face of Christ' (2 Cor. 4:6). This is the work of the Spirit of God. He reproves and convicts the careless sinner of his sin (John 16:8—11). He brings to new birth those who are dead in sins and trespasses (John 3:5—8; Eph. 2:1). He gives access to a holy God by application of the merits of Christ (Eph. 2:18). He sanctifies those thus redeemed, and assures them of God's eternal and unalterable favour for the sake of Christ (Eph. 1:13, 14).

Without the Spirit to apply the atonement, we should never know its efficacy. Without the Spirit to awaken us to the fact of an offended God, we should remain heedless, dead to all spiritual reality. Without the Spirit to stir our long-dead consciences and empower us to turn from idols and our sin, there would be no repentance (1 Thess. 1:9). Without His operation in our hearts, there would be no implanted faith, by which alone we may be saved (Eph. 2: 8, 9). Without His power, we could not be raised from spiritual death to new life in Christ (Rom. 8:13).

Christians may, and do, differ on the precise order of these things and the exact manner of the Spirit's work in salvation and the new birth. But all agree that it is His work to bring these things about and to change rebellious, careless sinners into those who live no longer for themselves but for Him who died for them and rose again. Without *this* common ground there would be nothing for us to argue over concerning His *further* work in the believer's heart!

Christians agree that there *is* a continuing work of the Spirit in the believer. Paul writes, 'The love of God has been poured out within our hearts through the Holy Spirit who was given to us' (Rom. 5:5). Jesus promised that the *Paracletos* would be with and in His disciples 'for ever' (John 14:16, 17). It is His gracious work to sanctify the believer, making him more and more Christ-like. 'We all', declares Paul, 'beholding . . . the glory of the Lord, are changed into the same image . . . as by the Spirit of the Lord' (2 Cor. 3:18, A.V.). Expressed in different terms, it is the Spirit's work to suppress our sinful tendencies

and to produce in our lives His 'fruit' of 'love, joy, peace,
patience, kindness, goodness, faithfulness, gentleness, self-
control' (Gal. 5:16—23). He helps us in our spiritual weakness (Rom. 8:26) and strengthens us with power in the
inner man, that Christ may dwell in our hearts in all His
fulness (Eph. 3:16—19).

God's Holy Spirit works, not only at the level of the
individual believer, but also among believers collectively,
that is, in the church. It was to the infant church that the
promise of the Spirit was fulfilled on the Day of Pentecost.
It was the testimony of the church that God authenticated
by the power of the Spirit, as recorded so eloquently in
the Acts of the Apostles. It is to the church that the Holy
Spirit apportions His enabling gifts, so that each member
of the body of Christ may contribute to the benefit of the
whole (Eph. 4:16). It is in the church that believers are
'built together into a dwelling of God in the Spirit' (Eph.
2:22).

To summarize, therefore, there is broad agreement among
Bible-believing Christians concerning the *facts* of the Holy
Spirit's work in the regeneration of the sinner (the new
birth), in the sanctification of the believer and in the edification and empowering of the church militant here on earth.
The differences which we shall consider in what follows are
all concerned with the precise *manner* in which the Spirit
operates in the believer and the church. If we bear this in
mind, we shall avoid the pitfall of exaggerating those differences and the sin of despising those with whom we feel compelled to disagree. The differences are important, otherwise
there would have been no need to write this book. They
must, however, be considered in the context of the common
ground and the responsibility to exhibit Christian charity to
all 'who have received a faith of the same kind as ours by the
righteousness of our God and Saviour, Jesus Christ' (2 Peter
1:1).

3. Four viewpoints, three questions

The promise of the Spirit

Throughout the Old Testament and the Gospels, references are found to a future coming or outpouring of God's Spirit. 'It will come about', declares God through the prophet Joel, 'that I will pour out My Spirit on all mankind' (Joel 2:28). Ezekiel prophesies, 'I will put My Spirit within you and cause you to walk in My statutes . . . you will be My people, and I will be your God' (Ezek. 36:27, 28). Just prior to His ascension, the risen Christ speaks to His disciples of the same events: 'Behold, I am sending forth the promise of My Father upon you; but you are to stay in the city until you are clothed with power from on high' (Luke 24:49).

The Gospels emphasize Christ's role in the matter. John the Baptist announces, 'He Himself will baptize you in the Holy Spirit and fire' (Luke 3:16). The Lord Jesus lends His own emphasis to this same point, saying, 'If I do not go away, the Helper shall not come to you; but if I go, I will send Him to you' (John 16:7). The prophecies culminate in the first chapter of Acts as Christ assures His disciples, 'You shall be baptized with the Holy Spirit not many days from now' (Acts 1:5).

In John's Gospel we read of the Helper, or *Paracletos*, who had been promised by God the Father and was to be sent forth by Him. But this would only occur after Jesus Christ had ascended to His glory and would be at His request and in His place (John 14:16). Peter sums up the situation perfectly in his sermon on the Day of Pentecost: 'This Jesus, God raised up again . . . Therefore . . . having received from the Father the promise of the Holy Spirit, He has poured forth this which you both see and hear' (Acts 2:32, 33).

There is probably no dispute at all among evangelical

19

Christians concerning these promises and prophecies as such. God undoubtedly did promise that there would come a time in history when His Spirit would be given to His people in a remarkable manner and that equally remarkable consequences would ensue. It is just as clear that this giving of the Spirit had, in God's plan, to await the coming of the Messiah and specifically, His death, resurrection and exaltation. The promises and prophecies were fulfilled (or, more accurately, *began* to be fulfilled) on the Day of Pentecost — an event fixed in human history just as plainly as was the birth of Christ. Paul, writing to the Galatians, emphasizes that God has a timetable for such events: 'When the fulness of the time came, God sent forth His Son, born of a woman . . .' (Gal. 4:4). In the same way, the coming or outpouring of the Holy Spirit was clearly part of God's schedule for the unfolding of His redemptive purposes in the context of human history.

The Lord's great commission to the church, to go into all the world and preach the gospel, turned upon the coming of the Holy Spirit. The disciples were not to undertake this task without Him. They had to wait in Jerusalem until they had received power, until the Holy Spirit had come upon them. Then, and only then, were they to become His witnesses 'both in Jerusalem and in all Judea and Samaria and even to the remotest part of the earth' (Luke 24:49; Acts 1:8).

The differences between evangelicals arise when we consider the significance of all this for the believer and the church today. Clearly we still live in the gospel era. In sending His disciples out to evangelize the world, the Lord Jesus promised, 'I am with you always, even *to the end of the age*' (Matt. 28:20) and since His presence with the church was to be implemented by the coming of the Holy Spirit (see John 14 to 16) it follows that the Spirit remains with His people to this day. The promise of the Spirit has been neither rescinded nor withdrawn. Dispute arises, however, as to the manner in which the Holy Spirit's presence, in the believer and the church, is to be manifested. Should we expect to see today the same manifestations of the Spirit as are recorded in the Acts of the Apostles? Should each Christian experience his or her own private Pentecost or baptism in the Spirit? Must we seek such an experience? Should we expect the Spirit to 'fall' upon gatherings of enquirers, as He fell upon Cornelius and his household in Acts 10:44? Were the gifts of the Spirit, or charismata, which were practised by the Corinthian church (prophecy, speaking with tongues, etc) intended for the early days of the church only, or should we expect to receive and practise such gifts today?

These and similar questions exercise many Christians and not infrequently lead to division among brethren. Because of their controversial nature, many of us prefer not to think about these issues, sheltering within the comfortable pre-conceptions of our own particular group or denomination. But these matters cannot be ignored because, as we have seen, the work of the Holy Spirit in and through the church is fundamental to the great commission. We can no more carry out the task of evangelizing the world (or even our own locality) without the Spirit's power than could the apostles in Acts. Similarly, the work of the Holy Spirit in the believer is basic to our assurance, sanctification and spiritual satis-faction. It was, after all, concerning the promise of the Spirit that Jesus cried, 'If any man is thirsty, let him come to me and drink.' The living water He offered to the Samaritan woman at Sychar was likewise a metaphor of the Spirit (John 7:37, 38; 4:10). It is impossible therefore for us to ignore or play down the subject of the Holy Spirit's work today if we are to enjoy the benefits of saving faith and prove effective in the cause of Christ.

There is no shortage of information on the subject of our enquiry. A number of recent books have been added to an already considerable literature setting out the arguments for or against one viewpoint or another, and a significant public debate is still in progress on the validity of the modern charismatic movement, the baptism or 'sealing' of the Spirit and the charismata. Very seldom, however, do authors or commentators review the biblical case for each of several conflicting views of the Spirit's work in the believer, and that is what we plan to do in this book. As we do so, it will become clear why equally honest, Bible-believing Christians can arrive at such different conclusions. We shall also see that some of the conflicting ideas arise from differences in

emphasis and some from fundamental disagreements on
doctrine, while others stem from a failure to take a large
enough view of the promise of the Spirit. Above all our
object will be to arrive at the true teaching of Scripture on
these matters and achieve a scriptural balance between
extremes. This may mean that we must reserve judgement
in some areas where the Bible itself gives no clear-cut
answers. We must not be 'wise above that which is written'.

The major viewpoints

Any attempt to codify the beliefs of a particular group,
denomination or movement is likely to be hazardous, and
this is certainly the case with the subject in question. To
state, for example, that Pentecostals adopt a certain position
on some point of doctrine may immediately uncover the
fact that *some* Pentecostals think differently. This problem
reaches almost unmanageable proportions when we consider
the modern Charismatic movement, for the movement
embraces such an enormous range of opinion that it is
almost impossible to set down definitive beliefs. In this book
we are chiefly concerned with evangelical opinions, so that
we shall not consider in detail the teachings, for example, of
Roman Catholic or Unitarian Charismatics. Even so, it
remains extremely difficult to state in unambiguous detail
what evangelical Charismatics believe about the Spirit's
work. This is not at this stage intended as a criticism. Many
followers of the Charismatic movement rejoice in the idea
that their experience of the Spirit of God transcends their
interpretation, or doctrine, of that experience. For such,
the absence of a clear doctrinal scheme to their movement
is a strength and not a weakness. They point to the powerful
unifying influence of common experience, which submerges
petty differences of human logic and barren doctrine, and
fulfils Christ's prayer that His followers 'might be one'. We
neither accept nor reject such arguments at this stage, except
to say that all experience must be tested by Scripture and
must be consistent with its teachings. A unity based upon
experience *alone*, and which ignores the teachings and
warnings of the Bible, is not the 'unity of the Spirit', in spite
of all appearances and claims.

At the other end of the spectrum stands what I will call the 'Traditional Reformed' viewpoint on the promise of the Spirit. Here, as might be expected, we find a clear doctrinal line and some well-ordered arguments against the Charismatic position. Some of these arguments, however, are not altogether convincing because they have a tendency to stray beyond the limits of Scripture itself. An example of this is the argument from church history that some manifestations of the Holy Spirit must, of necessity, be limited to the apostolic age and could not occur today. As a result of this, some 'Reformed' Christians have modified their ideas on the subject and have adopted a more generous approach to the tenets of Pentecostalism, without embracing them fully. So again we encounter the problem that many shades of opinion exist even within the doctrinally tidy 'camp' of Reformed theology.

In spite of these difficulties, I believe it will be helpful to the reader if the major viewpoints on the promise and work of the Holy Spirit are set out in parallel. This will enable us to see just where they diverge and conflict, as well as where they are in close agreement. It should be clearly understood, however, that a given group or church may hold opinions that are not confined to any one of the 'major viewpoints' I shall present. For example, it does not follow that all established Pentecostal churches have their teachings fully or adequately represented by the 'Old Pentecostal' viewpoint set out below. Each of the four major viewpoints described here should be regarded as a consensus or emphasis to which certain churches, groups or movements adhere more or less closely.

For convenience we shall give each of our four major viewpoints a name as follows:
1. The Old Pentecostal viewpoint;
2. The Neo-Pentecostal (i.e. New Pentecostal) or Charismatic viewpoint;
3. The viewpoint of the Reformed 'Sealers';
4. The Traditional Reformed viewpoint.

We shall look at these in turn. For added clarity the teachings of each viewpoint have been set out briefly in Table 1 (pp. 35—36) together with the main Bible references used to support the argument in question. In the table, each major

viewpoint is represented by a vertical column, while down
the left-hand side are printed the various issues or sub-
divisions that make up the global viewpoint.

The tabulated statements of doctrine are, of course,
highly abbreviated, and we shall therefore expand each of
the major viewpoints in the course of our study. At this
stage we are not going to discuss the *pros* and *cons* of the
arguments employed, but simply summarize them, so that
the reader may have a clear idea of the range of opinion and
the points of difference.

The Old Pentecostal viewpoint

The movement which gave rise to the Pentecostal churches
of today can be traced to the early years of the present
century, when some Christians began to seek a 'baptism of
the Spirit' accompanied by speaking with tongues, that is,
a contemporary experience parallel to that of Acts 2. Such
manifestations occurred in Los Angeles in April 1906 and at
All Saints' Parish Church in Sunderland in 1907, under
the preaching of T. B. Barratt, a Methodist minister from
Oslo. The movement spread rapidly around the world, led
mainly by laymen, and reached a peak in Britain between
1925 and 1935 in the ministries of Welsh evangelists Stephen,
George and Edward Jeffreys. One of the major aspects of the
movement has been the emphasis on divine healing, and
healing campaigns are still a feature of Pentecostalism today.
Although reluctant at first to create an organization or
denomination, Pentecostal believers set up the 'Elim Four-
square Gospel Alliance' in Ireland in 1915 and the 'Assemblies of God in Great Britain and Ireland' in 1924. These two
groups remain the largest in the British Isles, while in North
America the major grouping are the 'Assemblies of God —
USA'. The movement is particularly strong in North America,
Scandinavia and Brazil, where individual churches exist with
as many as 6,000 members and a global membership of over
two millions is claimed. The main (relevant) tenet of 'Old
Pentecostalism' (so called to differentiate it from Neo-
Pentecostalism) is that baptism in the Holy Spirit is an event
that follows conversion or regeneration, sometimes after an
extended interval. Indeed, many regenerate believers fail to

receive this baptism, as a result of ignorance or sin, and it is each Christian's responsibility to seek earnestly for the Spirit's baptism. Some Pentecostals maintain that prior to receiving this baptism the believer is not indwelt by the Holy Spirit, but has only 'the Spirit of Christ', an inner principle, which is not to be equated with the Spirit of God, a Person. The Holy Spirit only takes up residence within the believer at the instant of the baptism of the Spirit. The implied distinction between the Spirit of Christ and the Holy Spirit is of sufficient importance for us to take it up at length in chapter 5.

Other Pentecostals, while not making this particular distinction, do emphasize a change in the relationship between the Spirit and the believer at 'the baptism'. Prior to being baptized in the Spirit, they suggest, the believers have the Holy Spirit with them, but are not indwelt by Him. They point to John 14:17 in support of this view. 'He [the Helper] abides with you [present tense], and will be in you [future tense, i.e., after Pentecost].' We shall examine this idea in detail in chapter 5 but we should note here that the once-for-all historical event of Pentecost is not necessarily paralleled by the individual experience of believers since that event. Thus the situation of believers 'before' and 'after' Pentecost may not correspond in any way to a 'before' and 'after' situation in the lives of Christians since Pentecost.

The coming of the Holy Spirit to the believer in the 'baptism of the Spirit', Pentecostals teach, is manifested in various ways, but notably by speaking in tongues (that is, foreign or celestial languages unknown to the person speaking). Instances of outpourings or effusions of the Spirit accompanied by tongues are, of course, recorded in Acts 2:4, 10:46 and 19:6. Some Pentecostal churches insist that speaking with tongues (or *glossolalia*) is a necessary evidence that a baptism of the Spirit has taken place, while others accept other manifestations (e.g. prophesying, healing) as equally valid evidence, even in the absence of 'tongues'. The latter would point to 1 Corinthians 12:30 to show that the gift of tongues was not intended to be exercised by all Christians.

The consequences of the baptism of the Spirit are, according to Pentecostal teaching, various, ranging from

sanctification and the fruit of the Spirit, as defined in
Galatians 5:22 (love, joy, peace, patience, kindness, goodness, faithfulness, gentleness, self-control), to power for
service (Acts 1:8) and the gifts of the Spirit, such as tongues,
prophecy, healing, knowledge and so on, which, they believe,
are to be exercised to the full today (1 Cor. 12:1–11).

Christians lacking the Spirit's baptism are thus joyless and
ineffective, deprived of the 'more abundant' life that Christ
came to impart.

In Pentecostal thinking the fulness of the Spirit, referred
to frequently in Scripture, is the ongoing experience initiated
by the baptism of the Spirit.

The Neo-Pentecostal or Charismatic viewpoint

The modern Charismatic movement is now some twenty
years old and is distinguished from Old Pentecostalism by
having arisen quite outside the older Pentecostal denominations. This 'Charismatic renewal' is a widespread phenomenon, being found in traditional denominations such as
the Church of England, in the Roman Catholic Church
(where it has received a cautious welcome from the authorities) and many nonconformist churches, including evangelical
groups. A particular feature of Neo-Pentecostalism, however,
is the growth of numerous house groups where believers
gather in small numbers to share their charismatic experiences, often dissociating themselves from churches of any
kind. Such groups do not claim to *be* churches; they tend to
play down the necessity for conventional institutions with
their church order, ministerial offices and the like. They
claim to have rediscovered the simplicity of primitive
Christianity in their totally unstructured worship and
association.

It is obvious from what has already been said that 'Charismatics' differ among themselves on a wide range of issues.
The Catholic Charismatic will disagree sharply with the nonconformist on the whole subject of church doctrine; liberal
and evangelical Charismatics will have fundamental differences on the doctrine of Scripture; the house-group member
will argue with the Neo-Pentecostal churchman on the
whole question of the church and its place in the contemporary Christian scene.

Even evangelical Neo-Pentecostal believers, however, find difficulty in defining common theological ground. Calvinists and Arminians, fundamentalists and neo-evangelicals, house-group members and churchmen may all be found in the Charismatic movement. A second feature, therefore, distinguishing Neo-Pentecostalism from Old Pentecostalism, is the extreme variety of theological and ecclesiastical opinion represented by the former. This has, understandably, caused the traditional Pentecostal churches to view the Charismatic movement with some suspicion and disapproval, in spite of the similarities between their views on the work of the Holy Spirit.

What then, are the views of Neo-Pentecostalism? Its emphasis upon the baptism of the Spirit, as a post-conversion experience of transforming power, is similar to that of the Pentecostal churches. Also, like traditional Pentecostals, Charismatics seek and practise a number of the 'charismata' or gifts of the Spirit, such as tongues. There is, however, less emphasis upon healing, and the main thrust of the Charismatic movement lies in the enrichment of the spiritual life of the believer and the worship of the church. In the context of worship, Neo-Pentecostalism emphasizes the unity conferred upon Christians by the common experience of the Spirit's baptism, and points to Acts 10, where such a baptism finally persuaded Peter that the barrier between Jew and Gentile was abolished in Christ. In some circles, therefore, the Charismatic movement has been hailed as God's contribution to the Ecumenical Movement, but some evangelical Neo-Pentecostals are more cautious. It is difficult, however, for anyone involved in the modern Charismatic movement to ignore the fact that the movement is by no means limited to evangelical believers.

The coming of the Spirit at Pentecost is linked in Acts with the enduement of the disciples with power. 'You shall receive power', declared the risen Christ, 'when the Holy Spirit has come upon you.' This power would result in effective evangelization, great boldness and irresistible preaching (see Acts 4:31). Although the major emphasis of Neo-Pentecostalism seems to be on the enrichment of spiritual life, it is therefore natural that claims are made to additional effectiveness in witness resulting from the baptism of the

Spirit. Certainly the movement is often characterized by an increased zeal to reach others with the gospel.

The Reformed Sealers' viewpoint

In naming the third and fourth of our major viewpoints I have employed the term 'Reformed', and this may require some explanation. Basically, the word is descriptive of the theology of the Protestant Reformation. That is, Reformed teaching or doctrine embodies the interpretations of Scripture and the understanding of the Christian gospel set out by the Reformers of the sixteenth century and those who followed in their footsteps. Notable among the Reformers, in his ability to define and clarify Reformation teaching over against Roman Catholic theology, was John Calvin of Geneva. As a result of this, the term 'Calvinistic' is often used interchangeably with 'Reformed'. Because Calvin's name is frequently identified with controversy over the subjects of predestination and election, it is easy to forget that he was the great codifier and commentator of the Reformation and that his teaching reflected very largely the common beliefs of all the Reformers on such matters as grace, human works and salvation.

In using the expression 'Reformed' to describe our last two viewpoints, we are therefore simply relating them to the mainstream of conservative Protestant theology with its emphasis on the sole authority of Scripture and upon salvation by faith in Christ, through grace alone, without the aid of human works.

The essence of the Reformed Sealers' position is that many Christians, whose theological position is Reformed are nevertheless dissatisfied with the conventional Reformed position on the baptism and gifts of the Holy Spirit (see next section). While rejecting many of the tenets of Pentecostalism, therefore, they insist that the New Testament extends to the believer today the expectation of a baptism of the Spirit similar to that recorded in Acts. This baptism is the same thing as the 'sealing' of the Spirit referred to in Ephesians 1:13, 14: 'Having also believed, you were sealed in Him with the Holy Spirit of promise, who is given as a pledge of our inheritance . . .' It is because of the emphasis placed upon these verses that I have adopted the title 'Sealers' for those holding this viewpoint. Notable among these brethren, was the late Dr D. M. Lloyd-Jones who ably expounded their ideas in his book *God's Ultimate Purpose*, though he himself cited, in support of his arguments, Puritan divines like John Owen and Thomas Goodwin, as well as others such as Charles Hodge, the Princeton theologian and Charles Simeon of Cambridge.

The Sealers point out that the baptisms of the Spirit in Acts occurred, in certain cases, some time after the recipients had become Christians. Notably this was the case with the Samaritans converted under Philip's preaching (Acts 8:1–12). The apostles in Jerusalem, on hearing that 'Samaria had received the word of God', sent Peter and John, who prayed that they might receive the Holy Spirit. 'For', adds Luke, 'He had not yet fallen upon any of them; they had simply been baptized in the name of the Lord Jesus.' As Peter and John laid hands on the Samaritan believers, the Spirit was imparted to them in some discernible, though undefined manner (Acts 4:14–18). The Sealers also point out that Ephesians 1:13 can be translated, 'In whom also, after that ye believed, ye were sealed with that Holy Spirit of promise' (A.V.), suggesting that the sealing is an occurrence subsequent to regeneration.

The Sealers do not accept the Pentecostal assertion that baptism or sealing in the Spirit must be evidenced by speaking in tongues or other charismatic gifts. They tend to follow the conventional Reformed line that these miraculous gifts ceased with the passing of the apostolic age, though some lean more to a Pentecostal view on this question. In contrast to 'Holiness' teaching, they emphasize that the baptism or sealing is not the same thing as sanctification, which is a process commencing at regeneration and going on continuously in all believers. The baptism of the Spirit is, rather, a special visitation or effusion of the Holy Spirit upon the individual believer, in which his apprehension of God is enlarged, his heart melted and his whole being filled with a deep (sometimes almost intolerable) sense of the glory and goodness of God. Many biographical cases are cited in which notable servants of God have recorded such experiences. Fundamental to the Sealers' view is that the recipients of this baptism are permanently changed by the experience. This change concerns, in particular, their assurance of sonship and the power and authority of their witness or ministry. Concerning the first of these, they take Romans 8:15 to refer to the experience of sealing: 'You have received the Spirit of adoption as sons by which we cry out "Abba! Father!"' This verse, together with Galatians 4:6, they maintain, refers to a dramatic conscious awareness of the fatherhood of God and thus of the personal security of the believer. It is an assurance stemming from the immediacy of God, an 'inner witness of the Spirit' which is to be distinguished from assurance inferred from the promises of Scripture. With reference to 'power for service', attention is drawn to 1 Corinthians 2:4 where Paul testified that his speech and preaching were 'in demonstration of the Spirit and of power'. The Reformed Sealers thus diverge from both Old and Neo-Pentecostalism, with their emphasis upon the gifts of the Spirit or charismata, but urge all believers to seek the sealing or baptism of the Spirit as an unsurpassed inner and personal experience of God and spiritual power. Like the Pentecostals, however, the Sealers view the baptism or sealing of the Spirit as the first experience of the fulness of the Holy Spirit, which may thereafter be enjoyed by the believer again and again. Those who deny their teachings, claim the Sealers, may be guilty of 'quenching the Spirit' (1 Thess. 5:19).

The Traditional Reformed viewpoint

This viewpoint was presented at length by B. B. Warfield in his classic book on *Miracles* published as long ago as 1918. It has been defended recently by a number of authors writing to challenge the validity of the Charismatic movement. It is also the viewpoint adopted by the majority of Plymouth Brethren and others who would not call themselves 'Reformed' in the sense of 'Calvinistic'. The key to the Reformed Traditionalists' teaching is 1 Corinthians 12:13: 'For by (or in) one Spirit we were all baptized into one body, whether Jews or Greeks, whether slaves or free, and we were all made to drink of one Spirit.' This, they claim, represents the definitive teaching of the New Testament and must carry far more weight than the historical incidents of Acts in arriving at a theology of experience for the believer today. The book of Acts provides a faithful historical account of the apostolic era, but we must consult the Epistles to discover whether or not the phenomena of Acts should be expected today.

This verse in 1 Corinthians appears to teach that the baptism of the Spirit is something that has happened to *all* believers. In particular it refers to the individual Christian's *incorporation* into the church, the body of Christ. It is the spiritual reality of which water baptism is the outward sign. Baptism in the Spirit, then, is coincident with regeneration, as is the 'sealing' of the Spirit. Both occur as the Holy Spirit takes up residence in the new believer's heart, for 'if anyone does not have the Spirit of Christ, he does not belong to Him' (Rom. 8:9).

The baptism experienced by the disciples in Acts 2 was, according to this viewpoint, a once-for-all historical event. The subsequent effusions in Samaria and Cornelius' household were also unique occasions of special historical significance when the gospel was first received by 'half Jews' (the Samaritans) and Gentiles respectively. The Traditional Reformed viewpoint has some difficulty with the effusion recorded in Acts 19:1–6, where the recipients were certain disciples of John the Baptist, since there seems to be no clear historical significance to this episode.

The Traditional Reformed viewpoint thus rejects the idea that Scripture warrants a special post-conversion experience called the baptism of the Spirit. Every believer undergoes this baptism at his regeneration. Thereafter he may (indeed, is commanded to) be 'filled with the Spirit' (Eph. 5: 18), as an ongoing privilege and responsibility. Rather than quenching the Spirit by denial of a post-conversion baptism, this viewpoint emphasizes that all believers, at all times, may enjoy the fulness of the Holy Spirit and the consequent fruit of His indwelling in their lives and service. The special experiences cited by the Sealers as baptisms of the Spirit are no more than particular cases of 'fulness' and are without any 'once-for-all' significance. The believer, therefore, should lay hold upon the Spirit's fulness, rather than seek some illusory baptism.

Traditional Reformed people adopt an uncompromising

attitude towards the charismatic gifts of tongues, prophecy, healing and so forth. They regard these gifts as passing phenomena, provided to support the early church prior to the completion of the New Testament. The revelatory function of tongues, interpretation and prophecy was gradually replaced by the written words of the apostles in Scripture. The authority of the apostles and New Testament prophets likewise became vested in the written Word, so that the gifts became redundant. Similarly, the special miraculous phenomena given to authenticate the apostolic testimony became unnecessary as the written Word became established. Just as the apostles themselves were a transitional order, so the miraculous gifts were also transitional.

In support of these contentions, Traditional Reformed believers point to the fact that recorded instances of miracles decrease markedly towards the end of the narrative of the Acts and that, apart from 1 Corinthians, the Epistles make little or no reference to the charismata. In the case of the Corinthian church, Paul writes at length concerning the gifts of the Spirit, but does so almost entirely in terms of warning against their misuse and excess. He also highlights the fact that a church so replete with miraculous gifts had produced disorder and division, and was at the same time rife with immorality. The spiritual gifts were obviously no evidence that the Holy Spirit was honoured or His fruit borne by that particular church. In reply, of course, Pentecostals agree that abuse of spiritual gifts by the Corinthians provides a timely warning against excess, but maintain that this has no real bearing on the basic question of whether such gifts should be exercised today.

Three questions

Our task from this point onwards is to examine the teaching of the Bible concerning the promise of the Spirit and its fulfilment. In so doing we shall subject the various teachings reviewed above to the test of Scripture and, hopefully, form a balanced and constructive view on where they are correct, where they err, and where no definite conclusion can be reached.

Although the viewpoints reviewed briefly above differ in

many details, it seems to the writer that the major differences can be reduced rather simply to three basic questions.

The first question is as follows: '*Is the Christian believer indwelt by God's Holy Spirit from the moment of his regeneration?*' This question emphasizes the relationship between the believer and the Spirit and how this relationship was changed by His coming at Pentecost. We shall need to enquire whether the historical event of Pentecost has some analogy in the life of the believer today, that is, are there 'before' and 'after' experiences of the Spirit for the Christian now, similar to the 'before' and 'after' experience of the disciples who were present at Pentecost?

Further questions arise from Romans 8:9, which asserts that a person must 'have' the Spirit of Christ if he is a Christian at all. Is 'having' the Spirit of Christ the same as being indwelt by that Spirit? And, indeed, is the Spirit of Christ the same thing or Person as the Holy Spirit? All these issues will be considered in chapter 5.

The second question is, perhaps, the central one in the whole debate. *Is there some single post-conversion experience, namely the baptism or sealing of the Spirit, which every believer ought to seek and receive?* This opens up the main controversy between the Traditional Reformed position on one hand, and that of the Pentecostals, Charismatics and Sealers on the other. We shall, however, also need to enquire into the precise nature of any such baptism or sealing to see where these last three viewpoints differ among themselves. This question will lead us to re-examine the promise of the Spirit in both Old and New Testaments. What exactly was promised? What did happen at Pentecost? How far were the baptisms or effusions of the Spirit recorded in Acts a fulfilment of the promise — fully or partially? Were these historical baptisms essentially *corporate* experiences, or did they have a basically personal and individual character, even though received by groups of believers? How does baptism in the Spirit relate to the fulness of the Spirit on one hand, and the inner witness of the Spirit on the other? Is a baptism of the Spirit necessary for power in Christian service and ministry? The second question, therefore, leads to many subsidiary enquiries and we shall spend several chapters considering these matters.

Our third and final question concerns the spiritual or miraculous gifts (the charismata) such as tongues, prophecy and healing. *Are these gifts to be practised today or were they temporary provisions for the infant church made redundant by the completion of the New Testament Scriptures?* A subsidiary issue must be whether or not the manifestations of such spiritual gifts practised among Pentecostal and Charismatic groups today are genuinely the work of the Holy Spirit or arise from some other cause. We shall examine the scriptural testimony concerning spiritual gifts in chapters 10–12.

Table 1

We set out below, in outline, the main views on this subject currently held among evangelical Christians. This brief review does *not* cover the entire doctrine of the Holy Spirit, but concentrates on His ministry to the church and the individual believer, and even here covers only certain aspects of that ministry. It must also be realized that within each of the four main viewpoints set out here there are diversities of opinion which are not detailed.

	Old Pentecostal	Neo-Pentecostal or Charismatic	Reformed 'Sealers'	Traditional Reformed
1. *The position of the Old Testament saints with regard to the Holy Spirit*	Not indwelt by Spirit. He came upon them at certain seasons. For argument see 3 below.	? Probably agree with Reformed view.	Indwelt and filled for special service. (Exod. 31:3; Judg. 6:34;11:29;1 Sam. 16:13;Micah 3:8;Hag. 2:5).	Same
2. *The promise of the Spirit*	Promised (Ezek. 36:27; 39:29; Joel 2:28; Luke 24:49; John 7:39; Acts 1:8; John 16:7). *After* Christ's glorification *For* power in service, consolation, assurance, instruction. *To* glorify Christ (John 16:14).	Same	Same	
3. *The indwelling (receiving) of the Spirit*	Nature or Spirit of Christ received at regeneration. Gift of Holy Spirit quite different. (Rom. 8:9–11 and see 'Baptism' below.)	Both Old Pentecostal and Traditional Reformed views found.	Believer indwelt from regeneration. No distinction between Spirit of Christ and Spirit of God. (John 14:23; Rom. 8:9–11;1 Cor. 3:16; Gal. 3:2).	Same, except Rom. 8:14–16 and Gal. 4:6 also apply from regeneration.

4. The baptism of the Spirit Collective baptism at regeneration (1 Cor. 12:13). Personal baptism follows regeneration. 'Second blessing' (for argument see column 3). Must/may be signified by tongues (Acts 2:4; 10:46). To be sought. Christian not complete without it. *For power and joy in service.*	After regeneration (see column 3). May be signified by tongues. Christian weak and joyless without it. Brings unity (Eph. 4:3).	Same as 'Sealing with Spirit' (Eph. 1:13). *After* regeneration (John 20:22; Acts 8:14–17; 9:17; 19:5–6). *For power* (Acts 1:8; 1 Cor. 2:4) and assurance (Rom. 8:14–16; Rom. 5:5). To be sought (Luke 11:13). Experimental, but not signified by tongues.	At regeneration (1 Cor. 12:13). Not necessarily 'felt'. Not to be sought. All experience of Spirit after regeneration falls under 'fulness'.
5. The fulness of the Spirit Ongoing experience of the baptism of Spirit.	Both Pentecostal and Traditional Reformed views found.	Ongoing experience of the baptism of Spirit.	Embraces all variety of relevant Christian experience subsequent to regeneration. A Christian responsibility (Eph. 5:18).
6. The fruit of the Spirit (*Gal. 5:22–25*) Only found in those baptized by Spirit.	Same?	Produce of indwelling. Not necessarily linked to baptism in Spirit.	Produce of indwelling Spirit (Gal. 5:24). To be emphasized above, and distinguished from, gifts of Spirit.
7. The Gifts of the Spirit (*charismata*) Tongues, interpretation, prophecy, healing, to be practised today (1 Cor. 12:28; 14:16.) Test by Scripture to avoid counterfeit. Some recognize sovereignty of Spirit in giving or withholding.	Largely same	Gifts are not fruit or sign of spirituality (1 Cor.). Sovereign Spirit (1 Cor. 12:29). May adopt Traditional Reformed view.	Gifts not for this age (1 Cor. 13:10). Thus satanic or psychological if manifested today.

Part Two

4. The relationship of the Holy Spirit to believers – *I. Before Pentecost*

In this chapter, and the two that follow it, we shall be concerned with the *relationship* that exists between the believer and the Holy Spirit. Although at first sight this might not seem a controversial issue, it really underlies the whole debate. For example, Pentecostals, Charismatics and Sealers all affirm that, prior to baptism in the Spirit, a believer has an incomplete or unsatisfactory relationship with the Holy Spirit. Whether or not this is the case can only be resolved as we examine what Scripture does teach about our relationship to the third Person of the Trinity. The main questions to be answered in this and the succeeding chapters are as follows. What was the relationship between the Holy Spirit and believers *before* Pentecost? This obviously involves both Old Testament believers – like Abraham, Moses, David and the prophets – and the disciples of Christ themselves up to the Day of Pentecost. Then again, how was this relationship changed by the coming of the Spirit at Pentecost? These two questions are obviously set in a historical context, since all would agree, I think, that Pentecost marked the beginning of a new era in the outworking of God's redemptive purposes.

The remaining questions also concern 'before' and 'after' situations but in a personal rather than a historical context. This distinction is important because it does not follow automatically that the historical transformation wrought upon the church at Pentecost is, or even ought to be, mirrored by a transformation of similar nature in the experience of the individual believer today, that is, after Pentecost. Thus we need to ask first, what relationship subsists between the Christian and the Holy Spirit from the moment of regeneration and, secondly, should this relationship undergo some profound change at a subsequent time?

Before we can answer these various questions we must make a thorough examination of the Bible, both Old and New Testaments, to see what it actually teaches on these matters. It is not sufficient to choose one or two texts and build our theology of the Holy Spirit upon them. In a subject as complex and controversial as this we need to stand back and view the broad consensus of Scripture. We need to allow every relevant passage its due weight and, moreover, to view the work of the Spirit in the context of the larger design of God's redemptive acts and intents. Some references will be highly relevant, therefore, although they do not explicitly mention the Spirit, while those that do must be examined carefully in the light of their immediate context.

Our method of approach will be to look first at the relationship of pre-Pentecostal believers to the Holy Spirit, taking each relevant Scripture in turn and making a brief comment. In the next chapter we shall continue this procedure with reference to post-Pentecostal believers. Then in chapter 6 we shall attempt to summarize the biblical testimony concerning this great relationship and, only then, provide definitive answers to the questions posed above.

The believer before Pentecost

It is clear that believers before Pentecost, both Old Testament saints and New Testament disciples, lacked the fulfilment of the promise of the Spirit. Their relationship with the Holy Spirit was therefore, in some manner, incomplete. Even the apostles, who walked with Christ Himself, looked forward to the coming of the Helper (the *Paracletos*) who was to do so much in them, for them and through them (John 14—16).

When, however, we look more closely at the relationship that did exist between the Spirit of God and pre-Pentecostal believers, we find it to be much more extensive and profound than might at first be imagined. Let us consider what Scripture has to say about the situation before Pentecost.

certain people for certain jobs

Temporary or Permanent

The Old Testament era

First of all, certain people were 'filled with the Spirit of God' in Old Testament times for special service requiring ability above that of human art. Bezalel and his fellow craftsmen were so equipped for the construction of the tabernacle. 'I have filled him with the Spirit of God', the Lord told Moses, 'in wisdom and understanding' (Exod. 31:1—11; 35:31). Similarly, the seventy elders of Israel were endued with the Spirit that had hitherto rested 'upon' Moses so that they might share with him the burden of government. 'The Lord took of the Spirit who was upon [Moses] and placed Him upon the seventy elders . . . when the Spirit rested upon them, they prophesied' (Num. 11:16—29). It is clear from verse 29 ('Would that all the Lord's people were prophets, that He would put His Spirit upon them!') that the Spirit referred to throughout this passage was, indeed, the Spirit of God Himself. Although the prophesying was a temporary phenomenon in their case (v. 25), the task of ruling Israel, for which they were equipped by the Spirit, was an enduring responsibility. As with Moses, therefore, the Spirit's resting 'upon' them was no ephemeral or transitory experience, but rather signified a continuing relationship.

In contrast, there were occasions when the Spirit of God 'came upon' individuals in a purely temporary sense, as when Balaam, hired to curse Israel, actually blessed them instead (Num. 24:2). Interestingly, the statement, 'The Spirit of God came upon him' prefaces the last of three attempts that Balaam made to oblige his patron Balak. This suggests that the Spirit's visitation occurred on three separate occasions in quick succession and emphasizes that Balaam had no *enduring* relationship with God's Spirit but was simply wrought upon during the instant of prophecy. This does introduce an important note of caution into our interpretation of such Scriptures as these, namely that one cannot deduce the precise nature of a relationship between an individual and the Holy Spirit from the prepositions employed to describe it. Thus the Spirit was 'upon' both Moses and Balaam, but the relationship denoted by that preposition was very different in the two cases. For Moses it indicated an abiding and intimate relationship, whereas for Balaam it was a transitory and involuntary one.

We shall have reason to emphasize again later the danger of thinking that prepositions such as 'in', 'with', 'among' and 'upon' can *of themselves* be used to define the relationship existing between individuals and the Spirit of God. We always need to study the context of the statements in question, as well as other Scriptures, before drawing our conclusions.

Joshua, Moses' successor as the leader of Israel, is described in Numbers 27:18 as 'a man in whom is the Spirit'. This was true of Joshua *before* Moses laid his hands upon him and commissioned him in the presence of the whole congregation of Israel. We read later that Joshua 'was filled with the spirit of wisdom, for Moses had laid his hands upon him' (Deut. 34:9). We cannot be sure whether the 'spirit of wisdom' mentioned here was the Spirit of God, or simply a God-given attribute that characterized Joshua. This is of secondary importance, however. The significant thing to notice is that the Spirit was in Joshua even before the laying-on of Moses' hands, and this suggests that the younger man enjoyed an abiding relationship with the Holy Spirit which was not linked to a specific task or ministry. Subsequent to his commissioning, Joshua was *further* endowed with a spirit of wisdom, that is, was specifically equipped for his new responsibilities as the leader of God's people.

As we shall see, almost all the references to the Spirit being 'in' or coming 'upon' individuals prior to Pentecost refer to enduements of power or ability for special service (leadership, combat, judicial roles, the authorship of Scripture, prophecy, and so on). The fact that Joshua was indwelt by the Spirit before he was given such special responsibilities, and *before* he was granted the gift of wisdom to equip him for leadership, is therefore particularly significant.

Consider Hebrews 11

The Spirit and the believer in Judges

The book of Judges has much to say about the Spirit of the Lord (i.e., Yahweh, God's covenant name). In every instance recorded there, the terminology is the same, namely that 'the Spirit of the Lord came upon' the person in question. The first recipient of the Spirit in Judges was Caleb's nephew

Othniel (Judg. 3:9—11). In common with the judges who succeeded him, Othniel not only led Israel to military victory, and thence established peace, but apparently restored a semblance of godliness to the nation. The judges' leadership therefore contained a spiritual element, as implied by Judges 2:18, 19 and by the very fact that their function *was* to 'judge' the nation (3:10).

Othniel's appointment as judge dated from the time when 'the Spirit of the Lord came upon him', and the context implies that the same Spirit remained upon him throughout the forty years of his leadership right up to his death. This leads us to another important point. Just because the expression 'came upon' carries the suggestion of superficiality, we must not imagine that the experience of these Old Testament believers was, in fact, superficial or temporary. The Spirit of God not only 'came upon' Othniel when God appointed him a judge and leader of His people, but the same Spirit apparently remained upon him throughout his lifetime. We have already seen that the same was true of Moses, Joshua and, in all probability, the seventy elders also.

Judges continues in similar vein to recount how the Spirit of the Lord came in turn upon Gideon, Jephthah and Samson. In Samson's case the Spirit 'came upon' him repeatedly, suggesting superficially that in the intervals between these occasions (Judg. 13:25; 14:6; 14:19; 15:14) the Spirit may have departed from him. But the expression used of these specific instances is that the Spirit 'came upon him *mightily*' (literally 'rushed upon him') indicating a special enduement of power in the face of particular crises. These repeated enduements of the Spirit in Samson's case are not therefore inconsistent with the view that the Spirit of God rested upon the judges throughout their lifetimes, in spite of their failures and mistakes. (Compare, for example, Gideon's error in making the golden ephod (8:27) with his favourable epitaph in 8:35.)

Saul and David

The Spirit of the Lord 'came upon' both Saul and David after their anointing by the prophet Samuel. In Saul's case, the coming of the Spirit was evidenced by his prophesying and, according to Samuel, he 'became another man' (1 Sam. 10: 10). However, we are also told that after his disobedience to God, 'the Spirit of the Lord departed from Saul, and an evil spirit from the Lord terrorized him' (1 Sam. 16:14). For King Saul, therefore, the enduement of the Spirit was temporary and conditional upon obedience. It can be argued that this conditionality was an essential characteristic of the Spirit's relationship with the Old Testament saints, especially since Christ emphasized that after Pentecost, the Holy Spirit would be with His disciples 'for ever' (John 14:16). Of David we read, 'The Spirit of the Lord came mightily upon David from that day forward' (1 Sam. 16:13). David's relationship to the Spirit was therefore ongoing and, as far as we know, continuous right up to his death. However, even David had occasion to plead with God, 'Do not take Thy Holy Spirit from me' (Ps. 51:11). He feared that his adultery with Bathsheba, and the consequent web of deceit and murder with which he tried to conceal it, would cause the same withdrawal of the Spirit of God as Saul had suffered. We may therefore consider that David's relationship with the Holy Spirit, although in fact a permanent one, was *potentially* breakable. This concept of conditional enduement, in which God, as it were, reserved the right to withdraw His Spirit, could also cover the other cases of lifelong enduement that we noted previously (Moses, Joshua, the elders and the judges). It is not possible, however, to be dogmatic about this. It is interesting to notice that long after the Spirit departed from Saul (1 Sam. 16:14), and even as he pursued David to kill him, the Spirit came upon Saul again and he prophesied (1 Sam. 19:15–24). This strange enduement had already fallen upon three separate groups of Saul's messengers sent to capture David, and evidently had the effect of stopping them in their tracks. In this unusual incident, therefore, it seems clear that God's Spirit actually came upon Saul to judge, disable and humiliate him rather than to equip him for service as had previously been the case.

David's relationship with the Spirit of God was particularly profound because he was not only a leader of Israel, but also one of the authors of Scripture. At the end of his life, describing himself as 'the anointed of the God of Jacob and the sweet psalmist of Israel', David declared, 'The Spirit of the Lord spoke by me, and His word was on my tongue' (2 Sam. 23:2). Of Old Testament prophets such as David, Peter states that 'the Spirit of Christ [was] within them' (1 Peter 1:11). No clear distinction is therefore drawn by Scripture between the Spirit being 'upon' a man and the Spirit being 'within' him. It would certainly be mistaken to suggest that the preposition 'upon' described the Old Testament relationship between believer and Holy Spirit while the word 'in' or 'within' betokens a post-Pentecostal relationship. Such an idea is sometimes based on a particular reading of John 14:17, a verse which will be considered later in this chapter. Even of Christ Himself the Old Testament prophesies that 'the Spirit of the Lord will rest on Him' (Isa. 11:2; 42:1; 61:1). Rather, the use of various prepositions to describe the relationship between the believer and the Spirit appears to signify different aspects, emphases or even simply different metaphors concerning the relationship. Thus the favourite terminology of the Old Testament, namely that the Spirit 'came upon' God's servants, seems to be a metaphor related to anointing, an act in which oil was poured upon the head of the recipient. When, however, the writer wishes to indicate that the Spirit of God was working through the person concerned, as in Bezalel's construction of the tabernacle or the authorship of Scripture, it is more appropriate to use the metaphor of indwelling to describe the relationship.

What does emerge from these early Old Testament accounts is that the indwelling or supervention (coming upon) of the Spirit was, arguably, conditional upon continued obedience. We say, arguably, because there is little doubt that some Old Testament saints enjoyed the enduement of the Spirit from a certain moment onwards throughout their lifetimes, and in such cases conditionality is very difficult to prove. Others, however, like Saul and, as an extreme example, Balaam, experienced the Spirit's supervention only to lose it again, which certainly argues in favour of conditional endue ment. The matter is complicated, however, by the fact that David could sin grievously without the Spirit being taken from him, so that any conditionality in his case was certainly not that of perfect obedience, and by the further fact that there was a great difference between such characters as Saul and Balaam on the one hand and Moses and David on the other. It is possible to suggest that the former were essentially unconverted men whom God used temporarily, while the latter were truly regenerate believers having an abiding fellowship with God. In this case it is entirely possible that the essential relationship between the man and the Holy Spirit was quite different in the two cases, even though the same terms are employed in each case.

The testimony of the prophets

The prophetical books make some interesting references to the relationship between the national Israel and the Holy Spirit. God, we read, 'put His Holy Spirit in the midst of them' and 'the Spirit of the Lord gave them rest'. They on their part, however, 'rebelled and grieved His Holy Spirit' (Isa. 63:10, 11, 14). Haggai assures the post-exilic nation, ' "I am with you", says the Lord of hosts. "As for the promise which I made you when you came out of Egypt, My Spirit is abiding in your midst; do not fear!" ' (Hag. 2:4, 5.) This demonstrates clearly that the Holy Spirit was an active presence throughout Israel's chequered history, a presence demonstrated *par excellence* by the prophetic ministry itself. As Zechariah says, 'The Lord of hosts had sent by His Spirit through the former prophets' both His law and His words (Zech. 7:12).

Ezekiel describes the activity of God's Spirit in relation to his own prophetic experience: 'The Spirit entered me', he explains, 'and set me on my feet' (Ezek. 2:2). This attribution of almost physical effects to the influence of the Spirit continues throughout the book, with such statements as 'The Spirit lifted me up and took me away', 'The Spirit then entered me and made me stand on my feet', 'The Spirit lifted me up between earth and heaven', and 'The Spirit of the Lord fell upon me' (Ezek. 3:14, 24; 8:3, 11:5 etc.). Clearly, the language here is mystical and we do not suppose that Ezekiel actually underwent physical levitation and transportation. Nevertheless the dynamic imagery reflects the profound impact made upon the prophet by these infillings of the Spirit. Ezekiel's reference to the Spirit 'entering' him do not add substantially to the conclusion already drawn – namely, that on various occasions the Spirit of God came with power upon Old Testament saints for the execution of specific tasks of service or ministry. 'I am filled with power – with the Spirit of the Lord . . . to make known to Jacob his rebellious act,' proclaims Micah (Micah 3:8).

As pointed out already in the case of Samson, we cannot deduce from Ezekiel's repeated experiences of the Spirit's coming, that there was no *abiding* relationship between the prophet and the Holy Spirit. We see a similar pattern in Acts, after Pentecost, where the disciples, who experienced the Pentecostal infilling and were clearly indwelt by the Spirit, were filled anew during the prayer meeting recorded in Acts 4:23–31. It seems, then, that in both pre- and post-Pentecostal eras it was possible for God's servants to enjoy both an abiding relationship with the Holy Spirit and, superimposed upon this, occasional special infillings as circumstance demanded. Finally, we may notice that Ezekiel further enriches the store of metaphor employed to describe the Holy Spirit's dealings with believers. To the standard Old Testament terminology, according to which the Spirit 'came upon' men, he adds 'entered into' and 'fell upon' as further descriptions. There is no warrant for suggesting that these various expressions describe different operations of the Spirit. Rather they reflect the prevalent practice of Scripture in attempting to define intangible and spiritual experiences, namely, the use of a range of metaphors, similes and descriptions to deepen our understanding of the thing described.

New Testament testimony concerning the Old Testament saints

The New Testament clearly ascribes the authorship of Old Testament Scripture to the Spirit of God working through the prophets. We find quotations from the Old Testament introduced by such clauses as, 'David himself said by the Holy Spirit' (Mark 12:36, mg.); 'The Holy Spirit rightly spoke through Isaiah the prophet to your fathers, saying . . .' (Acts 28:25); 'Just as the Holy Spirit says' (Heb.

3:7); 'The Holy Spirit also bears witness to us; for after saying . . .' (Heb. 10:15). Elsewhere more general statements
are made: 'Brethren, the Scripture has to be fulfilled, which
the Holy Spirit foretold by the mouth of David . . .' (Acts
1:16). Describing the spiritual lessons of the Mosaic tabernacle, the writer to the Hebrews explains that by its construction and ordinances the Holy Spirit was 'signifying'
certain truths symbolically (Heb. 9:8). Finally, of course,
we have Peter's definitive statements concerning the authorship of the Old Testament. 'The prophets who prophesied
of the grace that would come to you made careful search
and enquiry, seeking to know what person or time the Spirit
of Christ within them was indicating as He predicted the
sufferings of Christ and the glories to follow' (1 Peter 1:
10, 11). Again, in his second Epistle, he writes that 'No
prophecy was ever made by an act of human will, but men
moved by the Holy Spirit spoke from God' (2 Peter 1:21).

The authors of Old Testament Scripture, therefore, were
uniformly indwelt and wrought upon by the Spirit of God
to produce those Scriptures, writing only that which God,
through the Spirit, intended and moved them to set down.

But, we may ask, what of the generality of Old Testament saints? Were only those indwelt by the Spirit who
were entrusted with special tasks such as writing Scripture,
judging Israel or building the tabernacle? This question is
not easy to answer. We know, of course, that Old Testament believers were characterized by their faith, just as are
New Testament believers. Hebrews 11 is evidence enough of
this, though we could also cite numerous other references,
especially from Romans and Galatians, to demonstrate this
fact. What relationship did these men of faith have to the
Spirit of God in Old Testament times? We know they
'pleased God' by their faith (Heb. 11:5, 6) and were made
righteous by it (Heb. 11:7), just like us who believe in Christ
today. Furthermore, we read that 'These all died in faith,
without receiving the promises, but having seen them and
having welcomed them from a distance' (Heb. 11:13). We
shall see later that the promise of the Spirit was one of the
promises made to faith and, indeed, could be construed as
the blessing promised to Abraham (see Gal. 3:14—18).
The same verses in Galatians remind us that the gift of

the Holy Spirit is, today, received by faith just as they, in the pre-Pentecostal era, received the *promise* of that still-future gift.

This point is elaborated at the conclusion of Hebrews 11. 'All these', asserts the writer, 'having gained approval through their faith, did not receive what was promised, because God had provided something better for us, so that apart from us they should not be made perfect' (Heb. 11:39, 40). We may say with some confidence, I believe, that the promise they did not receive was the promise of the Spirit, with all that it implies. This gift was promised to them and shown to them 'from a distance' but nevertheless withheld from them. Why? John provides the answer: 'For the Spirit was not yet given, because Jesus was not yet glorified' (John 7:39). Note that Hebrews makes it clear that one day these Old Testament saints *would* receive the fulfilment, just as they had already received the promise. We are not told that they could never be made 'perfect' or complete, but only that this could not happen 'apart from us'. We conclude therefore that they enter posthumously into the same relationship to the Spirit of God that post-Pentecostal believers enjoy in *life* and will stand equal to us in all respects in the final outworking of God's salvation.

None of this, however, answers the question: 'What was their relationship to the Holy Spirit during their lifetime?' It clearly was not that enjoyed by believers since Pentecost, but neither was the relationship non-existent, for we have already seen that the Spirit indwelt at least some of them.

Hebrews 11 provides some clues. For example, we are told that Gideon, Samson, David and the prophets, among others, 'conquered kingdoms, performed acts of righteousness, obtained promises, shut the mouths of lions . . . were made strong, became mighty in war . . .' and so on, 'by faith' (Heb. 11:33, 34). Yet in the Old Testament record, as we have seen, they achieved these things as a direct result of the supervention of the Spirit of the Lord. May we not conclude, therefore, that *all* men of faith in pre-Pentecostal times were indwelt by the Spirit of God and that their faith was evidence of this indwelling? Admittedly this conclusion is an inference from, rather than an assertion of Scripture, but it seems more consistent than the view that only *some*

Old Testament believers had the Spirit of God 'upon' or
'within' them.

This view is supported by one further reference, namely
2 Corinthians 4:13. 'Having the same spirit of faith', writes
Paul, 'according to what is written, "I believed, therefore
I spoke", we also believe, therefore also we speak.' This
somewhat obscure verse becomes clear when viewed in the
light of what we have said above. The apostle, quoting from
Psalm 116:10, is telling us that believing gives rise to speaking. (See also Rom. 10:8–10.) This was true for the writer
of the psalm and it was true also for Paul, and this should
not surprise us, Paul suggests, since he had 'the same spirit
of faith' as did the psalmist. We cannot be sure that the
'spirit of faith' referred to here means the Holy Spirit.
Indeed, the translators have decided not to capitalize the
word 'spirit', thus implying a general use of the word. However, since the original Greek makes no distinction between
'spirit' and 'Spirit', it is at least possible that Paul was referring here to the Holy Spirit, linking the possession and exercise of faith directly to the indwelling of the Spirit for
both Old and New Testament believers (that is, the psalmist
and Paul himself).

We conclude, therefore, that some pre-Pentecostal
believers were certainly indwelt by the Spirit of God and
that, arguably, all men of faith, in all eras, have been so
indwelt. The special, miraculous gift of 'faith' was imparted
by the Holy Spirit (1 Cor. 12:9); it would seem strange if
the general, saving faith possessed by all believers had some
different source.

The New Testament era before Pentecost

The passages we have studied from the Old Testament are
paralleled in the New by many references which throw
light on the Holy Spirit's relationship with believers prior
to the Day of Pentecost. First of all, we find a small company of the faithful, including Elizabeth and Zacharias, the
parents of John the Baptist, Simeon and, of course, John
himself. Both Elizabeth and Zacharias were 'filled with the
Holy Spirit' in sudden experiences which gave rise to prophetic utterance (Luke 1:41, 67). John the Baptist himself

was 'filled with the Holy Spirit even from his mother's womb' (Luke 1:15 mg.) and was the forerunner of Christ, in 'the spirit and power of Elijah' (Luke 1:17). Of Simeon we read that 'the Holy Spirit was upon him', and the context here suggests strongly an abiding relationship since we are told he was 'righteous and devout, looking for the consolation of Israel' (Luke 2:25, 26). The Spirit had revealed to him that he would see the Messiah before he died and, in a particular act of the Holy Spirit's guidance, 'he came in the Spirit into the temple', where he met Mary, Joseph and the infant Jesus (Luke 2:25—35).

In these references we see repeated the pattern we have already discerned in the Old Testament Scriptures — namely, that the Holy Spirit both dwelt within, or upon believers in a lasting relationship, and also came, or fell upon people in sudden supervention, giving rise to prophetical utterance or other supernatural activity. The same verb 'filled' is used by Luke to describe both the enduring relationship (as in the case of the Baptist, filled with the Holy Spirit 'even from' his mother's womb) and the instances of sudden supervention (as in the case of Elizabeth and Zacharias).

The Spirit and Jesus' disciples

Secondly, of course, we may consider the disciples of Jesus before Pentecost. We know that their comprehension of Christ's mission was elementary and confused. Although He had explained in detail what was to occur concerning His death and resurrection (see e.g. Mark 10:33, 34), we find them disillusioned and fearful after the crucifixion. They were 'foolish' and 'slow of heart to believe' (Luke 24:25), having completely forgotten, it would seem, such discourses as that of John chapters 14—16 in which Jesus announced His imminent departure and promised that the *Paracletos* would come. Although God the Father had revealed to Peter that Jesus was 'the Christ, the Son of the living God' (Matt. 16:16), the same disciple immediately demonstrated his ignorance of Jesus' mission by protesting at the idea of His death (Matt. 16:22—23). One can almost hear the sorrow in the Saviour's voice as He reproaches another of His apostles: 'Have I been so long with you, and yet you have not come to know Me, Philip?' (John 14:9.)

The disciples therefore stand in distinct contrast to those like Simeon who recognized so clearly the nature and work of the Messiah. Even John the Baptist, speaking under the influence of the Spirit of God, had a far clearer view of the mission of 'the Lamb of God who takes away the sin of the world' than did the disciples who lived so close to Him, though John also, of course, went through a period of doubt (John 1:32—36; Luke 7:19). It is no surprise, there-fore, to find that the Gospels have very little to say about the Holy Spirit in relation to the disciples of Christ. When He first sent them out to preach 'the kingdom of heaven', He gave them authority to cast out evil spirits and heal sickness. He also told them that, when arraigned before hostile courts, they would be given words to speak, assuring them, 'It is not you who speak, but the Spirit of your Father who speaks in you' (Matt. 10:20). It would be difficult from this single text to demonstrate that any abiding relationship existed between the apostles and the Holy Spirit prior to the resurrection, and it would appear that during this period the apostles' relationship to the Spirit was actually inferior to that of Simeon, John the Baptist and indeed Old Testa-ment saints such as Abraham, Moses and David. This may help to explain the post-resurrection incident recorded in John 20:21—22: 'Jesus therefore said to them again, "Peace be with you; as the Father has sent Me, I also send you." And when He had said this, He breathed on them, and said to them, "Receive the Holy Spirit. If you forgive the sins of any, their sins have been forgiven them . . ." ' Some commentators see this merely as an anticipation of Pente-cost. That is, there was no imparting of the Spirit there and then but rather a further promise, dramatized by the act of breathing on them. This is a possible interpretation, but the plain meaning of the account is that the disciples did indeed receive the Holy Spirit in some manner at that moment. Considering the depth and extent of the relationship we have found to exist between the Spirit and other pre-Pentecost believers, in the Old Testament and Gospels, it is not difficult to accept the more natural reading of this passage. On this view, the apostles would have been brought

at that moment into a relationship with the Spirit of God
such as, Moses, say, or Simeon had known long before.
Certainly the disciples portrayed in Acts 1 (that is still prior
to Pentecost) possessed a confidence and prayerfulness that
contrasts strongly with the fearfulness of these same men
before Christ breathed upon them behind their fast-locked
doors. *Some* transformation had certainly occurred even
before the Day of Pentecost.

It is clear, of course, that even at this stage 'the Spirit was
not yet given, because Jesus was not yet glorified' (John
7:39). This special giving of the Spirit awaited the Day of
Pentecost. But this was equally true for *all* pre-Pentecostal
believers both of the Old and New Testaments and, as we
have seen, many of them nevertheless possessed a clearly
defined abiding and empowering relationship with the Spirit
of God.

The interpretation of John 14:17

Finally in our consideration of the apostles before Pentecost,
we must return to the Gospel of John. We shall be looking
in greater detail at the important chapters (John 14 to 16)
later, since for the most part they refer to a future, that is,
post-Pentecostal relationship between the disciples and the
Spirit, and therefore do not concern us here. These particular
promises could not be made good until Christ had departed.
'If I do not go away, the Helper shall not come to you' (John
16:7). A coming of the Spirit which was conditional on the
departure (or glorification) of the Lord Jesus could not have
been the *kind* of coming or filling experienced by, say,
Moses, John the Baptist or the disciples in the locked
chamber.

However, one verse embedded in the discourse on the
Paracletos does appear to refer to the disciples' current situation and is therefore relevant to our present discussion. In
John 14:17 Jesus speaks of 'the Spirit of truth whom the
world cannot receive because it does not behold Him or
know Him'. 'But', continues the Saviour, 'you know Him
because He abides with you, and will be in you.'

Some Pentecostals argue that this statement defines both
a pre-Pentecostal relationship in which the Holy Spirit was

merely 'with' the disciples, and a deeper post-Pentecostal relationship in which He dwelt 'in' them. However, we have already seen that great caution is required in the use of prepositions to specify the nature of such relationships. We saw that in pre-Pentecostal times the Spirit 'came upon' people, 'filled' them, 'fell upon' them, dwelt 'in' them, spoke through them and in them and remained in their 'midst'. It was not possible to associate each of these different expressions with a different kind of relationship. Rather it seemed that a range of different metaphors was employed to enrich the description of something that cannot easily be expressed in human terms. Of Christ Himself, who surely had the most clearly defined relationship possible with the third Person of the Godhead, we read in various places that the Spirit came upon Him (Matt. 3:16; 12:18), led Him (Matt. 4:1), filled Him (Luke 4:1), empowered Him (Luke 4:14) and remained upon Him (John 1:32). We do not suppose that these different phrases betoken five different relationships, but rather that they express five different aspects of a single relationship.

Similarly, in John 14, the preposition 'with' is used of the *future* relationship of the *Paracletos* to the disciples ('. . . that He may be with you for ever'). It is unlikely therefore to be used in the very same sentence (v. 17) to refer exclusively and definitively to a *present* relationship. (The Greek words translated 'with' in verses 16 and 17 are different, but are correctly rendered by the one English word. Indeed, the word *para* translated 'with' in verse 17 also forms part of the name *Paracletos* given by Christ to the Holy Spirit in these chapters. It can hardly be claimed therefore to indicate an inferior level of 'with-ness' to that denoted by the word *meta* used in verse 16.)

The second question concerning verse 17 is whether a distinction between present ('He abides with you') and future ('He . . . will be in you') is really intended here. The whole sentence, beginning with verse 16, is cast in the future and the present tense phrase in verse 17 can be understood to emphasize the *character* of the awaited *Paracletos* as the one whose nature is to abide or remain, rather than to indicate a present relationship. This view is adopted by such commentators as Hendriksen. We commonly use the present tense in English to denote future events, as when we say, for example, 'We are going to Spain for our holidays,' meaning 'We will be going . . . ' Although Greek and English tenses cannot strictly be compared, this does show how loosely tenses can be, and often are, employed in spoken language.

On balance, therefore, it would seem unsafe to use John 14:17 to define a pre-Pentecostal relationship between the disciples and the Holy Spirit. Still less should it be used to define a *general* relationship between believers and the Spirit prior to some special experience or baptism of the Spirit. Such an interpretation is quite inadmissible since, as we have seen, the Spirit was *in* many of the Old Testament saints, particularly the authors of Scripture (1 Peter 1:11), centuries before the Pentecostal baptism took place.

Conclusion

A full discussion of our conclusions will be given in chapter 6 after we have considered the position of post-Pentecostal believers. For the sake of clarity, however, we pause here simply to list the points that have emerged from our study so far.

1. Believers before Pentecost received by faith the *promise* of the coming of the Spirit, but not its fulfilment. (This fulfilment awaited the death and glorification of Christ.) They therefore did not have the same relationship to the Holy Spirit that post-Pentecostal believers possess. In due course, however, they also will be 'made perfect' or complete along with us, entering posthumously into the fulfilment of the promise.

2. Whatever they lacked, pre-Pentecostal believers did possess a genuine relationship with the Spirit of God which is variously described. The Spirit came upon them, dwelt in them and spoke through them. These actions of the Spirit are normally associated with the idea of equipment for the service of God, but, in many cases at least, the relationship described was abiding and even lifelong. In Joshua's case the Spirit of God was in him *before* he was selected for special service.

3. There is the possibility that the relationship between the Spirit and the believer before Pentecost was conditional upon obedience, in contrast to the unconditionality of the post-Pentecostal situation. However, this cannot be established with certainty.

4.   On the other hand, it can be argued by inference from Scripture that *all* men and women of faith before Pentecost were indwelt by the Spirit, He being the source of their faith as He was the source of their power to serve God.

5.   Negatively, it is quite clear that the indwelling of the Spirit, the fulness of the Spirit and the power of the Spirit are all phenomena experienced by believers before Pentecost and cannot therefore be definitive of the post-Pentecostal situation. The promise of the Spirit, which awaited the glorification of Christ and the Day of Pentecost, must consist in *something quite different* from these experiences, even though they do feature prominently in the apostolic church.

5. The relationship of the Holy Spirit to believers – *II. After Pentecost*

In this chapter we continue our perusal of the Scriptures to establish what they teach concerning the relationship between the Spirit and believers. In the previous chapter we examined this matter as it affected believers prior to Pentecost. We now turn to the new era that was inaugurated by that historic visitation of the Holy Spirit.

The actual events of Pentecost, which divide this chapter from the last, and the whole question of the Spirit's baptism and sealing, will be considered later in chapters 7–9. We are involved here only with the relationship or relationships which may subsist between post-Pentecostal believers and the Holy Spirit.

The passages which concern us include both the bulk of the relevant New Testament references, especially in Acts and the Epistles, and also what I will call the 'promise Scriptures' which pre-date Pentecost but nevertheless look forward explicitly to its coming and its consequences. We have still to consider the full import of the various promises relating to the Spirit recorded in the Old Testament, the Gospels and Acts 1, and we shall do this in due course. Our interest at present is to learn what these particular passages teach about the relationship of the Holy Spirit to believers following the fulfilment of His promised coming at Pentecost.

The blessing of Abraham

In Galatians 3:14 the promise of the Spirit is linked by Paul with what he describes as 'the blessing of Abraham'. 'Christ redeemed us from the curse of the law', he explains, 'that in Christ Jesus the blessing of Abraham might come to the Gentiles, so that we might receive the promise of the Spirit through faith.'

Although the detailed interpretation of this verse is perhaps open to debate, the apostle seems to indicate here that the Spirit's coming was included among the several promises made by God to Abraham. In particular, Paul has in mind the promise that in Abraham's descendants 'shall all the families of the earth be blessed' (Gen. 28:14). The fact that the Galatians, as Gentiles, had *received the Spirit* (Gal. 3:2) was to Paul an evident fulfilment of this prophecy, even though, as recorded in Genesis, it contains no explicit reference to the Holy Spirit.

Paul's logic here is not difficult to follow. The 'blessing of Abraham' embraces all blessings that are received *by faith*, for this is how Abraham himself received the promises God made to him. The essence of the covenant with Abraham lay just here: it was a covenant consisting of promises to be received by faith, and stood in contrast to the Mosaic covenant of works. Paul, in fact, seems to go even further, to suggest that God's covenant with Abraham was not only *a* covenant, but *the* archetypal covenant of promises to be appropriated by faith. If this is so, of course, all blessings received under the gospel are embraced in the Abrahamic covenant of promise. Outstanding among such blessings, Paul reminds us, are the gift of the Spirit (Gal. 3:2), justification and sonship to God (Gal. 3:14).

It is interesting to notice that here in Galatians 3 these three distinct blessings are referred to almost in the same breath, and in the following chapter of the Epistle Paul proceeds to link them together even more closely. 'God sent forth His Son . . . in order that He might *redeem* those who were under the Law, that we might receive the *adoption* as sons. And because you are sons, God has *sent forth the Spirit* of His Son into our hearts, crying, "Abba! Father!" ' (Gal. 4:4–6). There is no suggestion here that the gift or reception of the Holy Spirit is separable in time from the gift of justification or the act of divine adoption. Indeed Paul appears to link the 'sending forth' of the Spirit into our hearts with the act of adoption as effect and cause respectively.

What we are beginning to see is that since Pentecost, the Holy Spirit's coming to the individual is an integral part of salvation and is ranked with justification and adoption as a key aspect of that salvation. We also see that the relationship between the Spirit and the believer is intimately associated with other relationships, namely those between the believer and Christ (he is *'in* Christ Jesus') and between the believer and God (he is a son of God). This involvement of the entire Godhead seems to be one of the major distinguishing features of the post-Pentecostal relationship, when compared with the pre-Pentecostal situation. Let us pursue it further.

The promise of the *Paracletos*

Perhaps the most important of the 'promise Scriptures' is Christ's Paracletic discourse in John chapters 14—16, and here we find an emphasis placed upon the threefold relationship of the believer to Father, Son and Holy Spirit. After announcing the promise in John 14:16 ('I will ask the Father and He will give you another Helper'), the Lord Jesus continues, 'I will not leave you as orphans; I will come to you . . . In *that* day you shall know that I am in My Father, and *you in Me*, and *I in you* . . . If anyone loves Me, he will keep My word; and My Father will love him, and We will come to him, and make Our abode with him' (John 14:18, 20, 23).

It is clear, not only from these specific words but also from the whole purpose and tenor of John 14—16, that the divine indwelling of Father and Son is mediated by the Holy Spirit. 'He', said Christ, 'will be in you' (John 14:17) and it is by His presence within that both Father and Son *also* indwell the believer. How else could Christ both depart from them *and* come to take up His abode with them? Likewise, it is by the Spirit that the believer abides in Christ, for it was 'in that day' of the Spirit's coming that the disciples were to know that they were in Him (John 14:20). This also explains why the parable of the vine and the branches, with its emphasis upon abiding in Christ and bearing fruit, is embedded in this discourse on the coming *Paracletos*. Again, therefore, we see that the relationship between the

individual and the Holy Spirit after Pentecost is inextricably
bound up with the believer's relationship to the other Persons
of the Trinity. Indeed it is a major work of the indwelling
Spirit to deepen the relationship between the believer and
Christ. 'He shall glorify Me', explains the Saviour, 'for He
shall take of Mine, and shall disclose it to you' (John 16:14).

It seems to the present writer that this element of fellowship between the individual and the whole Godhead is
altogether absent from the relationship between believers
and the Holy Spirit before Pentecost, even though some of
them were filled with the Spirit in a real and continuing way.
Perhaps this is why Jesus said concerning John the Baptist
(who was 'filled with the Holy Spirit even from his mother's
womb' Luke 1:15, mg.), that 'he who is least in the kingdom
of heaven is greater than he' (Matt. 11:11). Similarly, Paul
declares the mystery, or secret, which had 'been hidden from
the past ages and generations; but has now been manifested
to His saints . . . which is Christ in you, the hope of glory'
(Col. 1:26, 27). The indwelling of *Christ* by the Spirit was
denied to past generations, even though the indwelling of the
Spirit Himself *was* vouchsafed to some, such as Bezalel, John
the Baptist, the authors of Old Testament Scripture, and
possibly to all who embraced God's promises by faith.

If we are right in this understanding of the discourse on
the *Paracletos* in John 14—16, and of Galatians 3—4, some
very profound consequences follow. That is, the promise of
the *Paracletos,* or Helper, must be fulfilled for the individual
believer *at his regeneration* and not at some subsequent time.
No man is regenerate who has not received Christ; yet it is
only as the Holy Spirit is received, that Christ Himself is also
received and takes up residence in a man's heart. At this
juncture, too, the child-Father relation to God is established
and recognized by the new-born believer as it is evidenced
by the indwelling Spirit (Gal. 4:4—6). Thus it seems essential
that the Spirit be received at regeneration.

The Epistle to the Romans confirms this point: 'You have
received the Spirit of adoption as sons by which we cry out,
"Abba! Father!" ' (Rom. 8:15 mg.) It seems illogical to
suggest, as some Reformed Sealers do, that this inner assurance of the fatherhood of God is an experience that comes
later than regeneration, in a special giving or sealing of the

Spirit. To maintain this view requires us to suppose that we receive adoption as sons at regeneration but only receive 'the *Spirit* of adoption as sons' at some later juncture! Such an unnatural divorce would require some very strong scriptural evidence to render it acceptable. Galatians 4:6 states that the Spirit of God's Son is 'sent forth' into our hearts because we *are* sons and for no other reason. Like Romans 8, therefore, Galatians seems to envisage the coming of the Spirit of adoption as a concomitant of adoption and not as some separate and subsequent event.

A final point of some importance in John 14 is the statement in verse 16 that the *Paracletos* would be with the disciples 'for ever'. Not only would He be 'in' them, but His indwelling would be permanent. In our discussion of the Old Testament order we saw that, in some cases, the Spirit came upon men for a limited time and that His indwelling even of prophets like David may have been conditional. It was not possible for us to establish this point beyond doubt, simply because some of God's servants clearly enjoyed a lifelong experience of the Spirit's resting upon or dwelling within them. Nevertheless, if David's fear expressed in Psalm 51:11 was well grounded, the possibility existed of the Spirit's withdrawal even from such as him. Whether or not the Spirit's indwelling before Pentecost was conditional upon obedience, it is clear from John 14:16 that this is no longer the case since Pentecost. For believers today, the relationship with the Holy Spirit is permanent and indissoluble. Nor does this conclusion rest upon this text alone, for did not Christ declare only a few chapters earlier in the same Gospel, 'My sheep . . . shall never perish and no one shall snatch them out of My hand'? (John 10:28.) The permanence of His indwelling is therefore a major aspect of the post-Pentecostal relationship between the Spirit and the believer.

The promise of the Spirit in the prophetical books

The best known prophetic promise is, of course, that of Joel 2:28–31, which is quoted in Peter's Pentecostal sermon: 'And it will come about after this that I will pour out my Spirit on all mankind . . . even on the male and female servants I will pour out my Spirit in those days . . .' Peter tells us explicitly that Pentecost was, in part at least, the fulfilment of this promise. Three aspects of the prophecy concern us here, namely that the gift of the Spirit would be *abundant* ('I will pour out'), that it would be non-selective or *general,* as regards the nationalities and status of the recipients ('all mankind . . . sons and daughters . . . even on the . . . servants') and that it would be accompanied by special signs and experiences (prophesyings, dreams, visions, wonders in the sky and on the earth).

There was nothing new, of course, in prophesying, dreams and visions, and these aspects of the promise in Joel actually seem to link the promise of the Spirit with His Old Testament manifestations. It is as if God were saying that what the Jewish nation had seen in limited fashion would one day be given in abundance and without discrimination. What they had received in measure would then be dispensed without measure. Abundance, therefore, and generality would characterize the relationship of the Spirit to believers after Pentecost, and we are reminded of the way the apostle Paul marvels at the 'mystery of Christ', namely that even 'the Gentiles are fellow-heirs and . . . fellow-partakers of the promise in Christ Jesus through the gospel' (Eph. 3:4–6).

Isaiah refers to a future time when the Spirit would be 'poured out upon us from on high and . . . justice will dwell in the wilderness and righteousness will abide in the fertile field' (Isa. 32:15–18). The same theme is taken up again when, speaking through the same prophet, God says, 'I will pour out water on the thirsty land and streams on the dry ground: I will pour out My Spirit on your offspring, and My blessing on your descendants . . . This one will say, "I am the Lord's . . ." and another will write on his hand, "Belonging to the Lord" ' (Isa. 44:1–5).

These prophecies are similar in import to that of Joel, pointing as they do to an unprecedented abundance of blessing and the personal enjoyment of that blessing by a host of nonentities ('this one, another') who rejoice in belonging to God. This emphasis upon belonging is reminiscent of the New Testament concept of the sealing of the Spirit, since the act of impressing a seal signified, among other things, ownership by the sealer of the thing sealed. This matter will be considered further in chapter 7.

Finally among the prophetical books, we come to the important testimony of Ezekiel. We say 'important' because Ezekiel tells us very clearly of the new relationship that was one day to be established between God and His people, in and through the Holy Spirit. 'Thus says the Lord God, "I shall gather you from the peoples and assemble you out of the countries among which you have been scattered, and I shall give you the land of Israel . . . And I shall give them one heart, and shall put a new spirit within them. And I shall take the heart of stone out of their flesh and give them a heart of flesh, that they may walk in My statutes and keep My ordinances and do them. Then they will be My people, and I shall be their God" ' (Ezek. 11:17—20). 'I will give you a new heart and put a new spirit within you; and I will remove the heart of stone . . . And I will put My Spirit within you and cause you to walk in My statutes . . . And you will live in the land I gave to your forefathers; so you will be My people and I will be your God' (Ezek. 36:26—28).

In these passages, the prophet is plainly speaking of the national Israel but, as Paul explains in Romans 10—11, the *spiritual* blessings promised to Israel are to be fulfilled within the church of Christ ('There is no distinction between Jew and Greek . . .' Rom. 10:12). What therefore was promised to Israel must *also* logically be promised to the church at large, excepting, of course, the specifically territorial pro-phecies, which surely refer to the Jews alone. It follows then that Ezekiel's prophecies describe the relationship that would one day belong to all believers, including the national Israel when they turn to Christ in repentance and faith (Rom. 11:12, 15, 23, 26).

What then *is* the new relationship described by Ezekiel? It is simply that of the indwelling Spirit of God, bringing about the fruits of obedience and love ('a new heart'). Because God would dwell in them by His Holy Spirit, they would be His people, and He their God, in a manner that could never be true under the old covenant. Notice again that this indwelling of the Spirit was to be *universal* among the people of God and not selective of a chosen few. Once again we observe that the indwelling Spirit is a definitive characteristic of the new relationship between God and men ushered in by the gospel of Christ. It is the Spirit within that causes believers to 'walk in [God's] statutes . . . to observe [His] ordinances' (Ezek. 36:27). It is His indwelling that *creates* the relationship described by the words: 'My people . . . their God'. It is therefore not possible to envisage a situation in which men believe the gospel, are born of the Spirit, and follow Christ obediently without having received the Holy Spirit. It is only *by* that Spirit's indwelling, says Ezekiel, that they become God's people and can live in obedience to Him. As Romans 8:2–4 puts it, 'The law of the Spirit of life in Christ Jesus has set you free from the law of sin and death . . . that the requirement of the Law might be fulfilled in us who . . . walk . . . according to the Spirit.' We conclude that all who are regenerate, and are therefore God's people and children, are indwelt by the Spirit of God.

The Spirit and the believer in Acts

Many of the references in Acts will be better dealt with in the following chapter on the baptism of the Spirit, but we shall here consider a number of verses that bear directly on the relationship issue.

In Acts 1:8 Jesus tells His disciples, 'You shall receive power when the Holy Spirit has come upon you; and you shall be My witnesses . . .' Here Christ employs the familiar language of the Old Testament, according to which the Spirit 'came upon' the servants of God to equip them for special service. Since service is also in view in the first chapter of Acts it is not surprising that this terminology of 'anointing' is also employed there. By the same token, however, there is nothing in these words to indicate that Pentecost would be an event unparalleled in Old Testament times. Continuity with the pre-Pentecostal operation of the Spirit, rather than the uniqueness of the Pentecostal baptism, is emphasized in this passage, therefore.

In the account of the Day of Pentecost itself, of course, Peter makes it clear enough that this is the long-awaited visitation prophesied by Joel and others and not just another incident of Old Testament supervention. The words used to describe the disciples' experience are not, however, altogether unfamiliar in the pre-Pentecostal era, for, we read, 'They

were all filled with the Holy Spirit' (Acts 2:4). The same
expression is, of course, used both of Bezalel (Exod. 31:3)
and John the Baptist.

The disciples in Acts were 'filled' with the Spirit not only
on the Day of Pentecost but on several subsequent occasions.
Thus in Acts 4:31 we read, 'When they had prayed, the
place . . . was shaken, and they were all filled with the Holy
Spirit, and began to speak the word of God with boldness.'
Similarly, Peter was filled afresh with the Spirit as he was
brought before the Jewish authorities charged with preaching the resurrection of Christ (Acts 4:8), as was Stephen
when he faced the ultimate test of martyrdom (Acts 7:55)
and Paul as he met the challenge of the sorcerer, Elymas
(Acts 13:9).

In all these instances we find men who had previously
received or been filled with the Spirit (in Stephen's case we
are specifically told that he was habitually 'full of faith and
the Holy Spirit', Acts 6:5), being filled anew in the face of
some special need or demand. Clearly, the term 'filled with
the Spirit' can signify both a continuing condition and a
special visitation of the Spirit upon one who is already
habitually filled. We have already seen in our discussion of
the pre-Pentecostal situation that the supervention ('coming
upon') of the Spirit was imbued with this double significance
in Old Testament times. We may also notice that the special
fillings of the Spirit could be repeated several times in the
experience of a single person (for example Peter in Acts 2:4;
4:8; 4:31 and Paul in Acts 9:17; 13:9).

The abiding fulness of the Holy Spirit, as distinct from
these sudden and special fillings, is mentioned several times
in the book of Acts. We have already referred to Stephen,
who was chosen as a deacon because he was 'full of faith
and of the Holy Spirit'. This statement clearly implies a
continuing or habitual condition, but also suggests that
Stephen, together with his fellow deacons (Acts 6:3), might
have been outstanding in this respect. Similarly, Barnabas
is described as 'a good man, and full of the Holy Spirit and
of faith' (Acts 11:24), while the disciples at Antioch in
Pisidia were 'continually filled with joy and with the Holy
Spirit' (Acts 13:52).

The basic relationship of the Holy Spirit to the believer

revealed in these references seems to be that of a habitual indwelling fulness which may, however, have been enjoyed in varying degrees by different people. This latter suggestion can be inferred from the fact that certain individuals, like the deacons chosen in Acts 6 and Barnabas, were *recognizably* full of the Spirit and, by implication perhaps, others were not. Paul's exhortation to the Ephesians to 'be filled with the Spirit' (Eph. 5:18) is relevant at this point. Such an exhortation obviously implies both that Christians may indeed be filled with the Holy Spirit (the verb employed suggesting an ongoing condition) and that they may also neglect to be so filled. If Christians can be commanded or exhorted to be filled, we may reasonably claim that to be filled habitually with the Spirit is the norm for believers and that all children of God possess the indwelling Spirit so that this norm might be realized.

In contrast to this habitual fulness, the special 'fillings' discussed above seem to have been of a rather different kind, representing an initiative of the Holy Spirit Himself as and when particular demands were made upon God's servants. At such times the Spirit came upon these men in a manner very similar to the superventions experienced by Gideon, Samson, the Old Testament prophets, Elizabeth and Zacharias. These superventions equipped them for particular acts of prophecy or service, just as the special fillings of the Spirit recorded in Acts provided power in the face of demanding situations.

We cannot leave Acts without discussing one account which appears to contradict our earlier suggestion that the Spirit indwells all post-Pentecostal believers from the time of their regeneration. This account, which we will call the 'Samaritan episode', is found in Acts 8:5–24 and relates how the gospel was brought to Samaria through the preaching of Philip. This is one of the five accounts in Acts of outpourings or effusions of the Spirit, all of which we shall be looking at in the next chapter. We single out this episode, however, because it is the one undebatable case in which, *after* Pentecost, men received the gift of the Holy Spirit some considerable time after their conversion to Christ and baptism in His name. We read, 'They believed Philip preaching the good news about the kingdom of God and the name of Jesus Christ, [and] they were being baptized, men and women alike' (Acts 8:12). 'Now when the apostles in Jerusalem heard that Samaria had received the word of God, they sent them Peter and John, who came down and prayed for them, that they might receive the Holy Spirit. For He had not yet fallen upon any of them; they had simply been baptized in the name of the Lord Jesus. Then they began laying their hands on them, and they were receiving the Holy Spirit' (Acts 8:14—17). We are not told what visible manifestations attended the giving of the Spirit in this case but obviously there were some outward signs, since 'Simon *saw* that the Spirit was bestowed through the laying on of hands' (Acts 8:18)

Whatever the details may have been, we have here a clear instance of baptized believers who had not received the Spirit until the apostles laid hands upon them. Note that their failure to do so is in no way blamed upon them. They were not disobedient in any respect, nor were they ill taught or ignorant concerning the gospel. 'The gift of God', as Peter calls the Holy Spirit in verse 20, was simply withheld from these people, apparently as an act of sovereign intent. This passage cannot, therefore, be used to imply that Christians have to fulfil certain conditions before they receive the Spirit.

The explanation of this episode will be considered further in our next chapter. At this point, however, we may notice that the 'two-level' experience of these Samaritan believers is identical to that of the Lord's own disciples before and after Pentecost. The simplest way to reconcile the Samaritan episode with other Scriptures is, therefore, to view it as a 'Samaritan Pentecost', that is a once-for-all historical event wholly similar to the Day of Pentecost itself and having exactly the same significance for the Samaritans as did Pentecost for the Jewish church.

Pentecostals, Charismatics and Reformed Sealers would, of course, deny this strictly historical interpretation of the Samaritan episode and consider it rather as a typical example of the normal operation of the Holy Spirit coming first in regeneration and later in the baptism of the Spirit. We must defer consideration of this argument till later.

The Spirit and the believer in the Epistle to the Romans

The Epistles are of special significance to our enquiry because of their doctrinal character, which is distinct from the historical character of Acts. This does not mean, of course, that we cannot derive doctrine from Acts, for 'all Scripture is inspired by God and profitable for teaching . . .' (2 Tim. 3:16). Pentecostals and Charismatics sometimes protest, justifiably, when attempts are made to devalue Acts as a source of valid information concerning the work of the Holy Spirit in believers and the church. Nevertheless, the character of any part of Scripture always has a bearing on the use we make of it, and it evidently does not follow that events recorded historically must necessarily be normative for the church today. An obvious example is the uniqueness of the apostles, who were witnesses to the physical resurrection of Christ and thus, by definition, not a continuing order in the church (see chapter 11). Thus the Epistles are particularly inportant in establishing normative principles and doctrine, and none more so than Paul's letter to the believers at Rome.

We begin in Romans 5:1–5 where Paul summarizes the blessings of justification by faith. These blessings include 'peace with God through our Lord Jesus Christ', access into 'grace', the 'hope of the glory of God', perseverance, character and the ability to rejoice in tribulation. Developing the idea of the believer's hope in God, Paul continues, 'And hope does not disappoint; because the love of God has been poured out within our hearts through the Holy Spirit who was given to us' (Rom. 5:5). If we ask who Paul means by 'us', our question is answered by the very next sentence: 'For while we were still helpless . . . Christ died for the ungodly' (Acts 5:6). Paul is clearly speaking of all converted sinners.

Paul's meaning appears to be as follows. Hope is one of the great benefits of justification, for the believer looks forward to sharing the glory of his Saviour throughout eternity 'Whom He justified, these He also glorified' (Rom. 8:30). But some might consider this great hope to be mere wishful thinking, a self-delusion of future grandeur on the part of the Christian, since the thing hoped for is not yet possessed. If this were so, the believer would rightly be 'ashamed' of his hope (A.V.) or 'disappointed' with it (NASB). But this cannot be the case because God has given 'the Holy Spirit of promise . . . as a pledge of our inheritance' (Eph. 1:14; see also 2 Cor. 1:22; 5:5). This guarantees that our hope of future glory is not an empty dream but a secure anticipation. The reason Christians are not ashamed of their hope, therefore, is that 'the Holy Spirit was given to us', and manifests His presence unmistakably by pouring out the love of God within our hearts. Later, in Romans 15:13, Paul prays, 'May the God of hope fill you with all joy and peace in believing that you may abound in *hope* by the power of the Holy Spirit.' Romans 5:1—5 seems to propose unequivocally that all who have been 'justified by faith' (v. 1) have also had 'the Holy Spirit . . . given to [them]' (v. 5). Otherwise they would be saved but, at the same time, deprived of the Christian's great hope, whereas Paul declares, 'In hope we have been saved' (Rom. 8:24). Hope and salvation appear inseparable in Scripture and it follows that the pledge of the Spirit, which alone secures that hope, must also be a concomitant of salvation rather than a divine 'afterthought'.

The Spirit manifests His presence by pouring into our hearts the love of God, says Romans 5:5. It is clear that the believer is fully aware of the indwelling Holy Spirit. He is aware, particularly, of a divine love directed both towards Christ and the Father and also towards his fellow men, especially his fellow believers. This last-named love is, indeed, one of the evidences of regeneration. 'We know that we have passed out of death into life,' declares John, 'because we love the brethren' (1 John 3:14). We are driven to conclude that those who know nothing of the love of God 'shed abroad' in their hearts, (as the Authorized Version translates Romans 5:5), are not only lacking the 'sealing of the Spirit' or His baptism, but also lack salvation itself.

Romans 8

We come next to what is probably the greatest single dissertation upon the Holy Spirit in the New Testament, namely the eighth chapter of Romans. In the previous chapter Paul is concerned with the principle or law of sin which 'indwells' the human soul (Rom. 7:17) and how we, as believers, may escape its power. 'Who will set me free', he cries, 'from the body of this death?' (Rom. 7:24.) He provides his own answer in Romans 8:2: 'For the law of the Spirit of life in Christ Jesus has set you free from the law of sin and of death.' Thus the Holy Spirit is introduced into the argument in the role of an indwelling principle which liberates those who are 'in Christ' from that other indwelling principle, sin. As a consequence, the sinner, who was previously incapable of keeping God's law, is now able to fulfil the requirements of that law, not by human effort but by following the leading of the indwelling Spirit (or walking according to the Spirit, as Romans 8:4 puts it).

Paul then proceeds to enlarge upon the essential difference between regenerate and unregenerate people (Rom. 8:5—9). The regenerate man is no longer 'in the flesh', that is, guided by the law or principle of sin that indwells the natural mind and body. Rather he is 'in the Spirit' (Rom. 8:9). What does it mean to be 'in the Spirit'? An explanation follows immediately in the same verse: 'You are . . . in the Spirit if indeed the Spirit of God dwells in you.' The believer, therefore, is one who is distinguished from the unsaved person by one essential characteristic, namely he is indwelt by God's Holy Spirit. This assertion is reiterated by way of emphasis in the sentence that follows: 'But if anyone does *not* have the Spirit of Christ, he does not belong to Him.'

You will notice that I have assumed that the Spirit of God and the Spirit of Christ are one and the same, as indeed the natural reading of this passage would indicate. Verse 11 reinforces this understanding as it continues, 'But if the Spirit of Him who raised Jesus from the dead [that is, God] dwells in you . . .' It is hardly conceivable that Paul would confuse his readers by referring in such rapid succession to the 'Spirit of God', the 'Spirit of Christ' and the 'Spirit of Him who raised Christ', unless these different titles referred to the same Person throughout.

However, Pentecostals generally maintain that the Spirit of Christ is *not* the same as the Spirit of God. Some suggest that the Spirit of Christ is simply a principle imparted to the believer on conversion and that the Holy Spirit Himself does not indwell the Christian until the latter has, subsequently, received a 'baptism in the Spirit'. Others take a more moderate line, arguing that the Holy Spirit does come to the believer at regeneration, but only in the *role* of the Spirit of Christ. He then comes again in His own right, as the Holy Spirit, at and after the Pentecostal baptism.

However, neither of these attempts to make a distinction between the Spirit of Christ and the Spirit of God are really supportable. Firstly, as we have demonstrated already from John 14:16—24 and other Scriptures, Christ is in the believer only *by* the indwelling of the *Paracletos*, the Holy Spirit. To speak of Christ coming into the believer's heart without the *Paracletos* also coming is to make nonsense of the teaching of John 14. 'The Spirit of truth . . . will be in you. I will not leave you orphans; I will come to you . . . In that day you shall know that I am . . . in you' (John 14:17—20). We have also seen that other passages, such as those in Galatians 4 and Romans 5, see the indwelling of the Holy Spirit as part and parcel of the miracle of regeneration, and not as some separate event.

However, the issue is surely settled once and for all by two statements made by the apostle Peter. In 1 Peter 1:11 we are told that 'the Spirit of Christ' was 'within' the writers of Old Testament prophecy, testifying to 'the sufferings of Christ and the glories to follow'. In 2 Peter 1:21 we read that these same prophecies were made as 'men moved by the Holy Spirit spoke from God'. Unless we are to suppose that there were two distinct divine agents at work in the inspiration of the Scriptures, we must surely conclude that the Spirit of Christ and the Holy Spirit are simply different titles of the one Spirit of God. This should not surprise us, for He has many titles in Scripture. In Romans 8 alone He is variously called the Spirit, the Spirit of life, the Spirit of adoption, the Spirit of God and the Spirit of Christ, while elsewhere He is the Spirit of truth, the Spirit of grace, the *Paracletos* and the Spirit of the Lord.

Exactly the same conclusion can be deduced from Acts 16, where Paul and his companions were 'forbidden by the Holy Spirit' to evangelize in Asia and, attempting to enter Bithynia, were not permitted to do so by 'the Spirit of Jesus' (Acts 16:6,7). It would need a very tortuous argument to suggest that this episode of negative guidance involved two different Spirits.

Returning to Romans 8, we may now see how straightforward is the argument of verses 9-11 once we allow that only
one Spirit is in view here. Let us paraphrase the verses, simply
retaining 'the Spirit' but dropping His various descriptive
titles. The paraphrase then reads, 'However, you are not in
the flesh but in the Spirit, if indeed the Spirit dwells in you.
But if anyone does *not* have the Spirit, he does not belong to
Christ. And if Christ *is* in you, by the indwelling Spirit, even
though the body is dead because of sin, yet the spirit is alive
because of Christ's righteousness. And if the Spirit dwells in
you, God who raised Christ Jesus from the dead will also give
life even to your mortal bodies through His Spirit who indwells you.' Thus Paul asserts that those in whom Christ
dwells by His Spirit have spiritual life *now*, in spite of the
fact that their bodies are 'dead', that is, still subject to mortality and corruption (see v. 21). That is not all, however.
The indwelling Spirit is also the seal or guarantee of a future
physical quickening or resurrection of the believer, just as
Christ Himself was raised physically from the dead. ('As in
Adam all die, so also in Christ all shall be made alive. But
each in his own order: Christ the first fruits, after that those
who are Christ's at His coming' (1 Cor. 15:22, 23)). The Holy
Spirit Himself will be the agent of this resurrection, just as He
is now its guarantee.

Paul continues to develop his vision of the Christian's
future. The glory of this future resides in the fact that the
believer is a child, or son, of God. Almost the entire chapter
turns on this concept of sonship and it is the key which un-
locks the meaning of the argument. The chief consequence of
the Spirit's indwelling, quite apart from any gifts or quality
of life He may impart to the believer, is that the one who has
received Him is *thereby* confirmed to be a child of God. 'For
all who are being led by the Spirit of God, these are sons of
God. For you have not received a spirit of slavery . . . but the
Spirit of adoption as sons, by which we cry out, "Abba!
Father"! The Spirit Himself bears witness with our spirit
that we *are* children of God' (vv. 14—16 mg.,). Indeed the
passage seems to indicate that sonship is not only confirmed
by, but actually consists of, the possession of the indwelling
Spirit. It is 'because you are sons', says the apostle in Galatians 4:6, that 'God has sent forth the Spirit of His Son into

our hearts crying, "Abba! Father"!'. There is, of course, cause and effect here. We are sons, or children of God, primarily because God 'foreknew' and 'predestined (us) to be conformed to the image of His Son, that He might be the first-born among many brethren' (Rom. 8:29). The original or ultimate *cause* of sonship, therefore, is the electing love of God. The coming of the Spirit to a believer is a *consequence* of this election, as Galatians 4:6 explains. But it is equally true that the Spirit's indwelling is a cause of our sonship, albeit a contingent and effectual cause rather than an ultimate one. That is, the Spirit's indwelling makes *actual,* in time and in human experience, what God has previously determined would transpire.

To establish and confirm the sonship of the believer is, then, the most important purpose of the Spirit's indwelling and against this everything else that He does pales by comparison. But His other works in the believer are also important and we find many of them enumerated here in Romans 8. The second most significant work of the Holy Spirit is a consequence of the first — namely, that He will one day deliver God's children from the corruption of physical death. We have already considered this, but it does no harm to emphasize what is taught here. For, we read, 'The anxious longing of the creation waits eagerly for the revealing of the sons of God . . . in hope that the creation itself will be set feee from its slavery to corruption into the freedom of the glory *of the children of God'* (Rom. 8:19—22). The future deliverance of God's people from physical mortality and their glorification (see v. 30), will signal a new world order in which the whole creation will also be released from corruption into a freedom and glory, not of its own, but of the glorified church. In what way is this future work of the Spirit a 'consequence' of our sonship, as stated earlier? In the sense, surely, that Christ Himself could not be held by death (Acts 2:24), because of His divine nature. In the same way, those in whom the Spirit of God dwells and who, by consequence, have 'become partakers of the divine nature, having escaped' natural corruption (2 Peter 1:4), must also eventually be delivered from physical death and its effects *because of what they are.*

Thirdly, we see, flowing from His primary role as the Spirit of adoption, a sanctifying work of the Holy Spirit in the

believer. 'If, by the Spirit, you are putting to death the [sin-
ful] deeds of the body, you will live' (Rom. 8:13). Here the
believer has a part to play. He must recognize that he has an
obligation to live a life consistent with his new status as a son
of God, in spite of the fact that he still inhabits a body and
mind which are prone to sin (Rom. 8:12). It is he, therefore,
who must ever be 'putting to death' the sinful actions and
tendencies of his own 'old' nature. This is a large subject, but
all we have time to notice here is that the believer can do this
only 'by the Spirit' who indwells him. Once again we see that
'sonship' is the key to Paul's teaching on sanctification, since
it provides the motivation for a holy life. 'As obedient *children . . .*,' adjures Peter, 'be holy . . . in all your behaviour, because it is written, "You shall be holy, for I am holy." ' (1
Peter 1:13—17).

Fourthly, we see here the Spirit's work of assurance in the
believer. 'The Spirit Himself bears witness with our spirit that
we are children of God' (Rom. 8:16). A note of happy certainty is sounded in verse 15 as *by the Spirit* we are enabled
to cry out, 'Abba! Father!' This exclamation breathes a joy-
ful recognition that God is our Father and we are His children. It is uttered in the immediacy of the heart, an inner
witness by the Spirit of adoption that can no more be ra-
tionalized than it can be questioned. The child *knows* he is a
child because the indwelling Spirit reveals this to him, and he
exults in that knowledge. Again, therefore, assurance is
bound up with the relationship of sonship. It is because God
is our Father that we have certainty concerning the forgiveness of sin and our final salvation.

Fifthly, as we have already seen in Romans 5, we have
hope (that is, sure expectations) by the Spirit. Since we are
children, argues Paul, and are assured of this by the witness
of the Holy Spirit, we must also be heirs of God and fellow-
heirs with Christ (Rom. 8:17). It is sonship, and that alone,
which places us in this remarkable situation. No wonder Paul
declares, 'That the sufferings of this present time are not
worthy to be compared with the glory that is to be revealed to
us' (Rom. 8:18). As the apostle John states in simple but awe-
some terms, 'Beloved, now are we the sons of God, and it
doth not yet appear what we shall be: but we know that,
when he shall appear, we shall be like him' (1 John 3:2, A.V.)

Sixthly, it is in the context of this hope of future glory that we are told, 'The Spirit also helps our weakness' (Rom. 8:24–26). As we wait in weakness for the consummation of God's purpose for His children, for the 'revealing of the sons of God' (Rom. 8:19), as Paul puts it, we have the strengthening grace of the Spirit to keep and lead us. Likewise, during this period of earthly pilgrimage, we are assured by the same Spirit that 'God causes all things to work together for good to those who love God, to those who are called according to His purpose' (Rom. 8:28). We rest secure in the knowledge that God's purpose will bring all His children, *via* election and justification, to final glory along with Christ (Rom. 8:29, 30). Accordingly we 'overwhelmingly conquer' in the conflicts of life and discipleship (Rom. 8: 37), since nothing can come between the children and the Father's loving purposes in Christ (Rom. 8:38, 39).

The emphasis we wish to make here is that all these blessings are ours because of our sonship to God, and this sonship *consists* of the indwelling of the Spirit of adoption. The love of God, predestinating the believer to be conformed to the image of His Son (Rom. 8:29) is the ultimate cause of his sonship. But the gift of the indwelling Spirit is the contingent and effectual cause of the child-Father relationship. The Old Testament and pre-Pentecostal believers, though they 'gained approval through their faith, did not receive what was promised,' states Hebrews 11:39, 'because God had provided something better for us, so that apart from us they should not be made perfect'. We noticed in the last chapter the strong implication that they will eventually be made perfect, that is, they will eventually and posthumously attain the same status of sonship as do post-Pentecostal believers. But they did not attain it 'apart from us', that is, in their own earthly lifetime (apart, of course, from those who lived through Pentecost). John the Baptist serves as a good example here. Filled with the Holy Spirit throughout his life, he nevertheless never enjoyed the relationship with the Holy Spirit which makes the post-Pentecostal believer a son of God and a spiritual brother of Christ (Rom. 8:29). Thus the least in the kingdom of God is greater than John (Luke 7:28). But, implied Hebrews 11:39, he posthumously assumes this status of sonship *along with us* in the final

consummation of God's purposes. This is a very satisfying con-
conclusion, for while it shows clearly what the pre-Pentecostal
believer lacked, not having received the promise of the Spirit,
it also indicates that the heroes of faith, so celebrated in
Hebrews 11, do ultimately attain their full reward along with
ourselves, the heirs of the promise. And so it must surely be,
for it would be unthinkable that such as Abraham, held up
by the New Testament as a supreme exemplar of faith,
should finally be rejected by God or accorded a lower status
in His kingdom than the believers of today.

Finally, it is important to grasp fully the significance of
verses 29 and 30 of Romans 8. They tell us that God's redemption purpose, for each believer as well as for the church as a
whole, can be viewed as an unbroken (and unbreakable!)
chain. Beginning with God's eternal foreknowledge and predestination, it embraces the Christian's experience in time,
namely, his calling and justification by the gospel, and reaches
on to final glorification. This future state of glory is so secure
for the believer that Paul uses the past tense, speaking of it as
something already accomplished, as indeed it is, in the mind
of God. The final purpose of the whole chain of events is that
Christ 'might be the first-born among many brethren' (Rom.
8:29). God intends to gather around Him in the glory a vast
family of adopted children to whom He will have imparted
His nature by the indwelling of the Spirit of His Son. As in
the case of Christ Himself, this final glorification will be
attained *via* (and not without) a physical resurrection. Indeed,
although Paul asserts that we are already in this life the
children of God (v. 16), he also states (v. 23) that we are still
'waiting eagerly for our adoption as sons, the redemption of
our body'. This is not a contradiction, for the apostle sees
adoption as a *process*, begun in this life by the gift of sonship
and the Spirit of adoption, but consummated at Christ's
return by the resurrection or redemption of our physical
bodies in uncorruptible glory (see 1 Cor. 15:35—58). It is
clear, then, that the chain of God's purposes must be completed for every true believer. No link can be missing for any
of His children. Thus *all* the events and experiences described
by Paul in the earlier part of the chapter, being links in this
chain, must apply to every Christian. All believers must experience the power of the 'law of the Spirit of life' over-

coming the principle of indwelling sin (v. 4). All believers must be found 'putting to death the deeds of the body' (v. 13) with at least some degree of success. All believers must walk according to, or be led by, the Spirit (vv. 4, 5, 14). All believers are indwelt by the Spirit (vv. 9, 10). All believers receive the Spirit of adoption with His inner testimony to their sonship (vv. 15, 16). All believers are heirs of God (v. 17) and all will be raised physically, and delivered from corruptibility at Christ's return (vv. 18—23). All believers will share Christ's glory (v. 29). This, surely, is the essence of Paul's whole argument in Romans 8. It precludes any interpretation which applies some of the experiences related in this chapter to a special category of believers, namely, those who have received a baptism or sealing of the Spirit.

The Spirit and the believer in the Corinthian Epistles

In First Corinthians Paul introduces the subject of the Holy Spirit as early as the second chapter. He reminds his readers of the manner in which the gospel came to them. 'My message and my preaching', he declares, 'were not in persuasive words of man's wisdom, but in demonstration of the Spirit and of power, that your faith should not rest on the wisdom of men but on the power of God' (1 Cor. 2:4, 5). The Corinthians, then, had experienced the power of the Spirit working upon their hearts as they came to faith in Christ. But did they actually *receive* the Spirit at that time? It would appear so from what follows, for Paul continues, 'We have received . . . the Spirit who is from God, that we might know the things freely given to us by God . . . But a natural man does not accept the things of the Spirit of God . . . he cannot understand them, because they are spiritually appraised . . . but he who is spiritual appraises all things' (1 Cor. 2:12—15). We may first notice that Paul speaks inclusively: 'We have received'. This might, of course, be a reference to Paul himself (a kind of 'royal we'), but this is most unlikely here since the apostle uses 'I' and 'my' at the beginning of both chapters 2 and 3. The 'we' passages in chapter 2, therefore, would appear to refer to believers in general, and this is supported by the similarity in wording between verse 12 of the present chapter ('Now we have received, not the spirit

of the world, but the Spirit who is from God') and Romans
8:15 ('For you have not received a spirit of slavery . . . but
the Spirit of adoption').

Accepting, then, that Paul is here including his readers
when he says, 'We have received,' does he not thereby imply
that *every* member of the Corinthian church is included?
After all, some converts might well have been added to their
number between the penning of the Epistle and its delivery
and Paul could hardly know anything of their experience of
the Spirit! If the receiving of the Spirit is a post-conversion
experience, should not Paul have said 'Some of us have received . . .'? The contrast drawn in these verses is between
the believer, to whom the Spirit has revealed the things
'freely given to us by God', and the 'natural man who does
not accept the things of the Spirit of God'. The latter knows
nothing of the Spirit or of God, having no spiritual dimension to his make-up.

This argument might be thought to be weakened by the
opening verses of chapter 3: 'And I, brethren could not
speak to you as spiritual men . . . for you are still fleshly'
(1 Cor. 3:1–3). Is Paul not here drawing a distinction between two levels of Christian experience? Might this not
imply that experiences outlined in chapter 2 are true of those
who have not only been born again but have *also* 'received
the Spirit that is from God'? This alternative interpretation
is ruled out completely by the conclusion of chapter 3, where
Paul addresses these 'fleshly' Christians, with their jealousy
and strife, in withering terms. 'Do you not know', he thun-
ders, 'that you are a temple [or sanctuary] of God, and that
the Spirit of God dwells in you?' (1 Cor. 3:16.) This admoni-
tion is repeated later in the Epistle, apparently to those who
were flirting with sexual immorality: 'Flee immorality . . . do
you not know that your body is a temple of the Holy Spirit
who is in you, whom you have from God, and that you are
not your own? For you have been bought with a price' (1
Cor. 6:18–20). Here, then, is no superior, 'Spirit-filled' category of believers, but rather the weak, the sinful and the immature among the Corinthians. Yet it is of *these* that Paul
asserts the reality of the indwelling Spirit. He even suggests
that they may have forgotten that the Spirit dwells within
them. 'Do you not know . . .?' he cries. In chapter 6 he goes

further, to *use* the fact that the Holy Spirit is within them to stir up his readers to resist sin and to warn them of the dire consequences of profaning the 'temple of God' (that is, their physical bodies). He does not say, 'If you sin God will not give you the indwelling Spirit.' Rather, he argues, *'Because* God has given you the Holy Spirit you must not sin.' The implication is clear, therefore, that all who have been 'bought with a price' (1 Cor. 6:20) are temples of the Holy Spirit. Note also, comparing 1 Corinthians 3:16 with 6:19, that the Christian's body is a temple both 'of God' and 'of the Holy Spirit'. This is consistent with our earlier discussion on John 14—16, in which we argued that God the Father and God the Son indwell the believer *by* the Spirit and not independently of Him.

A further statement of interest is to be found in 1 Corinthians 6:9—11: 'Do you not know that the unrighteous shall not inherit the kingdom of God? . . . And such were some of you, but you were washed . . . sanctified . . . justified in the name of the Lord Jesus Christ, and in the Spirit of our God.' The reference is clearly to salvation, regeneration and cleansing from sin. Even the term 'sanctification', which normally refers to a progressive growth in grace, probably here signified the initial setting apart of these believers from their former lives of sin to the service of God. They had been washed from sin and justified, not only in the name of Christ, but also 'in the Spirit of our God'. What does this mean? Paul explains his terminology in Romans: 'You are . . . in the Spirit, if indeed the Spirit of God dwells in you' (Rom. 8:9). Assuming that the apostle is using these terms consistently (and there is no reason to suppose otherwise), this can only mean that the person who is washed from sin and justified in the name of Christ is thereby 'in the Spirit' and thus indwelt by the third Person of the Godhead.

Paul's discourse on the charismata or spiritual gifts occupies three chapters of 1 Corinthians, namely chapters 12 to 14, but will not be dealt with here since it relates more directly to the subjects of chapters 10—12. We move on, therefore, to 2 Corinthians, which has much to teach us about believers' relationship to the Spirit of God.

We begin in 2 Corinthians 1:21, 22, where the apostle explains the basis of the Christian's security: 'Now He who es-

tablishes us with you in Christ and anointed us is God, who
also sealed us and gave us the Spirit in our hearts as a pledge
[or down payment].' As we saw earlier, Paul's terminology
here is inclusive — that is, the things spoken of apply by implication to all believers. There is no suggestion that any
member of the Corinthian church might be excluded from
the benefits referred to, or that these statements are restricted
to a certain class of believers. The generality of Paul's intention can, in fact, be demonstrated from the text itself since
the word 'establish' means to make firm or secure. This is
not a reference to a feeling or assurance of security but to
the *fact* of our security in Christ. (The personal assurance
of this fact is the subject of the words that follow: 'Who also
gave us . . . a pledge'. The whole purpose of a pledge or down
payment is to provide assurance of the thing promised.) Thus
we see that Paul is addressing all those who have, as a matter
of *fact,* been made secure in Christ, and this is surely true of
every believer.

But if this is so, it follows that every believer has also been
'anointed' and 'sealed' by God, and given the Spirit in his
heart. Although anointing, sealing and the gift of the Spirit as
a pledge are here spoken of as three distinct blessings, it is
clear that they refer to three different aspects of the same
essential event, for elsewhere Paul refers to the believer being
'sealed in Him *with* the Holy Spirit of promise, who is given
as a pledge' (Eph. 1:13). Thus sealing and the gift of the
Spirit are one and the same, while anointing, by which the
believer posesses direct knowledge of spiritual truth, (1 John
2:20, 27), also relates to the ministry of the Spirit as explained in John 14:26 ('He will teach you all things . . .').
Thus we conclude that *all* believers are anointed and sealed
by the Spirit, and have the Spirit in their hearts as a pledge of
God's future intentions for them. This subject will be taken
up at greater length in chapter 7.

Moving on to chapter 3 of this Epistle, Paul describes the
Corinthian believers as his 'letters of commendation', not
written with paper and ink but 'with the Spirit of the living
God . . . on tablets of human hearts' (2 Cor. 3:1—3). The
apostle did not need men to authenticate his ministry, for
the Corinthians themselves were giving evidence of its power
and genuineness. It was a 'ministry of the Spirit' that he

exercised among them and as a result, Paul's converts enjoyed both the liberty and the transforming work of the Spirit of the Lord (2 Cor. 3:8, 17, 18). Not only, therefore, does the Holy Spirit indwell our hearts, providing knowledge of God, enabling us to serve Him and guaranteeing His promises; He also carries on a transforming work changing us into the image of Christ from one degree of glory to another, as we behold Him in the Scriptures (2 Cor. 3:15—18).

The Spirit and the believer in Galatians

The importance of this Epistle in any discussion of our subject is witnessed by the fact that we have already had cause to quote from Galatians in considering previous portions of Scripture. Let us now, however, take a longer look at the teaching of this letter.

The similarity between Galatians and Romans at certain points is quite unmistakable, and the reason is not difficult to discover. In Romans Paul deals with the profound difference between law and grace. By attempting to obey rules for human conduct, even God's own rules, no one can be justified in God's eyes. This is not because the law is at fault, but because we are moral captives to the principle of sin that indwells all the sons of Adam. No matter how good the law may be, therefore, we are incapable of keeping it, being ruled by sin. Indeed, the better the law we try to obey, the greater is our failure, because the greater is the antagonism of sin towards that law. The only answer to this problem is grace, namely that God gives to us as a free gift, a new and more powerful inner principle, which is able to neutralize and overcome the principle of sin. This new principle or power is 'the law of the Spirit of life'. It is mediated to us by the indwelling Spirit of God and received by faith. Such is the teaching of Romans.

Now the Galatians had embraced this gospel. They had, says Paul, 'begun by the Spirit' (Gal. 3:3). But certain false teachers had persuaded them that in addition to faith in Christ and reliance upon His indwelling Spirit, they also needed to keep the Jewish law if they were to be justified before God. They needed, therefore, to be told in no uncertain terms and with the considerable vehemence exhibited here by Paul, what he had already expounded in Romans: namely, that justification by obedience to law was both impossible and a contradiction of the gospel of faith. 'For if righteousness comes through the Law, then Christ died needlessly' (Gal. 2:21).

The first point to notice is that Paul is preoccupied, throughout the first five chapters of Galatians at least, with the means by which sinners obtain justification in the sight of God. Until verse 13 of chapter 5 he does not advance beyond this question. The subject of justification is his sole concern. This is important, for it is in this context that we read that the Galatians had 'begun by the Spirit', had 'received the Spirit by hearing with faith' and had been 'provided' with the Spirit (Gal. 3:2–5). These benefits, therefore, had been theirs from the beginning, from the time they first trusted in Christ, and the implication is that they received the Spirit of God as an integral part of their initial justification. As late in the Epistle as Galatians 5:5, the apostle contrasts those who seek to be justified by law with those who look for righteousness 'through the Spirit, by faith', suggesting that all true believers fall into the latter category. What is implied in Galatians 3 and 5, is made explicit in chapter 4, where the subject of adoption is raised. Remember that Paul is still dealing with the means of justification or redemption. 'When the fulness of the time came,' he writes, 'God sent forth His Son . . . in order that He might redeem those who were under the Law, that we might receive the adoption as sons' (Gal. 4:4, 5). Christ came, therefore, not simply to justify and redeem. Redemption was not an end in itself but rather a means to an end. God's ultimate purpose in sending Christ was not to redeem men but to adopt them as His sons! The picture is not difficult to grasp, for when a benefactor entered an ancient slave market to redeem a slave, he did not do so for the sake of the act of redemption itself. His purpose was to transform both the status and the expectations of the former slave. He had an eye to the slave's future quality of life and standing in society. Thus God's purpose is to transform the *status* of the sinner, liberating him from slavery to sin, exalting him to sonship and making him an heir of God. 'Therefore you are no longer a slave but a son; and if a son, then an heir through (the gracious act) of God' (Gal. 4:7, mg.).

The identical argument is employed in Romans 8:17, as we saw earlier.

Redemption, which by definition applies to every believer, is therefore the doorway to sonship. Redemption, or justification, is the work of God and sonship is the status secured for the believer by that work. 'And,' continues Paul, 'because you are sons, God has sent forth the Spirit of His Son into our hearts, crying, "Abba! Father!"' (Gal. 4:6.) There is no suggestion of delay here. The coming of the Spirit of adoption to the new-born child of God cannot, by any logic, be postponed. That would be like saying that a baby new-born into the human race had to live for some time before being imbued with a human spirit. There is not the slightest suggestion in Scripture that the adopted child of God is left in a kind of spiritual twilight awaiting the coming of the *Spirit of* adoption at some later stage in his development.

But even if we were tempted to divorce the act of adoption from the coming of the Spirit of adoption, Galatians 4:6 forbids us to do so. For it specifies one condition, and only one condition, for the sending forth into our hearts of the Spirit of God's Son: namely, that we be sons! Once that condition is fulfilled, says Paul, the Spirit comes to us. As soon as we are sons, just so soon does God send forth His Spirit into our hearts. We may again use the illustration of human birth. A new-born child begins to breathe once it has been delivered and the onset of breathing is announced by the baby's cry. There is a sequence of events, namely delivery followed by the commencement of breathing, but both events, as well as many others, are all part of a single process, that of live birth. So there is a sequence in spiritual birth. The process of redemption issues, without interruption, into sonship and forthwith the Spirit of adoption, the breath of God, enters the nostrils of the new-born believer. Immediately, His indwelling presence is announced to the believer's heart by the cry of 'Abba, Father'.

This, then, appears to be the import of Galatians 4. I do not say that an alternative interpretation is impossible, but I do say that it would be forced. What cannot be gainsayed is that no condition other than sonship is laid down for the sending forth of the Spirit into the believer's heart. It is also clear that this sending forth is a known and felt experience

for the believer, bringing, at the very least, an assurance of
his new status as a child of God.

Eventually, at verse 13 of chapter 5, Paul does move on
from justification to the life of faith. How should a Christian,
who has been justified, conduct himself in the church and in
the world? In answering this question the apostle uses arguments similar to those employed in Romans 8, and these can
be summed up in the words of Galatians 5:25: 'If we live by
the Spirit, let us also walk by [or follow] the Spirit.' The
opening 'if' does not convey doubt but rather bears the
meaning of 'since' or 'seeing that'. This is important teaching
for it implies that all believers *do* live by the Spirit in the
sense that they owe their spiritual life to His indwelling. It
also makes clear, however, that such persons do not necessarily 'follow' the Spirit in His gracious leading (Gal. 5:18).
There is nothing automatic about walking in the Spirit, for
otherwise there would be no need for Paul to exhort his
readers to do so, as he does repeatedly (Gal. 5:16, 25; 6:4, 9).
Those who 'live by the Spirit' have a solemn responsibility to
'walk by the Spirit', to produce 'the fruit of the Spirit' (Gal.
5:22) and to 'sow' to the Spirit (Gal. 6:8). Militating against
such a walk is, of course, the 'flesh' or principle of sin which
still resides in the believer and which constantly opposes the
leading of the indwelling Spirit (Gal. 5:17).

We conclude, then, that believers, by virtue of their regeneration, 'live by the Spirit'. That is, they enjoy spiritual
life in consequence of His indwelling. But the degree to
which His indwelling produces fruit in their lives is to some
extent their own responsibility. However, no Christian can
presume to accept salvation and neglect to follow the Holy
Spirit's leading in his daily life, since anyone who attempts
such a course of action is likely to discover he is not, after
all, a child of God (Gal. 5:19–21; 6:7, 8). The believer who
understands that he is indwelt by the Spirit of God and who
cultivates, or 'sows to', the Spirit is guaranteed victory over
the sin that also dwells within him (and which will remain
within him as long as he is in the body).

The Spirit and the believer in Ephesians

We have already had occasion to refer to Ephesians 1:13, 14 but let us now look more closely at these verses. In this chapter Paul defines, in great and glorious detail, God's purpose for His children. 'He chose us in [Christ]', declares the apostle, 'before the foundation of the world . . . He predestined us to adoption as sons through Jesus Christ to Himself' (Eph. 1:4, 5). This teaching is exactly the same as found in Romans 8 and Galatians 4:5—6, showing again that God's ultimate purpose is to cause every believer to inherit glory as a child of God and a co-heir with Christ Himself.

It is no accident that further teaching on the indwelling of the Holy Spirit is again found in the context of God's final purposes. This is the case both in Romans 8 and Galatians 4, and it begins to emerge with the added force of repetition that the indwelling of the Spirit is an essential and integral part of the whole plan of salvation. Indeed, the restatement of this fact in Epistle after Epistle only underlines what is perfectly clear from any single passage, namely that the gift of the Holy Spirit is the pledge or guarantee that God's final purposes will surely come to pass. 'Having also believed, you were sealed in Him with the Holy Spirit of promise, who is given as a pledge of our inheritance, with a view to the redemption of God's own possession, to the praise of His glory' (Eph. 1:13, 14).

Taking the teaching of Romans, Galatians and Ephesians together, therefore, we see a picture building up in which the gift to the believer of the indwelling Spirit fulfils a variety of functions.

1. He is the Spirit of promise, that is, His coming fulfils God's ancient and pre-Pentecostal promises.
2. He is the Spirit of God's Son, and in that capacity is the effectual cause of our sonship to God. 'You were sealed *in Him*' (Eph. 1:13).
3. He is the seal or mark of God's ownership of the believer. We are 'God's own possession' (Eph. 1:14).
4. He is the pledge or earnest of the promised inheritance, a kind of down payment guaranteeing that God's ultimate purpose will be fulfilled for every one of His children.

5. He witnesses within the believer's heart to this effect, assuring us of our status both as children and heirs of God.

6. He is the effectual cause, not only of our sonship, but also of our sanctification and our glorification.

It is little wonder, then, that after setting out these things Paul turns to prayer, asking that his readers might be enlightened to '*know* what is the hope of His calling', and 'what are the riches of the glory of His inheritance in the saints'. He wants them to recognize in full the nature of the salvation which God has provided in Christ and makes effective by His Spirit.

Chapter 2 of the Epistle develops the corporate aspect of our salvation, emphasizing particularly the unity of Jew and Gentile in the church. Through Christ, asserts Paul, 'both have . . . access in one Spirit to the Father' (Eph. 2:18). The apostle then presents, in the closing verses of the chapter, one of the classic metaphors of the church: 'The whole building, being fitted together, is growing into a holy temple in the Lord; in whom you also are being built together into a dwelling of God in the Spirit' (Eph. 2:19–22). Not only does the Spirit of God dwell in the individual believer, whose body is His temple or sanctuary (1 Cor. 6:19), but He also dwells in the church corporately. There is surely a continuity between these two pictures. The Spirit does not dwell in the church *independently* of His dwelling in those who make up the church. It is rather *because* He indwells believers that He also can be said to reside in the church. That is why Paul can make a natural transition from the teaching of Ephesians 1: 13, which plainly refers to the individual, to that of Ephesians 2:22, where the whole company of believers is in view. This is not to empty the concept of a corporate indwelling of its meaning. The corporate indwelling has a significance over and above that of the individual's experience. 'The church . . . is [Christ's] body, the fulness of Him who fills all in all' (Eph. 1:23), and that church has a corporate existence and a corporate role in God's purposes. The point to grasp is that the church consists of its members, just as a human family consists of the individuals that make it up. *It* exists because *they* are of the same flesh and blood. In the same way the church is the habitation of the Spirit because the individuals of whom it is composed are also, separately His sanctuaries, His temples. Any other interpretation of the Spirit's habitation of the church creates enormous problems because the *locus* or place of His residence has then to be defined apart from the members themselves.

It is appropriate, while we are considering the corporate relationship of Christians to the Holy Spirit, to refer forward to some verses bearing on this matter in chapter 4 of this Epistle. That chapter expands at length upon the unity and corporate nature of the church. It is Christ's body, and all that God has given by way of gifts to the church are for its blessing and edification. The particular point for us to notice, however, is Paul's statement that the unity that Christians have among themselves is 'the unity of the Spirit' (Eph. 4:3). This they are urged to 'preserve . . . in the bond of peace'. Notice that they are to preserve it, not to seek it or establish it, for it is something they already possess by virtue of their membership of the body of Christ. ('There is one body and one Spirit, just as you were called in one hope of your calling' Eph. 4:4.) This unity derives from the fact that each believer is 'in the Spirit', or indwelt by the Spirit. Heart answers to heart, therefore, as believers, all possessing the same Spirit of God, come together in the 'fellowship of the Spirit' (Phil. 2:1). Each child of God, being led by the Spirit of God, moves under His guidance in the same direction, sharing the same concerns and interests, serving the same Lord, interacting with his brothers and sisters in Christ in love and mutual joy. This, then, is the unity of the Spirit. But once again we are unable to ignore that other indwelling principle, namely sin, that wars against the Spirit, producing its evil fruit so eloquently described in Galatians 5:19–21. The jealousy, envy and dissension produced by sin will, in particular, disrupt and negate the unity of the Spirit if allowed to do so. Thus it is necessary for the Ephesians, and all Christians, to work at this task, or as Paul puts it, to be 'diligent to preserve the unity of the Spirit in the bond of peace', lest it be disrupted by sin.

In chapter 3 of the Epistle we again find Paul at prayer. This time he asks God that his readers might be 'strengthened with power through His Spirit in the inner man; so that Christ may dwell in [their] hearts through faith . . .' (Eph. 3:16, 17). At first sight this might suggest that Christ does not necessarily inhabit the believer's heart, for if He does, what need is there to pray for Him to do so? Some indeed suggest that such verses as Colossians 1:27 ('Christ in you, the hope of glory') do not apply to all Christians, but only to those who have received the baptism or sealing of the Spirit. Such a view, however, is not admissible in the light of 2 Corinthians 13:5. 'Test yourselves to see if you are in the faith; examine yourselves! Or do you not recognize this about yourselves, that Jesus Christ is in you — unless indeed you fail the test [or are disapproved]?' Here Paul states plainly that all Christians have Christ within and he cannot mean, therefore, that this is not the case when he prays in Ephesians 3. How, then, are we to understand the clause: 'That Christ *may* dwell in your hearts through faith'? The answer probably lies in the Greek word translated 'dwell', for it means literally to 'settle down in a home'. The word 'dwell' used of the indwelling Spirit in Romans 8 is a simpler word meaning to 'make home'. The word used in Ephesians 3:17 is a compound word which adds the dimension of permanance, settlement or rest. Paul does not therefore deny that Christ is already 'in' his readers' hearts, but rather prays that He may be thoroughly at home there. Expressed in terms of what was once a popular catch-phrase among Christians, he prays that Christ might not only be resident in their hearts, but President there also.

What is plain enough in this prayer is that Christ's indwelling is effected by the power of 'His Spirit in the inner man' (Eph. 3:16), and this accords with our previous conclusions that Christ and the Father come to the believer *by* the Spirit and not independently of Him. The Holy Spirit is here referred to in terms of the strength and power that He imparts as the believer seeks to enjoy the fulness of the indwelling Christ. It is surely in a further reference to the Spirit's indwelling that Paul adds his doxology: 'Now to Him who is able to do exceeding abundantly beyond all that we ask or think, according to *the power that works within us*, to Him be the glory' (Eph. 3:20, 21).

The fulness of Christian experience, then, is discovered as the Spirit of God, working powerfully in our hearts, makes actual to the believer Christ's indwelling and His surpassing love. It is by 'the power that works within us' that we come to know the breadth, length, height and depth of the love of Christ. That power is none other than the Holy Spirit. We have already seen Him as the indwelling principle working negatively in the conquest of sin (Rom. 8). We now see His inward power exercised positively in expanding the believer's capacity to lay hold upon and enjoy the fulness of God in Christ.

Our final text in Ephesians is a most important one. 'Do not get drunk with wine', exhorts the apostle, 'for that is dissipation, but be filled with the Spirit, speaking to one another in psalms and hymns and spiritual songs, singing and making melody with your heart to the Lord, always giving thanks for all things in the name of our Lord Jesus Christ to God, even the Father' (Eph. 5:18–20). We may notice here, for future reference, that the state of being filled with the Spirit is portrayed as a state of joy, even of exuberance. Perhaps it is with this in mind that it is contrasted with inebriation, for drunkeness brings a kind of false exuberance and liberty of spirit. It is one of the major claims of Pentecostals and Charismatics that their teaching leads Christians into the experience pictured here by Paul, and we must consider this claim in another chapter.

The Spirit and the believer in Thessalonians

First Thessalonians begins with a powerful introduction in which Paul recalls their response to his preaching when he first brought the gospel to them. 'Our gospel', he reminds them, 'did not come to you in word only, but also in power and in the Holy Spirit and with full conviction' (1 Thess. 1:5). As a consequence of this, he continues, 'You . . . received the word in much tribulation with the joy of the Holy Spirit' (1 Thess. 1:6). The role of the Spirit of God described here is twofold. Firstly, it was He who imparted such gracious power to the gospel preaching, causing the apostle's words to impact upon their hearts with the full force of spiritual conviction. But, secondly, their reception of those words was accompanied by a joy generated, not by their own emotions, but by the Spirit within them. It appears, then, that the fruit of the Spirit (love, *joy*, peace . . . see Galatians 5:22) began to appear in their lives from the very moment they received the word of the gospel. No wonder they 'became an example to all the believers in Macedonia and Achaia' (1 Thess. 1:7).

The gospel preached at Thessalonica must have contained reference to the unbreakable chain of divine purpose between justification and glorification, which we have had cause to notice so frequently in Paul's writings. This emerges as the apostle records how they had 'turned to God from idols to serve a living and true God, and to wait for His Son from heaven' (1 Thess. 1:10). Apostolic gospel preaching did not end with the forgiveness of sin and reconciliation to God, as is so often the case today. The *purpose* of God in saving men and women from their sins was emphasized, namely a full and final redemption, including the resurrection of the body at Christ's second coming (see 1 Cor. 15:53). It was natural, therefore, that they should not only turn from idolatry and serve God but also that they should look expectantly for Christ's return. Little wonder for, according to Paul, their future destiny was bound up with that return!

We have recalled this apostolic emphasis upon the total scheme of salvation because it constitutes the background to another important Scripture, this time in Second Thessalonians, where Paul writes as follows: 'God has chosen you from the beginning for salvation through sanctification by the Spirit and faith in the truth. And it was for this He called you through our gospel, that you may gain the glory of our Lord Jesus Christ' (2 Thess. 2:13, 14).

This is, of course, reminiscent of Romans 8 in its emphasis upon the unfolding purpose of God, from election, through calling and sanctification, to final glorification. But the chief reason for our interest is the role of the Holy Spirit in this process. It is by the Spirit, implies Paul, that they were sanctified or set apart as children of God. It does not seem sufficient to interpret this simply in terms of the sanctifying or purifying work of the Spirit in the believer, though no doubt that was also in Paul's mind. The word 'sanctified' is sometimes used in Scripture to signify the essential separation of the believer from the world and to God (see, for example, 1 Corinthians 1:2 and John 17:19, where Christ uses the word of Himself being set apart). Here, then, the Thessalonians' salvation is said to be *effected* or brought about through sanctification by the Spirit and faith in the truth. How does the Spirit sanctify or separate the believer to God? Surely it is by His indwelling, which transforms their status before God from being rebellious sinners to being sons and daughters of the Father. As Paul expresses it elsewhere in these Epistles, 'God has . . . called us . . . in sanctification' — not only unto sanctification. 'He who rejects this', continues the apostle, 'is not rejecting man but the God who gives His Holy Spirit to you' (1 Thess. 4:7, 8).

The Spirit and the believer in the Pastoral Epistles

The particular value of the Pastoral Epistles (1 Timothy, 2 Timothy and Titus) lies in the fact that they were addressed to pastors, or leaders, in the church of the Lord Jesus Christ. They therefore contain special emphases and insights that are not found elsewhere in the New Testament.

The first reference in the Pastorals to the relationship between the Spirit and the believer illustrates this point, as Paul adjures Timothy to 'guard, through the Holy Spirit who dwells in us, the treasure which has been entrusted to you' (2 Tim. 1:14). The treasure or, literally, 'good deposit', refers plainly to the gospel, of which, Paul declares a few verses earlier, 'I was appointed a preacher and an apostle and a teacher'. Although Timothy was not an apostle, he was a preacher and teacher of that same gospel (1 Tim. 4:13—16) and verse 14, which refers to the treasure that must be guarded, is preceded by the exhortation: 'Retain the standard of sound words which you have heard of me.' Paul is clearly speaking here of the doctrine he had imparted to his pupil.

Timothy, the preacher and pastor, therefore, had a special charge, namely to safeguard the purity of the apostolic gospel. But this could only be done 'through the Holy Spirit who dwells within us'. Human faithfulness and zeal were not adequate for the task. They would fail in the face of the battles and hardships that inevitably come the way of those who serve the Master, as the context makes clear (2 Tim. 1:11, 12; 2:1—7). The indwelling Spirit of God provides the faith, power and grace for the servant of God to triumph in this warfare. 'For God has not given us a spirit of timidity, but of power and love and sound judgement' (2 Tim. 1:7, mg.). In the light of verse 14, I have no doubt that the final phrase in this quotation is a reference to the indwelling Spirit who is the giver of spiritual power, who sheds abroad in our hearts the love of God, and who is the Spirit of truth.

The Epistle to Titus also contains an important reference to the work of the Spirit in the believer, where Paul writes as follows: 'He saved us . . . according to His mercy, by the washing of regeneration and renewing by the Holy Spirit, whom He poured out upon us richly through Jesus Christ our Saviour, that being justified by His grace we might be made heirs according to the hope of eternal life. This is a trustworthy statement . . .' (Titus 3:5–8). Paul himself underlines the importance of this statement, but the reader will already have recognized its significance because of the manner in which the outpouring of the Spirit is discussed in relation to salvation itself.

The first thing to notice is that the apostle here represents salvation as having two components, namely 'washing' and 'renewing'. Washing clearly refers to the forgiveness of sin, as reference to Ephesians 5:26, Revelation 1:5 (A.V.) and Revelation 7:14 will confirm. This cleansing is effected in the process of regeneration in which the believer dies to sin and is made alive to God (Rom. 6:6–11). The renewing is a work of the Holy Spirit in the believer which is both past ('He *saved* us by . . . the renewing'), and ongoing ('Put on the new self who *is being* renewed . . . according to the image of the One who created him', Col. 3:10). It seems very likely that renewing is another name for sanctification. As we pointed out earlier, sanctification is both the act of setting us apart to a new status, that of God's children, and the process by which we are made fit to enjoy that status. The work of renewal is thus identical to that of sanctification. Both are an essential part of salvation, as Paul makes plain in this passage, and this implies that all who are saved and regenerated have also been renewed (past tense) and are being renewed (present tense) by the Spirit. Although His indwelling is not mentioned directly, it is surely taken for granted that the work of renewal must be carried on from within.

Accepting then, as we must from Titus 3:5, that all who are saved are also renewed by the indwelling Spirit, what are we to conclude from the verses that follow? These state that the Holy Spirit, by whom all believers are renewed, was 'poured out upon us richly through Jesus Christ our Saviour, that being justified . . . we might be made heirs'.

Who does Paul mean by 'us'? On whom has the Spirit

been poured out richly? Superficially, there are three possible answers. Paul may be referring to himself and others who have had a similar experience; he may be referring to the church collectively, for example, at Pentecost; or he may be referring to all believers. The argument in verse 5, which shows the renewing of the Spirit to be an essential ingredient of salvation, must predispose us to the third of these alternatives. It would be odd if Paul actually meant, 'He saved us all, by means of washing us all and renewing us all by the Holy Spirit, whom He poured out upon some of us . . .' This interpretation involves a distinct change in the meaning of 'us' from a general significance in verse 5 to a limited one in verse 6. Nor can it be argued that Paul is referring to himself or a limited group of believers, throughout this passage, since he goes on to ask Timothy to 'speak confidently' to others about these matters so that 'those who have believed God may be careful to engage in good deeds'. Clearly Timothy's listeners must themselves have experienced these things if they were to apply them to their own Christian lives.

However, there is another, more convincing reason for thinking that Paul's statement concerning the outpoured Spirit applies to all believers. This is that, as always, the apostle points his readers forward to the purposes of God in salvation, as he continues: 'That being justified . . . by His grace we might be made heirs of eternal life according to hope' (Titus 3:7, mg.). This, clearly, applies to every Christian, yet our being made heirs is here represented as a *consequence* of the Spirit being 'poured out upon us'. Of course, the first cause of our being heirs is God's grace. But from that grace flow a sequence of secondary, contingent and effectual causes, namely salvation (v. 5), justification (v. 7) and the gift of the Holy Spirit (vv. 5, 6). Once again, we find sonship and heirship linked with the gift of the Spirit, as we did in Galatians 4 and Romans 8. And we would emphasize again that this is not a loose linking together of sundry benefits of the gospel. In Paul's thinking at least, there is a strong causal connection. The Spirit of adoption is the One who actualizes and confirms our sonship; He is the evidence, guarantee and 'down payment' in respect of our future inheritance; He secures our heirship;

He is the agent who will effect our future resurrection and glorification. Little wonder, then, that Paul speaks of Him being 'poured out upon us richly', for He secures immeasurable riches in Christ for every believer.

The Spirit and the believer in Hebrews

Of the several references to the Holy Spirit in Hebrews, that in Hebrews 2:4 will be considered later since it has reference to miraculous gifts rather than the relationship between the Spirit and the believer. Other allusions concern the Spirit's inspiration of Old Testament prophecy and, again, do not concern us here. This leaves two difficult but interesting references which must be considered because, at first sight, they suggest that the Holy Spirit once given to the believer might be withdrawn again. We have seen that this possibility did indeed exist in pre-Pentecostal times but it is quite contrary to the uniform teaching of the New Testament concerning the post-Pentecostal era.

The verses in question are as follows: 'In the case of those who have once been enlightened and have tasted of the heavenly gift and have been made partakers of the Holy Spirit, and have tasted the good word of God and the powers of the age to come, and then have fallen away, it is impossible to renew them again to repentance' (Heb. 6:4–6).

'How much severer punishment do you think he will deserve who has trampled under foot the Son of God, and has regarded as unclean the blood of the covenant by which he was sanctified, and has insulted the Spirit of grace?' (Heb. 10:29.)

If these passages stood alone, out of context, it would be necessary to understand them as references to converted or regenerate people. These folk are 'enlightened'. They have been made 'partakers of the Holy Spirit' and 'sanctified'. Yet they are eventually lost beyond recall and rejected by God. Some have tried to solve the dilemma by suggesting that these verses describe a hypothetical situation. This, however, is not at all convincing, since the writer introduces these statements to stimulate both godly fear and action in his readers who were tending to drift back into Judaism. If the dangers of apostasy so vividly portrayed here are merely hypothetical dangers, which do not actually exist, the exhortations are stripped of their power. Alternatively, the apostle is guilty of deceit, leading his hearers to believe that they are in danger when, in fact, they are not.

Fortunately, the context of both passages makes it clear that, in spite of the phraseology employed, they do not refer to regenerate people at all. First of all, in Hebrews 6, the verse quoted is followed immediately by an illustration in which the gospel is likened to rain and its hearers to soil. There are two kinds of soil and, under the same 'rain', one produces good crops but the other produces only thorns and thistles which must be burned. Clearly, the writer has in mind *one* gospel but *two* kinds of hearer, and the expressions employed in verses 4 and 5 ('have been enlightened', 'have tasted the good word of God', 'have been made partakers of the Holy Spirit' etc.) therefore refer to the gospel *preached* rather than the gospel *received.* Or, to put it another way, they refer to the externals of gospel hearing rather than the inward results of faith.

This presumption is reinforced by verse 9, which immediately follows the illustration of the two soils watered by the same rain. 'But, beloved, we are convinced of better things concerning you, *and things that accompany* (or belong to) *salvation,* though we are speaking in this way' (emphasis added). It is clear that the writer does not for one moment hold that those who are really saved stand in danger of apostasy. Of such, he is convinced of better things. What he is at pains to point out, however, is that the experiences detailed in verses 4 and 5, as long as they remain at the external level of enjoying the preaching, savouring the blessings of the gospel, and being present during times of great spiritual manifestations, do not necessarily imply or accompany *salvation.* It is possible to be swept along by enthusiasm and wonder at the sight of God's manifest working, and yet not be involved in the personal transaction of faith. This is clearly the message of Hebrews 4:2: 'Unto us was the gospel preached as well as unto them: but the word preached did not profit them, not being mixed with faith . . .' (A.V.). It is also Paul's theme in 1 Corinthians 10: 1–5 where he points out that all the Israelites passed safely through the Red Sea, were 'baptized' in the cloud and the sea, drank from the same spiritual Rock, and so on. But as long as these remained external experiences, no saving change was wrought upon their hearts.

The context of Hebrews 10 is no less explicit than that of chapter 6. Those who stand in danger of 'insulting the Spirit of grace' are those who 'go on sinning wilfully after receiving the knowledge of the truth' and for whom 'there no longer remains a sacrifice for sin' (Heb. 10:26). But, declares John, 'No one who is born of God practises sin . . . By this the children of God and the children of the devil are obvious; any one who does not practise righteousness is not of God' (1 John 3:9, 10). So then, one who knows the truth and continues wilfully to practise sin, demonstrates that he is no Christian, whatever profession he may make, and this is the thrust of Hebrews 10. The security of the true believer is, in fact, taught in the very same chapter, for Hebrews 10:14 states that 'By one offering He has perfected for all time those who are sanctified.'

Summarizing, therefore, we see that it is possible to be a 'partaker' of the Holy Spirit in a purely external sense which does not 'accompany salvation'. Such a possibility might arise, for example, if a person is present during scenes of revival and is impressed and moved and even carried along emotionally by what is happening around him. He may profess conversion and begin to practise the outward aspects of Christian discipleship. But his heart is unchanged and he continues in a course of sin. It is such people who 'insult the Spirit of grace', for they profess to know His transforming power, yet by their actions they deny this absolutely. Hebrews, therefore, does not actually contribute directly to our understanding of the relationship between the Spirit and the believer. But for a correct view of that relationship it is vital to understand the meaning of the verses considered in this section.

Peter's testimony concerning the Spirit and the believer

Peter addresses his First Epistle to a far-flung audience, those 'scattered throughout Pontus, Galatia, Cappadocia, Asia and Bithynia' (1 Peter 1:1). What he has to say about them, therefore, must be of very general application and this is particularly helpful in our present enquiry. His readers, Peter maintains, have all been 'chosen according to the fore-knowledge of God the Father, by the sanctifying work of the Spirit' (1 Peter 1:2). The purpose of this sanctifying work is that they might 'obey Jesus Christ and be sprinkled with His blood'. It is interesting to see, however, that Peter, like Paul, is unable to leave the matter there. He proceeds immediately to elaborate on the great privilege of Christians, namely 'an inheritance which is imperishable and undefiled and will not fade away, reserved in heaven . . . a salvation ready to be revealed in the last time . . . at the revelation of Jesus Christ' (1 Peter 1:3–7). It is clear that Paul's pre-occupation with the unbroken chain of redemption, from election to glorification, is shared by Peter. The Spirit's role in this chain of events is well-nigh continuous, as we have seen from the consensus of the Pauline Epistles. Peter's comment here is limited to the sanctifying work of the Spirit which, as we have seen before, may refer both to an initial 'setting apart' in regeneration and to the ongoing work of conforming the believer to Christ. Peter's major emphasis seems to be on the work of the Spirit in regeneration, since this is mentioned explicitly in verse 3 and by implication in verse 12 ('Those who preached the gospel to you by the Holy Spirit sent from heaven').

However, there can be no doubt that the passage contains other, less apparent, references to the work of the Spirit in the believer. 'Though you have not seen Him [that is, Christ] , you love Him', asserts Peter, 'and though you do not see Him now, but believe in Him, you greatly rejoice with joy inexpressible and full of glory' (1 Peter 1:8). Such rejoicing is plainly the fruit of the indwelling Spirit and this verse speaks of an exceptional depth of experience in the midst of severe trials.

Experience of this order would today be considered extraordinary and would be attributed by some to a special visitation of the Spirit not vouchsafed to all believers. Yet, as we have seen, Peter is addressing a general audience, having only their trials in common, and the conclusion is unavoid-able that he considers this inexpressible joy to be a norm of Christian living. Notice that his readers are *also* said to be 'distressed by various trials' (1 Peter 1:6). Their joy is not,

therefore, unattenuated but rather coexists with the sorrows
of life. It is a joy experienced in depth, not merely an outward exuberance. It is the fruit of the Spirit.

A remarkably similar allusion occurs in chapter 4 of the
Epistle. Warning his readers to expect a 'fiery ordeal', Peter
tells them that they share the sufferings of Christ and should
'keep on rejoicing'. 'If you are reviled for the name of Christ',
he continues, 'you are blessed, because the Spirit of glory
and of God rests upon you' (1 Peter 4:12—14).

Here Peter uses terminology concerning the Spirit which
is more familiar in the Old Testament than the New. The
Spirit rests 'upon' them rather than 'within' them, as is
normal in post-Pentecostal references. Again this emphasizes what we have already pointed out on numerous occasions, namely that the prepositions 'upon', 'with' and 'in',
used variously in Scripture to describe the relationship of
the Holy Spirit to the believer, can never provide a basis
for defining that relationship theologically. Each is a metaphor providing a particular idea or emphasis and each is used
of both pre- and post-Pentecostal situations.

The word 'rest' does not here have the connotation of
anointing, but rather suggests a clothing of believers in the
garb of glory. Reviled by men, they stand undefiled and
glorious in the sight of heaven, 'protected by the power of
God' (1 Peter 1:5) from all ultimate harm, their souls
entrusted to a faithful Creator (1 Peter 4:19).

The Spirit and the believer in John's First Epistle

John's First Epistle is much concerned with the believer's
relationship to God. It speaks of Christians abiding or being
in Christ, of being children of God, of 'having' both Christ
and the Father abiding in them. The tests of true discipleship are found here in abundance and, in particular, the
genuine believer is differentiated from the apostate by
having an 'anointing from the Holy One' (1 John 2:20).
Since the Father and the Son are referred to by their own
names in the verses that follow, it is not unreasonable to
suggest that John here uses the title 'Holy One' to signify
the Holy Spirit. This interpretation is supported by the
metaphor of anointing and also by the fact that this

anointing imparts knowledge: 'You have an anointing from the Holy One and you know all things' (1 John 2:20, mg.). This is obviously reminiscent of John's Gospel, where the disciples are promised the 'Spirit of truth' to guide them 'into all the truth' (John 16:13).

The anointing they have received, John continues, abides in them, teaching them about 'all things' (1 John 2:27). In particular, it teaches them that they 'abide in Him' and are 'born of Him' (1 John 2:27, 29).

The anointing, therefore, is both lasting and illuminating. Among other things it produces an inner knowledge of the believer's position in Christ. The apostate, in contrast, has no such anointing and no such inner witness, or so John implies in 1 John 2:19 and 20. These people 'went out from us' because they were never truly 'of us', explains the apostle. 'If they had been of us, they would have remained with us.'

The implication is clear that all true believers possess this anointing and the consequent knowledge of their standing in Christ. The anointing 'abides' in them, just as the 'seed' of regeneration also abides in them (1 John 3:9). It cannot be removed. It is an anointing of assurance and John underlines this repeatedly. 'We know . . . that He abides in us, by the Spirit which He has given us', he declares (1 John 3:24). 'By this we know that we abide in Him and He in us', he repeats, 'because He has given us of His Spirit' (1 John 4:13). It goes without saying that the same Spirit also bears witness to the believer concerning the facts of the gospel as well as the believer's standing. 'It is the Spirit who bears witness, because the Spirit is the truth . . . If we receive the witness of men, the witness of God is greater . . . The one who believes in the Son of God *has the witness in himself* . . . And the witness is this, that God has given us eternal life' (1 John 5:7–11).

The teaching of this Epistle on the Spirit's work in the believer is centred, therefore, upon the work of assurance. This assurance concerns both the basic facts of the gospel (e.g., that Jesus is the Son of God) and the believer's security, standing and endurance in Christ. It is an anointing of knowledge that is immediate rather than inferential and reminds us of Paul's teaching in Romans and Galatians, namely that the child of God cries out in spontaneous recognition of the fatherhood of God. It is interesting that John should also insist that assurance flows from the indwelling Spirit in this manner since in this Epistle he *also* gives a variety of external tests which permit Christians to *infer* the reality of their faith (e.g. the practice of righteousness, love, the confession of Christ and obedience, 1 John 3:10; 4:7, 15; 5:2). John's message seems to be that true assurance stems from the Spirit's witness in the heart but that this inner witness must be confirmed by the fruits of righteousness in the believer's life. The balance is excellent. The external tests protect us from the danger of self-delusion, while the inner witness protects us from legalism and assures the believing heart of the Father-child relationship which exists between God and the Christian. 'See how great a love the Father has bestowed upon us', cries John, 'that we should be called children of God, and such we are' (1 John 3:1).

6. The relationship of the Holy Spirit to believers – *III. Conclusions*

In the two previous chapters we have examined in some detail the many Scriptures in both Testaments which shed light on the relationship between the Spirit and the believer. The purpose of this present chapter is to summarize and reflect upon what we have learned as a result of this study. This will involve us in a certain amount of repetition but this is inevitable if we are properly to digest the embarrassing wealth of biblical evidence which bears upon our subject. One of the major causes of erroneous teaching and straightforward misunderstanding of the Spirit's work in the believer is our natural tendency to concentrate on a few 'proof texts' and neglect the balance of Scripture. Let us, therefore, attempt to draw the threads together and arrive at a truly biblical definition of this great relationship.

At the beginning of chapter 4 we posed four different but related questions. What was the relationship of the Holy Spirit to believers before Pentecost? How did Pentecost change this relationship? What relationship with the Spirit is established today at the believer's regeneration (or conversion)? Should this relationship undergo a subsequent change or transformation? The last of these questions must, in part, be deferred once again, until we have considered the sealing and baptism of the Spirit in the next two chapters. The first three questions may now, however, be answered with some degree of assurance.

1. What was the relationship of the Holy Spirit to believers before Pentecost?

Let us remind ourselves of the conclusions we reached at the end of chapter 4. We saw there that pre-Pentecostal believers

definitely lacked something in their relationship to the Holy
Spirit, since they lived in an era during which the promise of
the Spirit was unfulfilled. They were not ignorant of that
promise, however; indeed, they *embraced* the promise of God
by faith. But they saw it 'at a distance' as something that
would not be fulfilled during their own lifetime (Heb. 11:13).
Nevertheless through faith they remain heirs of the promise
of a heavenly country and there is little doubt from Hebrews
11:40 that their inheritance is identical to that which post-
Pentecostal believers anticipate, namely glorification, along
with Christ, as the children of God.

Throughout the pre-Pentecostal era, both in Old and New
Testament times, believers were wrought upon by the Holy
Spirit. He 'came upon' them, not only in sudden power for
service, but also in an abiding, resting, enabling manner. He
'entered into' the prophets and spoke through them. He
indwelt the authors of Scripture and filled such men as
Bezalel and John the Baptist in a continuing experience of
grace, strength and enablement. Indeed we have suggested
that every pre-Pentecostal believer, being an heir of the
promises through faith, was indwelt by the same Holy Spirit
of faith (cf. 2 Cor. 4:13) as are post-Pentecostal believers.

We have seen, of course, that the giving of the Holy Spirit
to these Old Testament saints may arguably have been conditional upon obedience. Yet even here it is clear that the
obedience required was not sinlessness (else David would
certainly have forfeited the Spirit's presence) but rather the
obedience of faith. This is what King Saul lacked and that is
why the Spirit of the Lord departed from him.

We see, then, that in their relationship with the Spirit of
God, some (if not all) pre-Pentecostal believers enjoyed much
of what is characteristic of post-Pentecostal experience,
namely indwelling, prophetical insight, miraculous and non-
miraculous power for service, wisdom and skill in spiritual
matters, fulness of the Spirit and the fruits of the Spirit
(they 'performed acts of righteousness', Heb. 11:33). This is
no overstatement and each of these assertions can be proved
from the Scriptures we have cited. We see therefore a very
large measure of continuity in the Holy Spirit's dealings
with God's people as individuals, before and after Pentecost.
This leads us to a most important conclusion, namely that,

whatever was withheld from the pre-Pentecostal church, it was not the things listed above, even though these feature strongly in the experience and teaching of the apostles. The long-awaited promise of the Spirit, the coming of the *Paracletos*, must have carried some wholly different and additional significance, something which had no counterpart for the pre-Pentecostal believer. What was given at Pentecost meant something so significant that, by virtue of it, the humblest recipient became 'greater' than John the Baptist, a man filled with the Holy Spirit even from his mother's womb! This leads us, then, to the second of our questions.

How did Pentecost change the relationship between the Holy Spirit and the believer?

There are three aspects of the giving of the Spirit at Pentecost which mark it out as unique. Firstly, there was an abundance and generality about the Pentecostal effulgence that was entirely new in God's dealings with His people. 'The promise', declared Peter, 'is for you and your children, and for all who are far off, as many as the Lord our God shall call' (Acts 2:39). This, of course, is a question of degree rather than essence, but it is an aspect emphasized particularly in Joel's prophecy. Secondly, the Spirit was given corporately to the infant church in a manner that appears to have been entirely novel and which we must examine in a later chapter. But these things alone are not sufficient to explain the total uniqueness of Pentecost, and for this we must examine how the individual's relationship to the Spirit was transformed at that point in history.

John, as is often the case, provides the key to this question. 'The Spirit was not yet given', he tells us, 'because Jesus was not yet glorified' (John 7:39). What was 'given' at Pentecost, and withheld from all previous ages, was something that *could not* be imparted until Christ had come, lived, died, risen and ascended to heaven. It was therefore a gift deferred in time because Christ's coming was fixed in time (Gal. 4:4). The essence of Pentecost lay, therefore, not in an enduement of power but in something intimately associated with the glorified Christ.

A further clue is found in Colossians 1:26, 27. Here Paul

speaks of 'the mystery which has been hidden from the past ages and generations; but has now been manifested to His saints, to whom God willed to make known what is the riches of the glory of this mystery among the Gentiles'. What is this mystery or secret of which Paul speaks? It is nothing less than 'Christ in you, the hope of glory' or, as Paul puts it later in the same Epistle, 'God's mystery, that is, Christ Himself, in whom are hidden all the treasures of wisdom and knowledge' (Col. 2:2, 3).

We should note in passing that Paul uses the word 'mystery', or 'secret', to signify different things. Thus in Ephesians 3:6 the mystery is the *inclusion* of the Gentiles in the promises, a rather different emphasis from that in Colossians 1. Elsewhere the word is used to signify God's whole will concerning our redemption in Christ (eg. 1 Cor. 2:7; Eph. 1:9, 10; 5:32; 3:19). Returning to Colossians 1:27, then, we see that the essence of the gospel mystery is Christ in the believer, giving rise to the 'hope' or expectation of divine glory. This is what believers in past ages were denied, what was not explicitly revealed to them — namely, that the Messiah, the Son of God, would not only come to earth to fulfil God's purposes, but that He would actually dwell within His people by the Spirit. This, the Scriptures emphasize, has tremendous implications for the believer's future glorification. 'Christ in you' constitutes the Christian's 'hope of glory'.

It is not that pre-Pentecostal believers were without hope. Abraham looked forward to Christ's coming, we are told, and rejoiced (John 8:56). Even Job, in the midst of his tribulation, could speak of the future saying, 'Without my flesh I shall see God, whom I myself shall behold' (Job. 19:26, 27). The Old Testament saints, surely, received the promises by faith, not simply on behalf of those who would follow them but also on their own behalf, expecting one day to participate personally in their fulfilment. The pre-Pentecostal believer lived in hope of 'a better resurrection' (Heb. 11:35), but he did not comprehend the full and amazing content of that hope, nor did he experience the foretaste of that hope vouchsafed now to those who have the firstfruits of the Spirit (Rom. 8:23).

For confirmation of these ideas, let us turn again to the Paracletic discourse of John 14 to 16. What was promised to the disciples (as something that still lay for them in the future) was not only the coming of the Spirit, but also that by His coming the Father and the Son would take up residence in their hearts. 'I will not leave you as orphans; I will come to you', said Jesus. '. . . If anyone loves Me . . . My Father will love him, and We will come to him, and make Our abode with him' (John 14:18, 23). It is not simply that the Holy Spirit would dwell within them, for that was true of pre-Pentecostal believers. The promise made here was that the Spirit's indwelling would result in Christ's indwelling and the Father's indwelling also. Before Pentecost, believers were indwelt and empowered by the Spirit. After Pentecost believers were to be indwelt by the divine Trinity in its entirety. No wonder Peter refers to 'His precious and magnificent promises', granted to us 'that by them [we] might become partakers of the divine nature' (2 Peter 1:4).

Notice that it is only by the granting (that is, fulfilment) of the promises that believers become sharers of the nature of God. The possession of the promises as such did not bestow this inestimable blessing upon men and women of faith before Pentecost. It is only the fulfilment at Pentecost of the ancient 'promise of the Spirit' that enables believers to enter into this entirely new relationship in which they become sharers of the glorious nature of the triune God.

The indwelling of Christ by the Spirit, which could not occur until the Son of God had come, suffered and ascended to His glory, brings a further benefit. Those indwelt by the Son of God are themselves children of God and therefore heirs of His glory. This is what Colossians means when it speaks of 'Christ in you, the hope (i.e. expectation) of glory'. Christ's presence within, by the Spirit, establishes for ever the believer's own sonship and thus his entitlement to inherit the glory of God. Pre-Pentecostal believers could only look forward to the day when they would, posthumously, enter into this same relationship with Christ and be made 'perfect' (Heb. 11:40). Post-Pentecostal believers, however, enter directly into this relationship, being 'born again to a living hope through the resurrection of Jesus Christ from the dead, to obtain an inheritance which is imperishable' (1 Peter 1:3, 4). This clearly could not be true of pre-Pentecostal believers during their earthly lifetime, for Christ had not then died and risen from the dead.

Let us then attempt to summarize what we have learned about the post-Pentecostal relationship between the Holy Spirit and the believer.

1. Believers since Pentecost have continued to enjoy everything that pre-Pentecostal believers experienced of the Spirit of God. The Spirit indwells them by faith, instructs them and empowers them for the service of God. That which was available to the pre-Pentecostal church in restricted measure, however, is shed upon the post-Pentecostal church without measure and without distinction of persons, race or status, upon 'as many as the Lord our God shall call'.

2. For the post-Pentecostal believer, to be indwelt by the Spirit is also to be indwelt by Christ and the Father. Unlike his pre-Pentecostal counterpart, he is inhabited by the Trinity and has become a sharer of the divine nature. This would seem to be the major difference between believers before and after Pentecost. It is also the essence of the promise of the Spirit, namely, that by the Spirit's indwelling the post-Pentecostal believer has his nature fused with the nature of God. This could not occur before the suffering and glorification of Christ since it is the life of the risen Christ that is imparted to the believer. It is in this sense that the Spirit was 'not yet given' before Pentecost. This fusion of human and divine natures in the believer is also the reason for the permanence of the Spirit's indwelling.

3. God's ultimate purpose is to glorify all believers with Christ ('We shall be like Him', 1 John 3:2). This will be true for Christians both individually and corporately as the church, the bride of Christ. For this ultimate purpose to be fulfilled, it is necessary for us to be adopted as children of God. This adoption is based upon God's electing love but is made actual by the coming into our hearts of the Spirit of adoption (or the Spirit of God's Son). Galatians 4 and Romans 8 particularly deal with this. Since the chain of redemption, from election to glorification, is unbroken (see Romans 8) it follows that every true believer must be subject to this work of adoption. There is no divorce or distinction between regeneration and adoption. They are different descriptions of the same essential event.

4. Adoption is not, however, completed at regeneration or conversion to Christ. It is a process which begins there but will only be completed, by the agency of the same indwelling Holy Spirit, at the resurrection when Christ returns (Rom. 8:32).

5. Meanwhile, the Spirit of adoption indwells the believer, assuring him that his future glory is secure and constituting, by His very presence within, a pledge or guarantee of that fact. He manifests His indwelling presence by pouring out within our hearts the love of God, so that the Christian is not ashamed of hoping for a future resurrection of glory (Rom. 5:5).

What is the believer's relationship to the Holy Spirit from regeneration onwards?

To some extent we have already answered this, our third question. We have seen that the Holy Spirit brings about the miracle of regeneration (we are 'born of the Spirit', John 3:5), but His work is not limited to this. Indeed, *adoption* cound be described as the most fundamental of all His works in the believer, since adoption is the means by which God's ultimate purpose for the redeemed will be fulfilled. Every believer is an adopted child of God. Adoption is achieved by the indwelling of the Holy Spirit, who brings Christ to dwell in our hearts and makes us sharers of the divine nature. Without the indwelling 'Spirit of adoption' we are not adopted. If we are not adopted, we are neither believers nor children of God.

It seems clear, then, that the indwelling of the Holy Spirit must begin at regeneration, for at regeneration we become sons and daughters of God, no less. And this new status is brought about by the indwelling of Christ by the Spirit.

The argument from adoption is conclusive enough, but the Scripture provides many other reasons for accepting that the Spirit's indwelling begins at conversion and not at some later time. We saw evidence from Ezekiel, Romans 5, Galatians and other Epistles that lead to the same conclusion. But perhaps the clearest statement of all is found in Romans 8. Here, those indwelt by the Spirit of God are said to be 'in the Spirit' and are contrasted with the unregenerate who are 'in the flesh'. A person is either one or the other; either in the Spirit or in the flesh. He cannot be both and he cannot be

neither one nor the other. Paul's analysis in Romans 8 leaves
no room whatever for a man to belong to Christ and yet not
be indwelt by the Holy Spirit. Even the carnal Christians of
Corinth, succumbing to division, jealousy, strife and immorality, were told that they were indwelt by the Spirit and
had been made 'one spirit' with the Lord (1 Cor. 6:17, 19).

Any teaching, therefore, that divorces the indwelling of
the Spirit from regeneration or conversion is unsupportable
from Scripture and based, at best, upon a misunderstanding
of the Holy Spirit's work in the believer. The best corrective
to such errors is to emphasize the doctrine of adoption. For,
once the New Testament teaching on this subject is grasped,
it becomes crystal clear that to be regenerate is to be adopted,
and to be adopted is to be indwelt by the Holy Spirit of
adoption. It also becomes clear that to be adopted as a child
of God is to be guaranteed a place in the physical resurrection and in God's heritage of glory. The indwelling Spirit
is Himself the pledge God gives us of His immutable purpose
in this matter and, at the same time, the agent by which that
purpose will be achieved.

Should the relationship of the believer to the Holy Spirit undergo a change at some time subsequent to conversion?

This, our final question, is really the subject of the third part
of this book and is developed in the next three chapters on
the sealing, the baptism and the fulness of the Spirit respectively. Even at this stage, however, it has become clear
that all the essential aspects of the believer's relationship
to the Spirit of God are established at regeneration. How can
we say this? Simply because adoption constitutes a Father-
child relationship between God and the Christian, within
which God will 'freely give us all things' (Rom. 8:32). Having
given us His Son, argues Paul, God cannot logically withhold
from us any spiritual provision. And Christ is 'given' not only
in the external sense of His death upon the cross for our redemption, but *also* (as the whole of Romans 8 testifies) to
dwell within our hearts by the Spirit of adoption.

It is very difficult to see, therefore, what *further* benefit
can be bestowed beyond that which every believer receives
when he or she is born of the Spirit. This is not to say, of

course, that the believer is instantly aware of all that has been given him in Christ. Indeed it is our common experience as Christians that we need to 'grow in the grace and knowledge of our Lord' (2 Peter 3:18), always discovering that there is yet much more to be discovered of the height, length, breadth and depth of His love. But our limited capacity to receive from God must not be interpreted as a limitation or withholding of His giving. Our need is not so much to seek what He has not yet given but rather to receive that which He has! We must explore this matter in greater depth in the chapters that follow.

Part Three

7. The sealing of the Spirit

The baptism and sealing of the Spirit

Before turning to the relevant Scriptures on these subjects, let us recapitulate the teachings of the four viewpoints presented in chapter 2. Pentecostals, Charismatics and Sealers all assert that Scripture defines a unique post-conversion experience, available to all believers but not received by all, in which the Holy Spirit comes upon the individual in power and blessing. The results of this 'baptism' or 'sealing' vary according to the viewpoint embraced. Pentecostals look for immediate outward and miraculous signs that a baptism has taken place, notably the sign of speaking in tongues. In the longer term, the Pentecostals expect baptism in the Spirit to result in greater power, joy and satisfaction in the Christian life and the acquisition of various spiritual gifts or powers (speaking in tongues, prophecy, healing gifts, etc.).

The Charismatics, though less formalized in their approach, adopt an essentially similar position over the baptism of the Spirit to that of the Pentecostal churches. Generally, they emphasize an enhancement of the depth and quality of spiritual life, a fuller understanding of spiritual truth, a greater unity with others who have experienced the baptism of the Spirit, and stronger zeal or devotion to Christ. Catholic Charismatics frequently claim a greater devotion to Mary and to the Roman Catholic Church as a result of their experience.

The Traditional Reformed position is totally at variance with these other viewpoints, claiming that the only baptism of the Spirit taught by the New Testament is that referred to in 1 Corinthians 12:13; 'By one Spirit we were all baptized into one body.' This baptism, they say, is the act by which God incorporates the believer into the church at his conversion (or better, at his regeneration). It cannot therefore be a

108

post-conversion event and the experiences related by those who believe that it is are either spurious or misinterpreted.

When we come to the more theological question of what actually *happens* on the occasion of a baptism or sealing of the Spirit, ideas are more confused. The Pentecostal churches have made the greatest effort to provide a 'theology' of baptism in the Spirit, but even there one finds sharp divisions of opinion. At one extreme some Pentecostals maintain that the Holy Spirit does not indwell the believer until after he has been baptized in the Spirit. Thus the Christian's experience today (they claim) is parallel to that of the disciples at Pentecost or the Samaritans in Acts 8. Baptism in the Spirit, they teach, is nothing other than the coming of the Holy Spirit to reside in the believer. Recognizing the problem raised for this opinion by Romans 8:9 ('If anyone does not have the Spirit of Christ, he does not belong to Him'), they draw a distinction between the Spirit of Christ and the Holy Spirit. The former, they suggest, is a principle rather than a Person, the Christ-life within rather than the Spirit of God. We have already seen, however, that this idea is contrary to Scripture. Christ and the Father are in the believer *by* the Holy Spirit, whose residence in the heart begins at regeneration and not at some later stage. The 'Spirit of Christ' is just one of the Holy Spirit's many titles.

A less extreme Pentecostal view is that the Holy Spirit does indeed dwell in the believer from the moment of new birth, but that He does so in the *role* of the Spirit of Christ. When a person is baptized in or by the Spirit, He comes afresh, as it were, in His own right. The question that arises here, of course, is whether there is any scriptural warrant for this teaching or whether it is a rationalization adopted to avoid the problem of Romans 8:9.

Charismatics seem generally less concerned with the theology of the Spirit's baptism and prefer to emphasize the experimental dimension. It is impossible, they say, to codify the work of the Spirit and the fact of baptism in the Spirit is so well established that it needs no further theological justification. They point to the events recorded in Acts and appeal to Peter's words: '*This is what* was spoken of through the prophet Joel' (Acts 2:16). Here is God's promise realized in human experience. Here is the Spirit outpoured.

To some extent the Reformed Sealers place a similar emphasis on the historical experiences of Acts and the validity of those experiences for Christians today. The Sealers, however, do attempt to provide a theological framework for their views in terms of the 'sealing of the Spirit', and this we must look at in this chapter.

One thing that these three viewpoints have in common is the idea that the coming of the Spirit at Pentecost has a valid parallel in the lives of individual believers today. This is a fundamental matter that we must examine in the next chapter.

The Traditional Reformed viewpoint denies that there is any unique post-conversion experience of baptism or sealing in the Spirit. This does not mean, however, that the Christian is to have no post-conversion experiences of the Holy Spirit. Indeed, claims this viewpoint, every believer from conversion onwards may know the fulness of the Spirit, including such special visitations of God as He may, in His divine wisdom, be pleased to give. Rather than suppressing or quenching the work of the Spirit in the believer, therefore, those who hold this opinion claim to open up the enjoyment of the indwelling Spirit to *all* believers at *all* times.

We shall approach our task in this part of the book by looking first, in this chapter, at the subject of the 'sealing of the Spirit', then in chapter 8 at the 'baptism of the Spirit' and finally in chapter 9, at the 'fulness of the Spirit'.

Although the 'sealing' and 'baptism' of the Spirit are considered by many to be different descriptions of the same event, it will be convenient to treat them separately, at least in the first instance. This is because the Scriptures which refer to 'sealing' make up a distinct and convenient group of references with which to deal at the same time. We must always remember, of course, that the Bible frequently does use different terms to describe the same thing. The purpose of this is not to confuse, but to enrich our understanding of the matter in question. To consider the sealing of the Spirit separately from the baptism of the Spirit is not, therefore, to prejudge the question of whether or not they refer to the same essential event. That question will be considered in due course.

The meaning of 'sealing'

It will be helpful, in spite of the lengthy quotation involved, to set out in full the verses which refer to the sealing of the Spirit. We shall then be able to see clearly the nature of these references, which are as follows.

'Now He who establishes us with you in Christ and anointed us is God, who also sealed us and gave us the Spirit in our hearts as a pledge' (2 Cor. 1:21, 22).

'We have obtained an inheritance, having been pre-destined . . . to the end that we . . . should be to the praise of His glory. In Him, you also, after listening to the message of truth, the gospel of your salvation — having also believed, you were sealed in Him with the Holy Spirit of promise, who is given as a pledge of our inheritance, with a view to the redemption of God's own possession, to the praise of His glory' (Eph. 1:11–14).

'Do not grieve the Holy Spirit of God, in whom you were sealed for the day of redemption' (Eph. 4:30, mg.).

Before examining these Scriptures, let us consider the significance of the verb used in these passages, 'to seal'. The same word is used of the sealing of Christ's sepulchre (Matt. 27:66) and also, in its noun form, of the seals on the book in Revelation 5:1–9, which had to be broken before it could be opened. Just as in English, therefore, the primary meaning of the word 'seal' is to close something (often a document) against unauthorized or premature disclosure. But there is also a derived meaning, again as in English, in which 'sealing' can also signify the act of impressing a seal, and the word is used in this sense in John 3:33 and Romans 15:28. In these two references the idea is that of 'setting one's seal' upon, or confirming, the testimony or action of another. An exactly similar variety of usage is found for the equivalent Hebrew word in the Old Testament Scriptures.

What, then, is the significance of the word in the passages we have quoted? Clearly, sealing is a metaphor in which the agent, God the Father, carries out some action, involving the Spirit, upon the believer. A careful reading of our verses shows that the Holy Spirit is the medium in which we are sealed. He is the seal; the One who does the sealing is the Father, and the one sealed is the believer.

This distinction is important. Reformed Sealers often speak as if the Holy Spirit Himself performs the act of sealing. But nowhere does Scripture say we are sealed by the Spirit. We read, 'God . . . sealed us and gave us the Spirit,' 'You were sealed . . . with the Holy Spirit' and 'The Holy Spirit . . . in whom you were sealed'. Grammatically speaking, in none of these cases is the Spirit the subject of the verb 'to seal', but always the indirect object. That is, the Spirit does not seal the believer. Rather, the believer is sealed by God in or with the Holy Spirit. The significance of this will emerge more clearly in the section that follows.

God's seal

The act of impressing a seal is clearly in Paul's mind in each of these passages, and we may therefore ask what such an act implies in normal and historical practice. Firstly, as we have seen, a document or package may be sealed up to be opened or revealed only at some future time, or by some properly authorized person. This aspect of sealing may well have been in the apostle's mind, especially in the light of Romans 8:19–23. The whole creation, we are told, together with the believer who has 'the first-fruits of the Spirit', waits eagerly for the 'revealing of the sons of God', namely the resurrection of their bodies and their adoption as sons (i.e. the completion of the adoption process). 'You were', declares Paul again, 'sealed for the day of redemption' (Eph. 4:30), while Peter speaks of 'a salvation ready to be revealed in the last time' (1 Peter 1:5). These Scriptures demonstrate that in this present age believers are, in a very real sense, hidden or concealed. Their true status is not apparent to the world (1 John 3:1). But they are sealed in this sense only until the 'day of redemption', when the children of God will be revealed for what they are.

Sealing is not, of course, to be viewed negatively. It does not merely prevent a premature consummation of God's purpose for His children. Rather the sealing is a guarantee that the promised consummation, though yet unrealized, will certainly take place. Thus the sealing of the Spirit is also 'a pledge of our inheritance, with a view to the [yet future] redemption of God's own possession' (Eph. 1:14).

This emphasis on guarantee is wholly consistent with our modern usage. When a written agreement between two parties is 'signed, sealed and delivered' we consider it to be binding on those parties. An obligation is laid upon those who have set their seal to the agreement to ensure that it is implemented. A signature is frequently sufficient to establish a binding contract. But when we wish to make doubly sure, we ask for both a signature and a seal. The sealing of a document imparts an added solemnity to the transaction, imposes an added burden of responsibility upon the parties and imparts an added assurance to them that the agreement will, in fact, be honoured.

Now the sealing of the Spirit differs from what we have just described in that it is a unilateral sealing. There are not two parties involved — namely, God and ourselves. We do not impress *our* seal to this promise; God alone does the sealing. If there *are* two parties, then they are God the Father and God the Son ('You were sealed in Him', that is, in Christ, says Ephesians 1:13). The undertaking that believers will receive their inheritance is a unilateral undertaking on the part of God, and to that He has set His seal. Nevertheless, our human analogy accurately represents the basic idea of commitment and obligation on the part of the one who applies his seal, and this is the idea that Paul seems anxious to convey.

God's trade mark

Two further lessons can be drawn from the metaphor of sealing. Firstly, a seal may be a mark of ownership, rather like a trade mark or even a cattle-brand, and this is the idea employed in Revelation 7:3, 4. This aspect may be in view when Paul refers to the redemption of 'God's own possession' (Eph. 1:14). The words 'God's own' have been inserted by the translators of the NASV, but the Authorized Version supports the idea projected here, referring to the 'purchased possession'. Believers are Christ's sheep, God's children, purchased with a great price — the blood of Christ (1 Peter 1:18, 19). They *belong* to Him. The Spirit of Christ, as we have seen from Galatians 4, is sent into the believer's heart because he is a son of God, and this also may be viewed as an expression of ownership on God's part. Seen in this light, the sending of the Spirit of adoption into our hearts can be equated with the sealing of the Spirit and this agrees with 2 Corinthians 1:22: 'God . . . sealed us and gave us the Spirit in our hearts.'

The second lesson is that sealing may be used to authenticate a document, demonstrating that it is genuinely what it claims to be. The indwelling Spirit, likewise, authenticates the believer's standing in Christ. This authentication is primarily inward, that is, it brings assurance to the believer himself. 'The Spirit Himself bears witness with our spirit that we are children of God' (Rom. 8:16). An outward authentication may also arise from the work of the Spirit, however, and this was clearly the case with certain of the effusions or baptisms of the Spirit recorded in Acts. At Pentecost the apostles' message was authenticated by the outward manifestation of the Spirit, while in the household of Cornelius the reality of their Christian faith was authenticated in Peter's eyes by the outpoured Spirit. The authenticating work of the Spirit will be considered at length in chapter 10.

The pledge of the Spirit

Returning to our verses on the sealing of the Spirit, we must now deal with a further aspect, namely that of the 'pledge', 'earnest' or 'down payment'. We have seen that the metaphor of sealing *of itself* implies a guarantee on the part of the one who impresses his seal. The giving of a 'pledge' or the making of a 'down payment' is really a separate or additional picture. We may illustrate this point as follows. Suppose you sign and seal an agreement to purchase a house. The agreement is legally binding upon you, but you may also be asked to pay a deposit on the property as an additional pledge of good faith. Notice that the sealing and the payment of a deposit are two distinct actions but remember also that they are both part of a single transaction.

In the same way, Paul distinguishes between the sealing of the Spirit and the 'down payment' or 'pledge'. 'God . . . sealed us *and* gave us the Spirit in our hearts as a pledge.' The distinction, however, is between the two different

metaphors employed (sealing and giving a pledge respectively) and we must not imagine that Paul is thinking of two
different *transactions* between God and the believer. There
is a single transaction with two (and indeed more) aspects,
and this is very important as we consider the debate between
the Reformed Sealers and the followers of the Traditional
Reformed position. The latter sometimes so emphasize the
sealing as a declaration or guarantee of God's intentions,
that they neglect the experimental reality of the pledge or
down payment. This must be felt by the believer, since the
pledge consists of 'the Spirit *in our hearts*'. (Indeed, a pledge
of which we had no cognizance could hardly be described as
a down payment at all!) On the other hand the Reformed
Sealers place so much emphasis on the experiential aspect
(embodied in the idea of the given pledge) that they fail to
recognize the sealing as a guarantee that must surely attach
to all believers. For *every believer* must be 'sealed for the day
of redemption' (Eph. 4:30). If this were not so, some Christians would have no part in that day, no part in the 'revealing
of the sons of God' or in 'the redemption of our body'
(Rom. 8:19, 23). That, surely, is unthinkable.

Sealing — the areas of dispute

We have already introduced the basic point of contention in
the previous paragraph. We now need to enlarge upon it and
examine the Scriptures in an attempt to resolve the matter.
Briefly, the Reformed Sealers view the sealing of the Spirit
as a post-conversion experience in which the Spirit comes to
the believer in overwhelming power, bringing a sense of love
and assurance to his heart and equipping him with particular
strength in, for example, preaching or other service. Their
doctrine of the 'sealing' is, in this respect, akin to the doctrine of the baptism of the Spirit held by Pentecostals and
Charismatics, except that the Sealers do not teach that outward signs, such as speaking with tongues, must accompany
the sealing.

  In contrast, the Traditional Reformed position is that
sealing, like baptism in the Spirit, is received by believers at
their regeneration and that it is coextensive with adoption
and the indwelling of the Spirit.

Much of the debate turns on Ephesians 1:13, which is translated in the Authorized Version as follows: 'In (Christ) ye also trusted . . . in whom also after that ye believed, ye were sealed with that holy Spirit of promise.' The implication of this rendering is, of course, that sealing occurs subsequent to believing and must therefore be considered as a second experience distinct from conversion. The further implication is usually drawn (but by no means justified) that sealing is not only removed in time from conversion but may never, in fact, be experienced by some believers. The reader will notice that this latter conclusion does not follow logically from the first, for it would be possible for a post-conversion experience to be, nevertheless, an *inevitable* experience for every Christian in the sovereign purposes of God.

However, let us return to the question as to whether Paul is speaking of a post-conversion event at all. The verb 'believed' used here is, in the Greek, an aorist participle indicating simple action without specifying whether that action is complete or incomplete, finished or ongoing. It cannot therefore be interpreted as a simple past tense. By common consent, the correct translation is of the form: 'Believing, you were sealed,' or 'Having believed, you were sealed.' An exactly similar grammatical form is found in such statements as 'Jesus answered and said' (i.e., 'Jesus, answering, said') which clearly does not mean He answered *before* He said. On the other hand, the same construction does sometimes imply sequence, as in Mark 1:31 which can be rendered: 'Having taken her hand, he raised her up,' and in Romans 5:1: 'Having been justified by faith, we have peace with God.'

In all such cases, however, we notice that the writers are emphasizing cause and effect, action and consequence. The two verbs employed in such clauses as we have quoted always denote linked or cognate action. Christ's 'saying' was part of His 'answering'. His taking the hand of Simon's mother-in-law was an integral part of the act of raising her up. Our peace with God can be viewed both as an inevitable consequence of the *event* of justification and an inseparable companion of the *state* of justification. Either or both of these emphases could be intended in Romans 5:1. In no case, however, do the two verbs in such constructions signify unconnected action. Applying this to Ephesians 1:13 ('Having believed . . . you were sealed'), we see that the grammatical form requires the two actions (believing, being sealed) to be either concomitant events or cause and effect. It is not admissible, therefore, to treat believing and being sealed as events *so loosely connected that one may occur without the other.*

The idea of sequence in the events should not present problems once we grasp the basic point that those events are linked together in an indivisible process. Thus on the Day of Pentecost Peter exhorts his hearers, 'Repent, and let each of you be baptized in the name of Jesus Christ for the forgiveness of your sins; and you shall receive the gift of the Holy Spirit' (Acts 2:38). Here we see a distinct sequence of events. They were to repent, then be baptized and finally they would receive the gift of the Spirit. Clearly such a sequence implies the passage of time, especially as a very large number of people were involved and the physical task of baptizing them must have been an imposing one. The work of conversion is not necessarily instantaneous, as many of us know from our own experience. Even Paul's conversion, dramatic as it was, was not accomplished in an instant. It was an extended process, beginning with conviction, and continuing through the visitation on the Damascus Road and his ensuing blindness to the laying on of Ananias' hands three days later (Acts 9:1–18). So it is with many, if not most, conversions to Christ. Each individual is wrought upon by the Spirit, who, says Christ, operates independently, mysteriously and in a sovereign manner in every act of regeneration (John 3:8). For both Peter's audience at Pentecost, and Paul in Damascus, the gift of the Holy Spirit was the final act in the process of their conversion. But it was part of that process, not an independent, disconnected experience, which might or might not be vouchsafed to them. Peter did not say, 'Repent, be baptized, receive forgiveness and then you may receive the gift of the Spirit'! Neither can we easily envisage a situation in which Paul was left, blind and Spirit-less, in Damascus. In both cases the coming of the Spirit was an integral part of the process of conversion, even though that process was extended in time.

In presenting this discussion of sequence in a person's coming to Christ, I have deliberately spoken of 'conversion' rather than 'regeneration'. The former word emphasizes the visible and experimental aspects of salvation, while the latter refers to the inward spiritual rebirth which causes the 'visible' transformation we call conversion. Scripture does not tell us at what specific point in the process of conversion a person becomes 'born again'. Indeed, it can be argued that regeneration is itself a process which may occupy a finite span of time, for regeneration is a metaphor based upon physical birth, which is by no means instantaneous. From the onset of labour to the safe delivery of the new-born child, the birth process may occupy many hours, and the Bible says nothing to indicate that the new birth is essentially different in this respect. We are not forced, therefore, to accept such arguments as 'The sealing of the Spirit must be a separate, post-conversion experience because, in Scripture, believing precedes water baptism, which in turn is followed by the gift of the Spirit'. It is more consonant with the teaching of Scripture to see the sealing of the Spirit as a part of the process of conversion or regeneration: a part which is just as indispensable to the process as are those other aspects we recognize as being inseparable, namely repentance, faith in Christ, confession (including water baptism) and the remission of sins. To these indisputable dimensions of the work of conversion we must surely add the sealing of the believer by the Spirit 'for the day of redemption' (Eph. 4:30). It is inconceivable that a man might be redeemed . . . with the precious blood . . . of Christ' (1 Peter 1:18, 19) without being sealed for that day of ultimate redemption of which Paul speaks in Ephesians.

We conclude, therefore, that sealing is an integral part of the process of conversion, an inevitable consequence of the Spirit's regenerating work in the believer. Let us now return to the passages we quoted at the beginning of this discussion to see if they confirm this view. In 2 Corinthians 1:21, 22 Paul spoke of his readers as those who were being established in Christ (present tense) but who had been both anointed and sealed (past tense) and had received the Spirit in their hearts as a pledge. This is wholly in accordance with our conclusion that, for the Corinthians as for all post-Pentecostal believers, the sealing of the Spirit was something that had accompanied their conversion to Christ. If Paul had thought of the sealing as an experience totally distinct from conversion, and one that any given believer may or may not have received at a particular time, he could not possibly have addressed a numerous readership, not all known to him personally, in these terms. Yet he states with confidence that the members of the church at Corinth had all received the sealing of the Spirit at some past juncture.

The same contextual argument holds good for the longer passage in Ephesians 1:11–14, for here Paul begins with the predestination of the believer and the inheritance that he *has already obtained* (v. 11). He goes on, without a break in his reasoning, to state that the Ephesians had also been sealed with the Holy Spirit of promise, who was a 'pledge of (their) inheritance' (v. 14). To suggest that some Christians have obtained an inheritance without receiving the pledge of that inheritance (as the Reformed Sealers do), seems to be the exact opposite of what Paul is teaching here. The apostle's message is that God has 'lavished' upon us the 'riches of His grace', has 'blessed us with every spiritual blessing' in Christ, has 'made known to us the mystery of His will' and has pre-destinated us to a gloriously secure inheritance (Eph. 1:3–11). It does not seem possible that this could be true for all believers and yet that some could be denied the seal and pledge which constitute both their title to it and their assur-ance of it. As he continues this passage, and prays for the eyes of their understanding to be enlightened, it is note-worthy that Paul does not ask that they might yet be sealed and receive the promised pledge. He treats those things as already accomplished. He asks rather that they may *know* that these things are so. The Greek verb used here signifies to see, perceive or be aware of some fact. The sense of Paul's prayer, then, is not that they might obtain 'the hope of His calling' but rather that they might become increasingly aware of what had already taken place, both in God's counsels and in their own hearts and lives.

8.   The baptism of the Spirit

Our title would be better rendered 'baptism in the Spirit', for it is quite clear from Scripture that the Holy Spirit is the medium of this baptism, while Christ is the One who baptizes (John 1:33). This is analogous, therefore, to the sealing of the Spirit, where we saw that God, the agent, seals the believer by the Spirit, who is therefore the medium of sealing or, more simply, the seal itself.

Both sealing and baptism are metaphors describing the work of the Spirit in the believer, but neither metaphor is intended to give a total picture of the reality, nor indeed can we ever fully define this work by human language. That is why a plurality of descriptions, similes and metaphors are employed in the Bible to define events and situations in the spiritual realm which, in many ways, defy any final definition. 'We see through a glass, darkly' (1 Cor. 13:12 A.V.).

We must eventually decide whether baptism and sealing refer to the same event, but before we can do this we must explore the significance of the former. That is the main purpose of this chapter. What is the baptism in the Spirit? How far can historical events like the Day of Pentecost be applied to the experience of believers today? Is baptism in the Spirit a personal or a corporate experience, or can it be both? What is its theological significance? That is, what part does it play in God's redemptive process for individuals and for the church? If we can find answers to these questions from Scripture we shall be well placed to consider the more practical issues. For example, should Christians seek a baptism of the Spirit if they have so far had no experience which can be described in these terms? Pentecostals, Charismatics and Reformed Sealers insist that they should. Indeed, the teaching of these groups centres upon this very point. The Traditional Reformed viewpoint denies the very existence of a unique post-conversion experience of spiritual baptism, maintaining that all believers are baptized in the Spirit at regeneration. This conflict we must seek to resolve by appeal to Scripture alone, for arguments based upon experience are suspect unless they accord with biblical teaching.

Our method of approach will be the same as we have adopted in earlier chapters. That is, we shall examine the relevant Bible passages chronologically and seek to draw from them such conclusions as they allow. We shall then try to summarize and reconcile these conclusions to give a consistent view of the biblical doctrine of baptism in the Spirit. Which are the relevant passages? These must include all specific references to our subject, of course, but will also cover the historic accounts of Acts and those 'promise Scriptures' that refer to the outpouring or effusion of God's Holy Spirit.

The meaning of baptism

Before beginning our examination of the relevant Scriptures, it will be helpful to consider what the word 'baptism' itself signifies. Most of the New Testament references to baptism are concerned with water baptism. The Greek verb *baptizo* means basically to 'immerse' or 'plunge'. In water baptism it therefore signifies the immersion of the subject in water, this outward action picturing the spiritual reality of burial and resurrection with Christ (see Rom. 6:11; Col. 2:12). The word can also be applied, by the association of ideas, to the pouring out of water. A person over whom a sufficient quantity of water is poured could be said to be immersed or drenched and thus 'baptized'. This usage does not, of course, convey the ideas of death and resurrection, but it does appear to be one of the main senses in which spiritual baptism is intended, and if this is so, then outpourings or effusions of God's Holy Spirit can properly be described as 'baptisms' in the Spirit.

In support of this identification of effusion and baptism, we may compare Christ's promise to His disciples just prior to Pentecost with Peter's words on that amazing day. 'You shall be baptized with the Holy Spirit', said Jesus, 'not many days from now' (Acts 1:5). When this event occurred,

however, the apostles' spokesman, Peter, did not refer to
'baptism' but instead identified their experience in terms of
Joel's prophecy. 'This is what was spoken of through the
prophet Joel: "And it shall be in the last days," God says,
"that I will pour forth of My Spirit upon all mankind"'
(Acts 2:16, 17).

Baptism in the Spirit, therefore, speaks of an abundance
of Spirit-given grace and power. This abundance, pictured by
'outpouring', implies both degree and extent. That is, the
Spirit is given both in great measure and to a wide variety
of persons. We have already noticed the latter point in
referring to the generality of the gift of the Spirit at and
after Pentecost and we need not, therefore, elaborate that
matter. The question of the degree or intensity of the gift
of the Spirit will, however, be considered further in what
follows.

What we have said so far defines the essence of baptism
but does not exhaust the content of the word. Water baptism has other connotations, including the ideas of washing
away sin (Acts 22:16.) (The verb *baptizo* is used to describe
the ceremonial washing of the body in Mark 7:4 and Luke
11:38) and of initiation. The idea of initiation is important
to our subject and we will pause here to consider it.

Water baptism in New Testament times was invariably
the first outward profession of faith in Christ. It thus rapidly
became the rite of initiation into the Christian church and
this usage persists to this day. But even before Pentecost,
the word baptism was used metaphorically to signify an
initiation. 'I have a baptism to undergo,' said Christ Himself,
'and how distressed I am until it is accomplished!' (Luke
12:50. See also Mark 10:38, 39). Even today we use the
expression 'baptism of fire' to signify an unwelcome first
experience. The idea of initiation is therefore always present
in New Testament thinking on baptism in the Spirit, and
explicitly so in some instances, as we shall see.

To summarize, therefore, the word 'baptism' expresses
four ideas, namely immersion, outpouring, cleansing and
initiation. Each of these aspects of baptism is found associated in Scripture with the work of the Holy Spirit. That
is, the baptism in the Spirit, as set forth in the Old and New
Testaments, embraces all of these ideas, not just one of

them as we might at first suppose. We find believers variously being immersed in the Spirit, having the Spirit poured out upon them, being initiated or incorporated into the church by the Spirit and being washed of their sins in the Spirit. Do these different operations of the Holy Spirit constitute a single baptism or is there more than one kind of baptism in the Spirit? This is just one of the questions we must eventually decide.

The questions to be answered

It will help to focus our attention on the major issues if we here summarize the questions we need to answer in the course of this chapter. They are as follows.
1. Are the sealing of the Spirit and baptism in the Spirit different names for the same event?
2. Is there only one baptism in the Spirit, or is the same expression used of more than one kind of spiritual experience?
3. Was the baptism of the Spirit a corporate experience of the early church, in which we share by spiritual descent, or should every believer experience his or her own spiritual baptism?
4. If baptism in the Spirit is personal to each believer, when does it occur? At conversion, or at some later stage?
5. Should Christians seek a baptism in the Spirit if they are not conscious of having received such an experience hitherto?

We shall return to these questions, hopefully with answers to most of them, in our conclusions at the end of the chapter. Let us now turn to the Scriptures.

The outpouring or effusion of the Spirit

This is perhaps the aspect of baptism in the Spirit that springs most readily to mind, simply because it is the aspect emphasized upon the Day of Pentecost. Many of the 'promise Scriptures' dwell upon this feature of the future giving of the Spirit, though other such Scriptures ignore it almost completely. For example, the Paracletic discourse of John 14–16 makes no mention of outpouring or effusion but dwells rather upon the inward working of the coming 'Helper'. We must never forget that Pentecost was not only the fulfilment of Joel's prophecy, but also of Christ's promise of the *Paracletos*.

Nevertheless, there can be no doubt that the fulfilment of God's ancient promise of the Spirit would be recognized by such an abundant manifestation of His coming that it could best be described by the metaphor of outpouring. Isaiah prophesies, 'The Spirit [will be] poured out upon us from on high . . . and righteousness will abide' (Isa. 32:15–17), and again, 'I will pour out My Spirit on your offspring, and My blessing on your descendants' (Isa.44:1–5). Joel, of course, adds the celebrated promise: 'I will pour out My Spirit on all mankind' (Joel 2:28) and Peter asserts that Pentecost was the fulfilment of this prophecy. A particularly important reference is Zechariah 12:10: 'I will pour out on the house of David and on the inhabitants of Jerusalem the Spirit of grace and of supplication, so that they will look on Me whom they have pierced.' The significance of this verse, and what follows, is that it must refer to the Jewish people and cannot be transferred to the church as a whole. We shall see presently why this is so important to our study.

In the New Testament we find John the Baptist predicting that Christ would baptize His followers 'with the Holy Spirit and fire' (Matt. 3:11; Mark 1:8; Luke 3:16; John 1:33), while the Lord Jesus Himself confirms John's testimony in Acts 1:5: 'John baptized with water, but you shall be baptized with the Holy Spirit not many days from now.'

In what sense was the Spirit of God 'poured out' on the Day of Pentecost? Firstly, there were miraculous manifestations or visible signs. The tongues of fire that rested upon the disciples symbolized the purifying work of the Spirit, the power of utterance and, possibly, the zeal of God. There was the rushing wind, whose sound brought the baffled and curious crowd to where the disciples were assembled. There was the proclamation of God's glorious works in foreign dialects and tongues. All this added up to an event which could not be ignored. Secondly, and more important than the outward signs, there was an abundance of power in the preaching of Christ crucified and risen.

Men were convicted of their sin in a remarkable manner and degree. Thirdly, in consequence, there was an abundance of repentance and faith, as three thousand souls pressed into the kingdom of God. In each of these aspects of the Day of Pentecost we find an abundance of grace that justifies the use of the term baptism or outpouring.

But the effusion of the Spirit did not begin and end with Pentecost, and there are four other episodes of 'outpouring' recorded in Acts. In the fourth chapter we read, 'And when they had prayed, the place where they had gathered together was shaken, and they were all filled with the Holy Spirit, and began to speak the word of God with boldness' (Acts 4:31). This effusion of the Spirit followed the infant church's first experience of persecution. The disciples' response was one of prayer and determination to overcome the opposition to the gospel preaching. They prayed, therefore, for boldness and requested that attesting miracles be granted to them (Acts 4:30). The Spirit's effusion was God's answer to their prayer.

The third recorded outpouring of the Spirit occurs in what we will call the 'Samaritan episode'. Philip, the deacon-turned-evangelist, went down to Samaria and 'began proclaiming Christ to them' (Acts 8:5). He performed miracles of exorcism and healing and a great number received the gospel and were baptized. Interestingly, however, in this case, an effusion of the Spirit was withheld. 'He [the Spirit] had not yet fallen upon any of them', we read, 'they had simply been baptized in the name of the Lord Jesus' (Acts 8:16). This is in distinct contrast to the situation at Pentecost when Peter commanded his hearers, 'Repent, and . . . be baptized in the name of Jesus Christ . . . and you shall receive the gift of the Holy Spirit. For the promise is for you and your children, and for all who are far off, as many as the Lord our God shall call to Himself' (Acts 2:38, 39). The Samaritans had, to all appearances, fulfilled these conditions and yet had not received the gift of the Spirit. It was necessary for two of the apostles to come specifically from Jerusalem and lay hands on the Samaritan converts before they received the Holy Spirit in a visible and experimental manner. We shall explore the reasons for this presently.

The fourth effusion of the Spirit took place in Cornelius' household and is recorded in Acts 10. Cornelius, of course, was a Gentile and Peter had to be prepared beforehand by a dream to secure his willingness to take the gospel of Christ to non-Jews. To have any dealings with Gentiles, especially in matters of religion, was anathema to the sincere Jew and an enormous barrier of prejudice had to be overcome. Eventually, however, Peter found himself preaching to Cornelius and his household, and as he proclaimed Christ an extraordinary and quite unexpected effusion of the Spirit engulfed the gathering. 'While Peter was still speaking . . . the Holy Spirit fell upon all those who were listening to the message. And all the circumcised believers who had come with Peter were amazed, because the gift of the Holy Spirit had been poured out upon the Gentiles also. For they were hearing them speaking with tongues and exalting God' (Acts 10:44–46). Obviously in this case, water baptism in the name of Christ took place *after* these people had received the Spirit of God, and this contrasts with Acts 2:38 and the Samaritan episode.

The last effusion of the Spirit found in Acts is described in the nineteenth chapter. The background to this event is that a Jew named Apollos had arrived in Ephesus 'teaching accurately the things concerning Jesus' in spite of the fact that he was 'acquainted only with the baptism of John' (Acts 18:25). We cannot be sure just how much Apollos knew at this stage. At first it might seem from this quotation that he was familiar with the life and teachings of Jesus. However, that would contradict the statement that he knew 'only' the baptism of John. Christ's disciples, after all, baptized many people in Jesus' name during His three-year ministry, and Apollos had obviously never heard of that. Furthermore, those whom Apollos had taught were not even aware (until Paul told them) that John had pointed forward to the One who would follow him, namely Jesus (Acts 19:4, 5). It seems clear therefore that Apollos had not heard of Jesus of Nazareth at all, but, being 'mighty in the Scriptures', was teaching accurately the messianic prophecies concerning Christ. It was only after Priscilla and Aquila had taken him aside and 'explained the way of God more accurately' that he taught that '*Jesus* was the Messiah' (Acts 18:26, 28).

When Paul arrived at Ephesus he found a group of twelve men who had clearly received instruction from Apollos and submitted to the baptism of John. They were 'disciples' of John but not of Jesus, since they had clearly never heard of Him (Acts 19:4, 5). After Paul had explained the gospel to them they were baptized afresh, in the name of Jesus, and when the apostle laid hands upon them we read, 'the Holy Spirit came on them, and they began speaking with tongues and prophesying' (Acts 19:5, 6).

What do the effusions of the Spirit teach us?

The first thing that we need to understand is the historical uniqueness of the Day of Pentecost. It was an event fixed in human history just as plainly as the incarnation of Christ, His death and resurrection. It could not occur until Jesus Christ had been glorified. Until it happened, the disciples were forbidden to proclaim what they already knew to be true. At Pentecost, the gospel floodgate was opened and a new era ushered in.

Although most would agree with this, the full implication is not always understood. The historical uniqueness of Pentecost means that it cannot be taken as a pattern of subsequent Christian experience. This is true in two senses. Firstly, we should not expect Pentecost to be repeated. It was the birth-day of the church militant and that will never recur. Secondly (and this is perhaps more difficult to grasp) we cannot use the experience of those disciples who lived through the Day of Pentecost as a general pattern for Christian experience. Because those disciples received the long-awaited gift of the Spirit some time *after* they had trusted in the risen Christ, it does not follow that believers subsequently should experience a delay between trusting Christ and receiving the gift of the Spirit.

Indeed, Peter's sermon on that very day makes clear that repentance and the confession of Christ in water baptism were henceforth to be the conditions for the bestowal of the Spirit: 'Repent, and let each of you be baptized in the name of Jesus Christ for the forgiveness of your sins; and you shall receive the gift of the Holy Spirit' (Acts 2:38).

This principle, enunciated by Peter, is surely the pattern

we would expect to be followed thereafter, rather than the atypical sequence of events experienced by those who, as believers, lived through the historically unique occasion of Pentecost. And this accords with what happened in Cornelius' household and at Ephesus. In the case of Cornelius, it is true, the Spirit was given before water baptism was administered, but this only signifies a still closer link between the giving of the Spirit and the act of believing on Christ. It was while Peter was yet speaking that the effusion took place. Why was the condition of water baptism (or confession, see Romans 10:9) waived in the case of Cornelius? Surely because the Gentile had already demonstrated his willingness to confess fearlessly the true God. He was, records Luke, 'a righteous and God-fearing man, well spoken of by the entire nation of the Jews' (Acts 10:22). In greeting Peter's arrival he was able to say of his whole company, 'We are all here present before God to hear all that you have been commanded by the Lord' (Acts 10:33). It does not seem too much to suggest that the attitudes of heart and mind that existed among this God-prepared audience already constituted a form of repentance and confession, so that the way was open for the Spirit to be given without further ceremony. Only the facts about Christ needed to be rehearsed before them, and this, of course, Peter did.

At Ephesus, again, we find that the outpouring of the Spirit followed immediately upon the hearing of the gospel of Christ and baptism in His name. Remember that these men, though called disciples, were followers of John and Apollos and had not even heard of Christ. Their hearts were prepared, of course, by repentance but the gospel of Christ was just as new to them as it was to the multitudes at Pentecost. At Ephesus a further ingredient is present, namely the laying-on of the apostle's hands. This was also a feature of the Samaritan episode which we will consider in a moment. All that we can usefully say concerning this is that God sometimes chose to use apostles as intermediaries in the bestowal of gifts, even of the gift of the Spirit. That such human intervention was not a necessary condition for the gift of the Spirit is evident from Acts 2:38 and the case of Cornelius. Why should God sometimes employ such

human agency? The most obvious answer, apart from the
sovereignty of God, is that it was desirable in some situations
to establish the authority of the apostles so that their subsequent teaching would be received the more readily as being
from God. Perhaps this need was greater in the case of those
not well versed in Scripture and who had no former alle-
giance to the Jewish faith. The Jews at Pentecost and the
God-fearing Cornelius did not therefore stand in the same
need of such demonstrations of authority as did the Samaritans with their corrupt religion or the ignorant Ephesians.

This brings us to the Samaritan episode, which does not
fit easily into the pattern discerned so far, namely that the
post-Pentecostal effusions of the Spirit followed immediately
upon belief and confession. In the case of the Samaritans,
faith in Christ and baptism in His name produced joy (a fruit
of the Spirit) but no manifest outpouring. The latter had to
await the apostolic delegation from Jerusalem and the laying-
on of their hands. What was the reason for this?

The main thing to realize is that although the Samaritan
episode is at variance with other post-Pentecostal effusions,
it corresponds closely to Pentecost itself! Like the disciples
awaiting the Day of Pentecost, the Samaritans had believed
in Christ, confessed Him and were rejoicing in Him. Like
those disciples, they yet awaited the bestowal of the Spirit,
the fulfilment of the ancient promise. Was this, therefore,
a Samaritan Pentecost, divorced in time from the Pentecost accorded to the Jewish church, but essentially of the
same character? And was the effusion of the Spirit in Cornelius' house at Caesarea a Gentile Pentecost, differing
only because there was no interval between the 'hearing of
faith' and the outpouring of the Spirit? Peter certainly draws
a close parallel between Pentecost and the events at Caesarea, referring to the latter as a fulfilment of Christ's promise of baptism in the Spirit (Acts 11:16).

This attractive idea can neither be proved nor disproved in
any final sense. It seems logical and not inconsistent with
any Scripture teaching, that the promise of the Spirit should
be fulfilled in separate stages for those who were Jews ('you
and your children'), those who were half-Jews (the Samaritans) and those who were Gentiles ('all who are far off').
On this view, each of these three effusions of the Spirit was

a unique historical event, not to be repeated. If this is so, the two-level experience of the disciples (before and after Pentecost) and of the Samaritans (before and after their visitation from on high) was also historically unique and cannot form a pattern for future generations.

Although we cannot be dogmatic about the uniqueness of the Samaritan episode in the way that we can be dogmatic about Pentecost itself, this interpretation does clear away the contradiction between Peter's assertion in Acts 2:38 and the happenings in Samaria. It also enables us to reconcile the historical accounts in Acts with the clear teaching found in the Epistles, namely that sealing and baptism in the Spirit are part and parcel of regeneration and not subsequent events.

To say that Pentecost, the Samaritan episode and (perhaps) Cornelius' experience were historically unique events, in which the promise of the Spirit was fulfilled in stages, accords with the pattern of the Lord's commission: 'You shall be My witnesses both in Jerusalem, and in all Judea (i.e to the Jews) and Samaria (i.e to the Samaritans), and even to the remotest part of the earth (i.e to the Gentiles)' (Acts 1:8). Again this correspondence does not constitute final proof that this interpretation is the correct one, but it adds credence to the suggestion.

The idea that the promise of the Spirit was fulfilled in three distinct stages, rather than one, may seem rather forced at first. Traditionally, we think of Pentecost itself as the single event which ushered in the age of the Spirit. We must remember, however, that the Pentecostal baptism was inaugural or initiatory. (The idea of initiation is implicit in baptism, as we have seen.) Something new began at Pentecost, but it certainly did not finish there! Take Joel's prophecy, for example. Although Peter could confidently identify Pentecost as its fulfilment, it is obvious that some of Joel's predictions did not come about on that day. There is no record of women prophesying, for example, nor were there 'wonders in the sky above . . . blood and fire and vapours of smoke' (Acts 2:19). The sun was not 'turned into darkness' nor the 'moon into blood'. These events will happen 'before the great and glorious day of the Lord', but they did not take place at Pentecost (Acts 2:20). Similarly, those promises of outpouring which, like Zechariah 12:10, seem to apply to the national Israel have not yet been fulfilled. Paul looks forward to the day when the Jews as a people will be grafted back into the 'olive tree' of the elect. But this will not take place until 'the fulness of the Gentiles has come in' to the church of Jesus Christ (Rom. 11:25—29).

It is clear, therefore, that the promises associated with the outpouring of God's Holy Spirit were not all fulfilled at Pentecost. Indeed some still remain to be realized. Pentecost was indeed the inauguration of the era of the outpoured Spirit, but it was only a beginning. It is not at all forced, therefore, to suggest that God chose to initiate different representative groups (Jews, Samaritans and Gentiles) into this era on different occasions. Indeed, this served to emphasize the universality of the gift of the Spirit, as highlighted by Joel's reference to 'all mankind'. It was the effusion of the Spirit upon Cornelius and his friends that finally convinced the Jewish believers that Christianity was for all men, regardless of racial background! (Acts 10:45—48; 11:1—18.)

On the balance of the evidence, therefore, we conclude that these three effusions of the Spirit were all inaugural events, unique in history, and that the two-level (or 'before' and 'after') experience of the Jews and of the Samaritans cannot be used as a pattern for subsequent Christian experience.

The continuance of effusions of the Spirit

To accept that Pentecost, the Samaritan episode and the effusion of Acts 10 were unique does not mean that all outpourings of the Spirit are unrepeatable. The effusion of Acts 4, when the Holy Spirit was poured out afresh upon the disciples who had already experienced Pentecost, and that of Acts 19 in Ephesus, do not have the character of unique historical events. The effusion promised to the national Israel that we discussed in the previous section also indicates that we still live in an era when the Spirit of God may be poured out upon men. And this, surely, is just what takes place in the revivals of true religion so amply recorded in church history. Indeed many Christians alive today have had direct personal experience of such revivals, small or great, in various parts of the world. At such times the power of God is present to a remarkable degree. Sinners are mightily convicted of their sin and large numbers are swept into the kingdom of God. Eventually the revival subsides, but normally leaves an impression upon the church that lasts for a considerable time. Although such revivals are by no means usually accompanied by miraculous signs, such as speaking with tongues, there is no obvious reason why such manifestations should not occur exceptionally under the influence of effusions of the Spirit. The question of such miracles will be considered later, in chapters 10—12.

The outward and inward significance of the outpouring of the Spirit

We must now come to grips with one of the most difficult questions raised by the effusions of the Spirit recorded in Acts. How do these outpourings relate to the experience of the individual believer, then and now?

We have already suggested that the two effusions in which existing believers were raised to a new level of spiritual experience (Pentecost and the Samaritan episode) were historical watersheds. Prior to these occasions the recipients of the outpoured Spirit were one with the Old Testament saints, having faith in God by the Spirit but not the indwelling of Christ by the Spirit. To these men, Jews and Samaritans respectively, the effusions marked not only a visible and corporate giving of the Spirit but also the personal fulfilment of John 14—16, that is an individual reception of the indwelling *Paracletos*. This is undeniably true of Pentecost and, as we have argued, a plausible and consistent interpretation of the Samaritans' experience.

It is clear, however, that the effusion of Acts 4 represented something quite different, since the recipients on this occasion were the same company who had received the historic visitation at Pentecost (both the original disciples and those who had been baptized in the name of Jesus on that day). There is no question of a change of relationship with the Holy Spirit in Acts 4. This effusion was a new filling and empowering of believers who were already indwelt by the *Paracletos*. This is important, for it shows that an effusion of the Spirit is not necessarily associated with a change in spiritual status on the part of the believer. Thus in revival the Holy Spirit may come powerfully upon believers, raising them to new heights of boldness and new might in preaching, without any suggestion that they had previously been deficient in their participation in the Spirit. And what is true of revival, affecting a whole community, may surely be true of the individual also. Thus a personal infilling of the Spirit, a private revival as it were, can take place without our having to interpret this in terms of a changed relationship with the Spirit of God.

This is where, in the writer's view, the Reformed Sealers and others are mistaken. In contemplating the testimonies of certain notable men of God, who record overwhelming experiences of the love and power of God poured upon them by the Spirit, they feel obliged to ascribe these to a changed relationship with the Spirit (for example, a 'sealing' in the Spirit). But if the disciples of Pentecost could undergo the effusion in Acts 4 without such a change, why should we suppose that any such effusion (personal or corporate) today must indicate a new standing with the Spirit of God?

It is, of course, quite proper to refer to such an effusion as a baptism of the Spirit, for that term can be used of any event in which the Spirit is poured out upon believers. But we must beware of calling it *the* baptism of the Spirit, as if it were a one-and-only occurrence that raises its recipient to some new status or relationship with God. We have seen already that Peter was 'filled with the Spirit' on a variety of occasions subsequent to Pentecost. Each such happening could be described as a 'baptism', without any corresponding change in the apostle's spiritual condition. Effusions or baptisms of the Spirit, therefore, can occur without their denoting any transformation in the relationship between the believer and the *Paracletos*. When used in the sense of 'outpouring', baptism does not necessarily signify initiation or the beginning of something new.

It will be argued that a Christian's first such experience of the outpoured Spirit constitutes the baptism of the Spirit with its implication of a change of spiritual status. We may again, however, refer to Acts 4. It is unlikely that those gathered at prayer in that account were limited to the original hundred and twenty disciples. Three thousand had been

converted on the day of Pentecost, and had received the gift
of the Holy Spirit, after the original effusion, with its manifestation of tongues and other wonders. These converts had
not, as far as we can tell, been partakers of the outward
signs vouchsafed to the disciples (see Acts 2:39–41). We read
only that they 'received his [Peter's] words' and 'were baptized' with water. Many of these must also have been at the
prayer meeting when the fresh outpouring of the Spirit took
place, for the very next verse asserts that 'the multitude of
those who believed were of one heart and soul' (Acts 4:32,
mg.). For any such converts therefore, Acts 4 was their first
personal experience of an effusion of the Spirit, yet they
had already received 'the gift of the Holy Spirit' (Acts 2:38).

Cornelius and the Ephesian disciples

In the remaining two effusions or baptisms recorded in Acts
the subjects were, as we have seen already, non-Christians.
In Cornelius' household the Spirit was poured out in the very
moment of their believing on Christ. There is no conflict
between the experience of Cornelius and his friends and the
teaching of the Epistles, which, as we shall see, view baptism
in the Spirit as a part of the process of new birth. It is true
that an effusion of the Spirit does not necessarily, or even
normally, accompany regneration (see the case of Lydia, for
example, Acts 16:14). But we have already seen from our
discussion on Acts 4 that a visible effusion of the Spirit is
not necessarily to be equated with reception of the gift of
the Spirit. Cornelius' gathering received simultaneously both
the gift of the Spirit and an effusion of the Spirit. So did the
disciples at Pentecost. But the converts on the day of Pentecost received the gift of the Holy Spirit without an effusion,
while the prayer meeting of Acts 4 received an effusion without receiving the gift (they had that already!).

The effusion in Cornelius' home was necessary, if for no
other reason than to convince Peter and the Jews that the
Gentiles were to be full participants of the grace of God in
Christ. Peter lays great emphasis upon the fact that he had
seen, with his own eyes, the Gentiles receive the selfsame gift
as was poured out upon the Jewish church at Pentecost
(Acts 10:47; 11:17). It was clearly crucial that a visible outpouring should occur upon the Gentiles.

The Ephesian effusion of Acts 19 is somewhat more obscure in its purpose. It certainly cannot be held to be historically unique, as can the events at Pentecost, in Samaria
and in Caesarea. On the other hand it was by no means typical of what happened when the gospel was preached with
saving effect. Indeed it is the only recorded instance in Acts
of an effusion of the Spirit upon the newly baptized! This
event was therefore an atypical occurrence, attributable to
the sovereignty of the Spirit of God, and possibly related to
the unusual level of miraculous signs that typified Paul's
ministry at Ephesus. This in turn was a consequence of the
unusual power of the black arts in that city (Acts 19:11, 18,
19). The explanation of the Ephesian effusion may therefore
lie in a particular need for authenticating miracles to establish
Paul's apostolic authority in the eyes of these converts and
others. This matter is relevant also to the Samaritan episode
where also the Spirit was poured out only after the apostles
had laid hands on the recipients. We shall return to the question of authenticating miracles in chapter 10.

A further aspect of the Ephesian incident can profitably
be discussed at this point. It has been suggested that the
sequence of events recorded there shows that baptism in the
Spirit is a post-conversion experience. The argument runs as
follows. These disciples believed the gospel as Paul explained
it to them. They must have been regenerate at that stage, for
the apostle would not have baptized unbelievers. Since they
received the Holy Spirit after water baptism (and the laying-
on of hands) it follows that their spiritual baptism took place
some time after their regeneration. Exactly the same argument could, of course, be applied to Acts 2:38, for Peter
states that the gift of the Spirit would be received after, and
as a consequence of, water baptism (or confession of Christ).

The fallacy in this argument lies in its attempt to make
regeneration an instantaneous event rather than a Spirit-
effected process. Nowhere does Scripture insist that regeneration is accomplished in a moment. Human birth, to which
Jesus likened regeneration (John 3:5, 6), is a process lasting
several hours. There is, of course, a moment when the baby
draws its first breath and utters its first cry, but this is the
culmination of perhaps hours of labour. Furthermore, Christ
warns us in the same passage of John's Gospel against trying

too hard to codify the work of the Spirit in regeneration. 'The wind blows where it wishes, and you hear the sound of it, but do not know where it comes from and where it is going; so is everyone who is born of the Spirit' (John 3:8). The important thing about regeneration is that once the Spirit of God begins the process, its safe completion is guaranteed. The process involves conviction of the sinner, repentance, despair of self-help, appreciation of the cross and of the resurrection, a cry for mercy, the act of faith and the assurance of pardon. But the degree to which these different aspects are experienced by the sinner, and even the order in which they fall, fluctuate from case to case. The time-scale over which they occur can vary enormously. How long did Saul of Tarsus kick against the goads of conscience, for example? At what point was he born again? Was it in the dust of the Damascus Road, when he called Christ 'Lord'? Or was it three days later when he regained his sight and was filled with the Spirit? (Acts 9:1–19.) Surely it is idle to speculate on these matters. We recognize that over a period of three days this man was wrought upon by the Spirit of God and brought to new birth. It was not instantaneous, nor should we expect it to be.

The sequence of belief, baptism and reception of the Spirit was not, of course, always followed in Acts. Cornelius demonstrates this fact. Surely we see here the sovereignty of the Spirit, acting freely as He wills in the manner of men's regeneration, now one way, now another. Sequence, therefore, does not imply divorce between the act of believing and the receipt of the Holy Spirit. Nor, as we have seen already, are effusion and reception of the Spirit the same things, though they may coincide, as with Cornelius and the Ephesian disciples.

Baptism and the effusion of the Spirit in the Epistles

Having considered at length the evidence from Acts, we now turn to the limited number of references in the Epistles that bear upon our subject. In contrast to Acts, there is little said in the Epistles about baptism in the Spirit, the concept of 'sealing' being much more evident.

In Romans 5, a passage we have examined previously, the

idea of effusion is applied to the inward experience of the believer. 'The love of God', asserts Paul, 'has been poured out within our hearts through the Holy Spirit who was given to us' (Rom. 5:5). Admittedly this verse refers to an effusion of the love of God by the Spirit, rather than an outpouring of the Spirit Himself. But the distinction is probably more apparent than real, since an effusion of the Spirit is only known and recognized by the effects it produces. We should remember that Paul had never himself been the subject of a corporate outpouring of the Spirit, such as his fellow apostles had known. He came upon the scene after Pentecost, Acts 4, Samaria and Caesarea. He had, of course, witnessed the Ephesian outpouring, but though it was given through his agency he was an onlooker of the actual effusion. He did, however, know what it was to be filled personally with the Spirit and it is not surprising that he should emphasize here the inward, in contrast to the outward, manifestation of the outpoured Spirit. As we have already shown in chapter 5, Romans 5 teaches that this inward effusion of the love of God is an integral part of regeneration, since it is the ground of Christian hope. If this verse speaks of a baptism in the Spirit, therefore, it is a baptism that accompanies conversion and not some subsequent event.

Although it does not mention 'baptism' by name, our next verse is of interest because it refers to 'washing'. 'You were', states the apostle, 'washed . . . sanctified . . . justified in the name of the Lord Jesus Christ and in the Spirit of our God' (1 Cor. 6:11). This text identifies three related but distinct operations of the Holy Spirit in the salvation of sinners. There is a washing from sin, a sanctification (setting apart) to God and a justification in His sight. Our interest centres in the word 'washed' from a Greek verb meaning to 'wash off' or 'wash away'. The only other New Testament use of this verb is in Acts 22:16 where Paul recalls the words of Ananias to him at his conversion: 'Arise and be baptized and wash away your sins, calling on His name.' The verb is clearly associated in Paul's mind with the washing of baptism, and to be 'washed in the Spirit' is therefore to be baptized in the Spirit. This, at least, seems highly likely to be the writer's intention. The use of baptism to signify cleansing from sin is certainly one of the several ideas implicit in the term, as we saw at the beginning of this chapter.

If this is so, then baptism in the Spirit stands alongside sanctification and justification as an aspect of a believer's regeneration. Indeed, it precedes these other aspects in Paul's statement. While this does not necessarily imply an order in time, it certainly signifies that baptism in the Spirit is an integral part of every Christian's regeneration.

Our next Scripture also refers to washing, the Greek this time referring to a vessel for washing, or 'laver'. The washing is not so likely this time, therefore, to be a reference to baptism, though this cannot be ruled out altogether. The text is Titus 3:6, which we have already considered at some length in a previous chapter. 'He saved us . . . by the washing of regeneration and renewing by the Holy Spirit, whom He poured out upon us richly through Jesus Christ our Saviour, that being justified by His grace we might be made heirs of eternal life' (marginal reading). When we looked at this Scripture in chapter 5 we saw that it argued powerfully for the coincidence of regeneration and the gift of the Spirit. The 'renewing of (i.e. produced by) the Holy Spirit' is just as much part of God's saving work as is 'the washing of regeneration'. This view is reinforced by the fact that the Spirit is said to be 'poured out upon us' in order that 'we might be made heirs of eternal life'. The argument is very similar to that in Romans 8 and Galatians 4, namely, that sonship, and the attendant status of heir, is bestowed upon believers by the indwelling Spirit of adoption. If the outpouring of the Spirit is a *means* by which we become heirs, it must accompany the acquisition of that status, not follow it. If all Christians are heirs, then all must have had the baptism of the Spirit.

What we did not discuss previously, however, was the term 'poured out', which speaks of baptism in the Spirit. It follows immediately from what we have already said that this baptism accompanies regeneration. The Spirit is not given at regeneration and 'poured out' in some subsequent and unconnected 'baptism'. Rather, the giving of the Holy Spirit in regeneration *is* an outpouring or baptism.

In what sense is the Spirit poured out richly in regeneration? Is Paul speaking of his own experience, or stating a principle applicable to all? No doubt both of these things are true. Paul plainly speaks out of the fulness of his own experience. But one needs only to re-read the eighth chapter of Romans to see how rich are the blessings and provisions made for all believers in God's scheme of redemption. The fact that so many Christians fail to appreciate and rejoice in these blessings does not in the slightest diminish the richness of God's giving. It is for us to enter into the riches of the glory that God has made ours by His indwelling Spirit! We must see more of this in the chapter that follows.

The teaching of 1 Corinthians 12:13

Our final Scripture is a most important one since, unlike many others, it is truly definitive of spiritual baptism rather than merely allusory or illustrative. It is for this reason we have kept it till last and devoted a separate section to it.

The text is embedded in Paul's dissertation on the charismata or spiritual gifts, which covers the twelfth to the fourteenth chapters of First Corinthians. These chapters will engage our attention in chapters 10 to 12 rather than here, but a single statement stands out as having a direct bearing upon our present discussion: 'For even as the [human] body is one and yet has many members,' argues the apostle, 'so also is Christ. For by [or in] one Spirit we were all baptized into one body, whether Jews or Greeks, whether slaves or free, and we were all made to drink of one Spirit' (1 Cor. 12:12–13).

The body referred to here is the church of the Lord Jesus Christ, as is made clear in verses 27 and 28 of this chapter. Nor is the picture limited to Corinth for Paul is speaking of the global church ('God has appointed in the church, first apostles . . .' 1 Cor. 12:28). When, therefore, he declares that 'by one Spirit we were all baptized into one body . . .' he is speaking of believers universally, 'whether Jews or Greeks, whether slaves or free', wherever they may be found. Not only do we have here a universal baptism in the Spirit, but a universal partaking of the Spirit: 'We were all made to drink of one Spirit.' What does this mean? This is an unusual figure of speech, but we may recall how the Lord Jesus spoke in similar terms to the Samaritan woman at Jacob's well. 'Everyone who drinks of this water', He said, 'shall thirst again, but whoever drinks of the water that I shall give him shall never thirst; but the water that I shall give him shall become in him a well of water springing up to eternal life' (John 4:13, 14). Again, in John 7:37, He cried, 'If any man is thirsty let him come to Me and drink', and the evangelist adds by way of explanation, 'This He spoke of the Spirit, whom those who believed in Him were to receive' (John 7:39).

It would seem, then, that Paul is here employing a double metaphor of the Spirit's coming to the believer. One metaphor, that of baptism, speaks of an outward occurrence; baptism is something done to us. Drinking, on the other hand, refers to an inward partaking of the Spirit.

It is clear from the context that baptism in the Spirit here refers to our initiation into the body of Christ, the church. It is universal among believers, the very point of Paul's argument being that no one who truly trusts in Christ is excluded from the body. Whoever we might be, whatever our religious background, nationality or status in society, we were joined to the same church by the same Holy Spirit.

Why, then, does Paul add his second metaphor at this point: 'We were all made to drink of one Spirit'? Surely because to view baptism in the Spirit as an initiation which every believer undergoes at his conversion might drain it of its experimental content. Here lies a serious criticism of the Traditional Reformed position which places great emphasis upon this particular text. Baptism in the Spirit, they sometimes argue, is our spiritual initiation into the church of Jesus Christ. It is not therefore an experience at all but a fact accomplished when we are born again. 'Not so,' says Paul in introducing his second metaphor. There is indeed an outward, almost ritual character about this universal baptism in the Spirit. By it we are declared members of Christ in God's sight, just as water baptism serves that purpose in the eyes of men. But at the same time we are made to drink of the Spirit! That is, we partake inwardly and experimentally of the water of life, the Spirit of grace. God's love is poured out in our hearts by His coming and we feel and know that God is our Father.

Some may object that many Christians have no spectacular conversion experience and that it is not even necessary for a person to feel anything intensely at that time. I believe we must re-evaluate this very common line of reasoning. One of the basic reasons for the rise of the Charismatic movement is the lack of genuine spiritual experience among Christians generally. The need for a 'second blessing' or a post-conversion baptism of the Spirit surely arises only because 'conversion' is for many devoid of any deep sense of God and of His power and love. New Testament teaching, such as the text before us now and many others, is that our factual incorporation into the church of Jesus Christ should be accompanied by a genuine experience of the Spirit within. We are made to drink of the Spirit. This experience may come to different individuals in different ways. For some, it will be an overwhelming experience of the love of God in Christ. For others, it will be a more gentle savouring of that same love. To some the Spirit of God comes as a flood upon dry ground (Isa. 44:3), but to others as 'the dew upon Israel' (Hos. 14:5, A.V.). To one, the majesty of God will appear most brightly; to another, His tenderness. A third may be most deeply affected by Calvary, a fourth by the rising in glory of the Son of God. But to each one, regeneration brings some experience of the love and joy of the indwelling Spirit.

I feel we must seriously doubt any conversion which is devoid of spiritual experience, devoid of such a baptism in the Spirit. The conversion which is merely intellectual or emotional, however orthodox, fails the test of Scripture. The baptism of the Spirit in 1 Corinthians 12:13 is certainly initiatory and attaches to every believer at his conversion. It is not, however, an unexperienced formality.

Is there more than one kind of Spirit baptism?

It has been suggested, because the baptism presented in 1 Corinthians 12 appears so different to that of Pentecost (with its corporate nature and miraculous effects), that there must be more than one kind of baptism in the Spirit. There is, some argue, a non-experimental incorporation into the body of Christ and a separate, experimental reception of the outpoured Spirit. This argument cannot really stand up to the full exposition of 1 Corinthians 12:13, as we have just seen, since Paul there includes both the initiatory and experimental aspects of Spirit baptism in a single event. We do, however, agree that in a different sense, there is more than

one kind of baptism in the Spirit. The personal baptism occurs upon our incorporation into the body of Christ, that is,
at our conversion. It is not only a 'ritual' baptism but a
genuine experience in which the love of God, in greater or
lesser measure, is poured out in our hearts by the Holy Spirit
who is given to us at that time (Rom. 5:5). The effusions or
baptisms of the Spirit recorded in Acts are more complex.
The Pentecostal effusion, together with those at Samaria and
Caesarea, served a double purpose. They constituted the
personal baptism in the Spirit for those involved, but they
also served as outward, visible and representative fulfilments
of the ancient promise of the Spirit. The effusion in Acts 4
had no unique personal connotation but was a new baptism
of power upon those who had already received the gift of the
Holy Spirit and is therefore the archetype of revivals of
religion. Finally, the events at Ephesus, in Acts 19, clearly
involved the personal initiatory baptism of the Spirit for the
twelve men concerned. But this was, atypically, accompanied
by miraculous signs as part of an unusual level of attestation
of Paul's ministry, demanded by the special situation in
Ephesus (Acts 19:11, 19).

We see, therefore, three types of baptism in the Spirit. Of
the first kind were the historically unique effusions, which
marked the fulfilment of the promise of the Spirit and were
inaugural of the church militant. Secondly, there is the
personal baptism in the Spirit experienced by every beliver
on his incorporation into the body of Christ. There is an intimate connection, of course, between these two kinds of
baptism. The first gave birth to the church militant at a point
in history and also, neccessarily, served as the personal baptism of those involved. The second, personal type of baptism
now causes believers to be added to the already established
body of Christ. In both types of Spirit baptism, therefore,
the church and the believer's membership thereof are
central.

The third type of baptism (effusion or outpouring) of the
Spirit also concerns the church, but does not involve any
change of spiritual status on the part of the believer. This is
the kind of effusion experienced by the church in Acts 4 and
involves a renewal of spiritual power and effectiveness. We
call such events today 'revivals', and the history of the church

abounds with examples. We cannot exclude the idea that an individual, as well as a community, might experience this kind of renewal and we shall see more of this possibility in the chapter that follows.

Our questions answered

At the commencement of this chapter we set down a list of questions that needed answering. We are now in a position to offer those answers.

1. *Are the sealing of the Spirit and baptism in the Spirit different names for the same event?*

Having explored the nature of both, we should now be able to reach a conclusion on this matter. This must surely be that it is misleading to equate sealing and baptism. For one thing we have identified three different categories of baptism in the Spirit, and sealing would only be equated with what we have termed personal baptism, as opposed to the historically unique baptisms and 'revival' baptism. There is a similarity between sealing and personal baptism in that both occur as part of the process of regeneration and both result from actions of the Holy Spirit. There, however, the similarity ceases. Sealing is the work by which the believer is made secure, kept safe until the 'day of redemption'. The Spirit comes to the believer as a pledge or guarantee that he will certainly partake of glory with Christ. The believer is also thereby authenticated as a true child of God and assured of this fact in his heart.

Baptism in the Spirit is a quite different metaphor, which speaks of washing from sin, the abundance of God's grace to the converted sinner and his initiation into the body of Christ, the church. There is an emphasis in baptism upon the experience of the outpoured love of God, whereas sealing carries the implication of a legal transaction which secures the status of the new-born saint. While sealing and personal baptism are both aspects of the regenerating work of the Spirit, it is therefore needlessly confusing to equate them.

2. *Is there only one baptism in the Spirit?*

Our answer is a definite negative. There are three categories
of event described in the New Testament under the metaphor
of baptism in the Spirit. There were the unique historical
baptisms, providing visible and miraculous evidence that the
ancient promise of the Spirit had been fulfilled. There were
revival baptisms in which the Spirit was poured out afresh
upon those who had already received the gift of the Spirit.
There is the personal baptism of every believer, which occurs
as part of the process of regeneration. Of necessity those who
believed in Christ before the relevant historical baptism had
their personal Spirit baptism on those historical occasions
(Pentecost, Samaria, Caesarea).

3. *Was the baptism of the Spirit a corporate experience of
the early church, in which we share by spiritual descent, or
should every believer experience his or her own spiritual
baptism?*

Our previous answer applies here also. We do indeed all
share in the historically unique events recorded in Acts since
they marked the giving of the Spirit in a manner which persists today. Since those events, every believer has the gift
of the Spirit, namely the indwelling of Christ and the Father
and thus a sharing of the divine nature. Equally, however,
every believer has his or her own personal baptism in the
Spirit at regeneration, and this is an experienced reality bringing love, joy and assurance to the heart. Furthermore, both
individuals and the church at large are permanently open to
revival baptism, namely an outpouring of the Spirit which
does not change their spiritual status but which renews and
empowers them for the service of God. So teaches Acts 4.

4. *If baptism in the Spirit is personal to each believer, when
does it occur — at conversion or at some later stage?*

The definitive personal baptism in the Spirit occurs at conversion as part of the process of regeneration. Revival baptisms or effusions of the Spirit may occur at any time after
conversion and may do so on more than one occasion.

5. Should Christians seek a baptism in the Spirit if they are not conscious of having received such an experience hitherto?

Every true believer, teaches the New Testament, *does* experience the baptism of the Spirit at conversion (see particularly Titus 3:5, 6). A professing Christian who has had no experience of the love of God shed abroad in his heart, and whose belief is merely intellectual, should examine both his heart and the Scriptures to see if he is indeed born again. If he remains in doubt he should seek spiritual counsel and not rest until he has a Spirit-given assurance of salvation and eternal security.

The true believer will, without difficulty, recall a time when his heart was melted by the love of God and when the Holy Spirit taught him to cry, 'Abba, Father', in joyous recognition that God is his Father. The earliest such occasion was his baptism in the Spirit, and before that event he was not regenerate, whatever intellectual belief he might have had. Believers, however, are exhorted constantly in the New Testament to enter more deeply into the riches of God's grace and it is right that all Christians should seek a fresh revival-type baptism of the Spirit of God. It must be recognized that in this matter the Holy Spirit exercises sovereignty and that we cannot expect, as of right, to receive remarkable effusions and revivals. It is proper, however, to pray for such, just as the disciples prayed, and received the outpouring of Acts 4.

It is wrong, however, to become joyless and inactive while waiting upon God for such effusions. The disciples were told to tarry for Pentecost, but not for Acts 4! Since Pentecost, the Spirit of God has not been withdrawn and does not have to be awaited. The revival effusion of Acts 4, in fact, occurred just because the apostles had been actively proclaiming the gospel and had run into severe opposition as a result. It was for boldness to overcome this resistance that they prayed, and it was boldness they received. To await passively an outpouring of the Spirit is to guarantee that none is received. We must be 'steadfast, immovable, always abounding in the work of the Lord' (1 Cor. 15:58) if we are to know God's blessing outpoured.

While revival baptisms are granted sovereignly by God, there *is* something of the power of the Holy Spirit constantly available for every believer. This is His fulness, and it is the subject of the chapter that follows.

9.   The fulness of the Spirit

In this chapter we shall be concerned less with events in the life of the believer and more with his condition or spiritual state. The events of personal baptism and sealing in the Spirit lie in the believer's past, having taken place at his regeneration. At that time also, he was adopted as a child of God and heir of glory, and the Spirit of God was poured out upon him in the abundance of God's mercy and grace.

But what of the present? Is the believer intended to live simply in the strength of past memories, or perhaps in hope of that other baptism, the Spirit's outpouring in revival? Surely not. These things have their place, of course. It is good for us to remember God's past gracious dealings with our souls, especially when we are passing through seasons of doubt and spiritual darkness. When the psalmist was 'so troubled that he [could] not speak', he 'considered the days of old' and 'remembered [his] song' in the night-time of distress (Ps. 77:5, 6). It is also good to stir ourselves from complacency and spiritual laziness by recalling God's past goodness, and Peter applies this stimulus to his readers. 'I shall always be ready to remind you of these things', he asserts, 'to stir you up by way of reminder' (2 Peter 1:12, 13). Likewise, looking to the future, it is right to pray for revival and the outpouring of the Spirit. We should surely pray that God would 'rend the heavens and come down' upon His people and His work. But this prayer must always be conditional upon the sovereign will of God concerning the times and the seasons of such blessings.

The New Testament makes it clear, however, that believers are to live neither in the past nor even in the future, but in the present. We are to 'be steadfast, immovable, always abounding in the work of the Lord' (1 Cor. 15:58). As a Christian, I am to live 'the life which I now live in the flesh . . . by faith in the Son of God', for 'Christ lives in

146

me' by His Holy Spirit (Gal. 2:20). Above all, I am to bring forth the fruits of the Spirit in a life of holiness and service to God.

These demands that Scripture makes on the believer are frankly superhuman, that is, beyond the capacity of fallen human nature. How may they be met? The answer lies in the provision made available to the Christian by the indwelling Spirit. Superhuman requirements can only be satisfied by superhuman resources. But through the indwelling Spirit Paul could soberly claim, 'I can do all things through Him who strengthens me' (Phil. 4:13). Nor is this capacity limited to spiritual giants like the apostle, for he himself prays for his readers that God 'would grant you, according to the riches of His glory, to be strengthened with power through His Spirit in the inner man . . . that you may be filled up to all the fulness of God' (Eph. 3:16−19).

Here, then, lies the secret of victorious Christian living, and this secret is expressed in one word, 'fulness'. The Spirit, dwelling in the believer's 'inner man', empowers or enables him to know the fulness of the living God. Nor need we distinguish between the fulness of the Spirit and the fulness of God for the post-Pentecostal believer. For we have seen that, since Pentecost, God the Father and God the Son indwell the Christian *by* the Holy Spirit. In this chapter, then, we shall explore the New Testament teaching on the fulness of the Holy Spirit and the fruit of the Spirit which stems from it.

Fulness of the Spirit before Pentecost

As a preliminary to our main study we should notice that fulness of the Spirit is not a post-Pentecostal concept. We have seen how Bezalel was 'filled with the Spirit of God in wisdom, in understanding, in knowledge and in all kinds of craftsmanship', to execute the design and construction of the tabernacle (Exod. 31:3). Joshua was described by God Himself as 'a man in whom is the Spirit of God' and is subsequently said to have been 'filled with the spirit (or Spirit) of wisdom' (Deut. 34:9). John the Baptist was 'filled with the Holy Spirit even from his mother's womb' (Luke 1:15, mg.), while both Elizabeth and Zacharias were filled

with the Holy Spirit before their respective prophecies
(Luke 1:41, 67).

This should not surprise us since we have demonstrated
in previous chapters that pre-Pentecostal believers were
indwelt by the Spirit of God. They lacked the promise,
namely the indwelling of Christ and the Father by the
Spirit. Nevertheless, being indwelt by the Spirit, they could
be filled with Him, for fulness is simply a measure of the
intensity of His influence and working in believing hearts.
Thus pre-Pentecostal believers could be filled to the full
with the blessing that *was* available to them, just as post-
Pentecostal Christians may be filled with that greater and
more extensive gift bestowed at Pentecost. There is no
difficulty, therefore, in the fact that fulness of the Spirit
spans both Old Testament and New Testament eras.

Another aspect of the fulness of the Spirit arises from
our pre-Pentecostal Scriptures — namely that the expression
is used equally of a habitual condition and of an occasional
experience. Thus Bezalel and John the Baptist are described
as habitually or continually filled with the Spirit, while
Elizabeth and Zacharias were filled specifically to enable
them to prophesy. Earlier, we saw a similar double usage
applied to the Spirit's supervention ('coming upon') in Old
Testament Scripture and we shall come across the same thing
in New Testament references to fulness. This is at first rather
confusing, but can be understood as follows. The indwelling
of the Spirit is a habitual condition. The fulness of His
indwelling may therefore equally be habitual, but it may also
be occasional or periodic. A further possibility exists. It may
be possible for one who is habitually filled with the Spirit to
be lifted to new heights of enduement for some specific and
occasional act of service. Habitual fulness and specific filling
would then, temporarily, co-exist. We must always remember
that 'fulness' of the Spirit is a metaphor and subject therefore
to a certain flexibility of use. A bucket of water which is
already full cannot then be 'filled', but such restrictions do
not apply to metaphors. This is especially the case if habitual
fulness signifies a state of fellowship or communion with
God, while occasional fillings refer to sudden enduements of
power or grace in the face of specific needs. This will become
clearer as we proceed.

Jesus and the fulness of the Spirit

The relationship of the Holy Spirit to Jesus of Nazareth has not so far formed part of our enquiry. This relationship between the incarnate Son of God and the third Person of the Trinity was, by definition, unique and has no direct bearing on the subject of this book. Because, however, it is bound to raise questions in the mind of the Bible reader, we pause here to consider the statement in Luke 4:1 that 'Jesus, full of the Holy Spirit, returned from the Jordan and was led about by the Spirit in the wilderness for forty days.' At His baptism, it will be remembered, the Holy Spirit descended upon Christ 'in bodily form like a dove' (Luke 3:22). This did not, however, mark the first coming of the Spirit to Jesus, for His physical humanity had actually been conceived by the same Spirit (Luke 1:35).

On the other hand, the descent of the Spirit at Jordan does not seem to have been purely symbolical, for it was from that moment that Jesus was 'full of the Holy Spirit'. Something occurred at Jordan that inaugurated Christ's public ministry and thereafter characterized His teaching and the miraculous signs He wrought. This is emphasized in the same chapter of Luke's Gospel. 'Jesus returned to Galilee' after the wilderness temptation, 'in the power of the Spirit, and news about Him spread through all the surrounding district' (Luke 4:14). As He began His teaching ministry He chose to read these significant verses from Isaiah: 'The Spirit of the Lord is upon Me, because He anointed Me to preach the gospel to the poor . . .' 'Today', continued Jesus, 'this Scripture has been fulfilled in your hearing' (Luke 4:17–21).

It is clear that the fulness of the Spirit was, in Christ's case, an anointing for public ministry. It speaks not so much of the unique relationship between Christ and the Spirit, which was surely established at His conception, but of the Father's attestation of His Son. It was at Jesus' baptism, and at the very moment the Spirit descended like a dove, that a voice from heaven proclaimed, 'Thou art My beloved Son' (Luke 3:22). As Christ Himself reminded the Jews, 'The Father who sent Me, He has borne witness of Me' (John 5:37).

The basic idea, found especially in John 5, is that the Father was working and witnessing alongside Christ Himself. 'My Father is working until now, and I Myself am working . . . Whatever the Father does, these things the Son also does in like manner . . . If I alone bear witness of Myself, My testimony is not true. There is another who bears witness of Me . . . The witness which I receive is not from man' (John 5:17, 19, 31, 32, 34). This divine witness, continued Jesus, was to be seen in the miracles He performed, namely 'the works which the Father has given Me to accomplish' (John 5:36).

I suggest that the Father bore witness by the agency of the Holy Spirit, who filled Jesus for this very purpose. The change that He underwent at His baptism was not a change in status. A sinner's status is transformed to that of child of God when the Spirit enters him in regeneration. But no such transformation could apply to the incarnate God Himself! Rather, the Son of God was joined, at His baptism, by the Spirit of God, so that *together* they could minister and witness to the gospel which He brought. Thus Christ's ministry, in word and act, was not His alone but a conjoint ministry between Himself and the Father (acting through the Spirit).

We shall see later that there are similar aspects in the ministry of the apostles and their companions — that is, God also bore them witness by the power of the Holy Spirit (Heb. 2:4). In this sense, then, the case of Christ's fulness of the Spirit is relevant to the believer's position, even though the relationship between Christ and the Spirit was totally unique to Him.

The fulness of the Spirit in Acts

We have already suggested that fulness of the Spirit has two distinct aspects, namely fulness as a habitual state and occasional fillings for special service. By 'occasional' we do not of course mean 'infrequent' but episodic, that is, experienced on specific occasions. We have also remarked that these two aspects of fulness are not mutually exclusive and that episodic fillings can occur in those already and habitually filled with the Spirit. This pattern, discerned already in pre-Pentecostal days, is apparent throughout the Acts of the Apostles.

The first episodic or occasional filling recorded in Acts took place on the day of Pentecost itself, when the disciples 'were all filled with the Holy Spirit and began to speak with other tongues as the Spirit was giving them utterance' (Acts 2:4). The particular need or service involved on that occasion was, of course, the declaration that the age-old promise of the Spirit was being fulfilled before the eyes of the astonished Jews (Acts 2:15, 16). Acts 4 records two episodic fillings: the first concerning Peter alone, as he faced his accusers and preached Christ to them (Acts 4:8) and the second a corporate filling of the church at prayer (Acts 4:31). In both cases the result of the filling of the Spirit was boldness and power in preaching the gospel. A further instance of occasional filling is that of Paul facing the opposition of Elymas in Acts 13:9.

In all of these episodic fillings there is some special, and clearly identifiable, requirement for a powerful manifestation or enabling of the Spirit. These needs, by their very nature, were short-lived and the filling of the Spirit was similarly short-lived. Indeed, Peter, in particular, experienced such episodic fillings on a variety of occasions, which indicates plainly their limited duration. We may notice in passing that occasional fillings with the Spirit probably occurred frequently even when they are not so described. One can envisage Peter being so filled in dealing with Ananias and Sapphira (Acts 5:1—11), and surely Cornelius and his company were 'filled' when the Holy Spirit 'fell upon' them.

Habitual fulness of the Spirit also features plainly in Luke's chronicle of the early church. The first case is one where some doubt arises whether occasional or habitual fulness is in view. Saul of Tarsus, blinded and at prayer, three days after his Damascus Road experience, is addressed by Ananias. 'Brother Saul,' says the disciple, 'the Lord Jesus . . . has sent me so that you may regain your sight and be filled with the Holy Spirit' (Acts 9:17). The reason for including this incident among the 'habitual' references is simply that Paul's future apostolic ministry is described in the same passage. 'He is a chosen instrument of Mine,' God tells Ananias, 'to bear My name before the Gentiles

and kings and the sons of Israel' (Acts 9:15). The fulness of
the Spirit was an ongoing requirement for this ministry and
it seems natural to suppose that Ananias was alluding to this.
We cannot be sure of this, however.

The other cases of habitual fulness are much more clear-
cut. The first deacons chosen by the early church were to
be 'men of good reputation, full of the Spirit and of wisdom'
(Acts 6:3). The habitual nature of this fulness is evident
since it is linked with the enduring qualities of reputation
and wisdom, both of which must have been characteristic of
the people concerned. Furthermore, of course, fulness of the
Spirit viewed as a qualification for office could not have been
merely episodic. In harmony with this, those chosen included
Stephen, 'a man full of faith and of the Holy Spirit' (Acts
6:5). Once again, by linking the characteristic of 'faith'
with the fulness of the Spirit, the writer implies that both
were conditions that typified the man at all times.

Stephen presents an interesting case history. Being identified as one full of the Spirit, he is also said to have been 'full
of grace and power' to perform 'great wonders and signs
among the people' (Acts 6:8). This latter fulness seems to
fall into the episodic category since it equipped Stephen for
special service. Finally, as he faced the ultimate test of
martyrdom, we read that 'Being full of the Holy Spirit, he
gazed intently into heaven and saw the glory of God and
Jesus standing at the right hand of God' (Acts 7:55). In
Stephen's case it is not easy to see the separation between
habitual and occasional fulness, but it is clear enough that
habitual fulness characterized his short but radiant life of
service to Christ.

Our next example is less spectacular but perhaps, by the
same token, more typical. Barnabas, we read, 'was a good
man and full of the Holy Spirit and of faith' (Acts 11:24).
As a result of his encouragement and counsel to the church
at Antioch, 'considerable numbers were brought to the Lord'
and taught (Acts 11:24, 26). Barnabas did no miracles, nor
did he found the church in that city. His role throughout
most of Acts is subservient to that of the apostle Paul.
Nevertheless, he was habitually and characteristically full
of the Spirit.

Finally, at the close of the thirteenth chapter, we read,

'The disciples were continually filled with joy and with the Holy Spirit' (Acts 13:52). The disciples in question were those of Pisidian Antioch, where Jews, proselytes and Gentiles alike had been brought to Christ, but where considerable opposition had also arisen from the Jews. There was nothing unusual in this, however; Paul and his companions were to endure many such experiences. What is said of the believers in Antioch cannot be attributed to any special factors, therefore, and we must conclude that their 'continual' or habitual fulness was a normal condition, not an extraordinary one. Once again we should remember that habitual fulness of the Spirit was not necessarily limited to those specifically mentioned in these terms in Acts. The situation at Antioch might well have been the norm.

On the other hand, we cannot avoid the implication that all members of the early church were not filled with the Spirit in this habitual manner. For had they been, it would have been pointless to specify such fulness as a condition or qualification for selection as a deacon (Acts 6:3). Just as all believers would not have been 'full of wisdom', so all were not 'full of the Spirit', otherwise the latter criterion for selection would have been useless. Similarly, Barnabas would hardly have been described as a man 'full of the Holy Spirit and of faith' had he not possessed these attributes in a degree that set him apart from other believers. We conclude, then, that while habitual fulness of the Spirit is a norm for Christian experience (a standard to be sought and claimed by faith), it was by no means possessed by all, even in New Testament times. We shall see later that this conclusion is borne out by the teaching of the Epistles.

The demonstration of habitual fulness

Before we leave this subject, there is one other thing to notice. In virtually every reference to habitual fulness, mention is made of some other attribute which keeps it company. The deacons were to be 'full of the Spirit and wisdom'. Stephen was 'full of faith and of the Holy Spirit', as also was Barnabas. The disciples at Antioch were 'filled with joy and with the Holy Spirit'. The reason for this is that fulness of the Spirit is manifested or made observable by the spiritual character of the individual. It is not a state which is self-evident, but one which so affects the visible actions and attitudes of the believer that he or she is marked out. In some, it was the high degree of wisdom that was most evident, namely the ability to make spiritual judgements and recommend courses of action which were honouring to Christ. In others it was the boldness of their faith in God that excited attention, while Barnabas is noted for his simple goodness as well as for his faith. In some, like the disciples at Antioch, the fulness of the Spirit was particularly evidenced by joy in the Lord, and one is reminded of Paul's assertion in Romans 14:17: 'The kingdom of God is not eating and drinking, but righteousness and peace and joy in the Holy Spirit. For he who in this way serves Christ is acceptable to God and approved by men.' Similarly, in the ensuing chapter, Paul prays, 'May the God of hope fill you with all joy and peace in believing, that you may abound in hope by the power of the Holy Spirit' (Rom. 15:13).

Such quotations could be multiplied, but these should suffice to emphasize our point. Fulness of the Spirit is made apparent, both to the individual and to others, by the fruit it produces in the life. The fruits we have noticed so far include wisdom, faith, goodness, joy, peace and hope, all of which can only 'abound' in the believer 'by the power of the Holy Spirit' (Rom. 15:13). We shall obviously take this matter further when we consider the subject of the fruit of the Spirit later in the chapter. What we have said already, however, should show that there is an intimate connection between habitual fulness of the Spirit and the production of His 'fruit'. That is, the evidence of habitual fulness is to be sought, not in spectacular experiences, but rather in terms of Christian character. Notice, however, that the characteristics in question will be plainly visible and even outstanding; we must not use this observation to devalue the fulness of the Spirit!

Fulness of the Spirit in the Epistles

We have already seen in Romans 15 that fulness of the Spirit is sometimes mentioned indirectly in terms of the character or fruit that His presence produces. Other Scriptures may be

cited to confirm this idea. In Romans 15:14, the verse
following the one quoted just now, Paul writes, 'I myself also
am convinced that you yourselves are full of goodness, filled
with all knowledge, and able also to admonish one another.'
The fulness of these things, it is implied, is also to be experienced 'by the power of the Holy Spirit', along with the joy,
hope and peace mentioned in verse 13. Likewise, Paul surely
has in mind the fulness of the Holy Spirit when he expresses
his confidence in verse 29 of the same chapter: 'I know', he
declares, 'that when I come to you, I will come in the fulness
of the blessing of Christ.'

To the Corinthians, the apostle writes of being 'filled with
comfort . . . overflowing with joy' in the midst of affliction
and conflict (2 Cor. 7:4). Of the Philippians he writes, 'I am
confident . . . that He who began a good work in you will
perfect it until the day of Christ Jesus . . . so that you may
approve the things that are excellent . . . be sincere and
blameless . . . having been filled with the fruit of righteousness' (Phil. 1:6—11). In Colossians, Paul prays that his
readers might 'be filled with the knowledge of His will in all
spiritual   wisdom   and   understanding'.   This   fulness   is
requested that they might 'walk in a manner worthy of the
Lord . . . bearing fruit in every good work'. Such a life of
abundant grace becomes possible as believers are 'strengthened with all power according to His glorious might' (Col.
1:9—11).

In none of these references is the fulness of the Spirit
mentioned directly. But in each case we see a fulness of
spirituality recounted or enjoined. Whether it be joy or
comfort, the fruit of righteousness, or the knowledge of
God's will, it is present in such degree and such abundance
that the picture of fulness is the only appropriate one to
use. From what we have already concluded, there can be
little doubt that such fulness can only derive from the fulness and strengthening of the indwelling Holy Spirit Himself.

The most direct statement concerning the fulness of the
Spirit is, however, to be found in Ephesians, in verses that
we cited briefly at the beginning of this chapter. So important are these references that we shall devote a separate
section to them.

Be filled with the Spirit

Let us begin in Ephesians 5, for this celebrated injunction casts much light on the practical application of our subject. 'Do not get drunk with wine', warns Paul, 'but be filled with the Spirit, speaking to one another [or yourselves] in psalms and hymns and spiritual songs, singing and making melody with your heart to the Lord; always giving thanks for all things in the name of our Lord Jesus Christ to God, even the Father' (Eph. 5:18—20).

One thing is plain; habitual fulness of the Spirit is a Christian privilege and duty. First of all it is clear that a person can only be filled with the Spirit if he is first indwelt by the Spirit, for fulness is simply a particular degree of containment. When Paul exhorts believers to be filled, therefore, he implies that they already possess the Spirit within their hearts. Secondly, it appears that Christians may fail or neglect to be filled with the Spirit, for otherwise no exhortation would be needed. Thirdly, Paul's command shows us that it is our duty to be in a state of spiritual fulness. This is not an optional extra for the believer, something he may choose or refuse at his whim. To be filled with the Spirit is the norm to which the child of God should conform.

This is important. It would be easy to write that fulness is the height to which we should aspire, but this is not the impression we receive from this text. A pinnacle of spiritual experience is something we might expect to achieve on rare occasions. But Paul's injunction refers to something continuous or normal. The tense of the Greek verb could be rendered, 'Be being filled with the Spirit.' It is to be a norm, not a pinnacle. As frequently as a drunkard might become inebriated, so frequently ought believers to be filled. Indeed, the contrast with drunkenness may have a greater force, suggesting that unless we are filled with the Spirit we shall be prone to fall into sin.

The fulness of the Spirit that is a Christian duty is not, of course, the episodic or occasional filling we noticed in Acts. Such episodes were, and no doubt still are, given in the face of special needs. To a great extent, episodic fillings are granted sovereignly by the Spirit and do not lie in the capacity of man to bring about. Paul's command to 'be being' filled refers to the habitual fulness which also features plainly in Acts and which is our chief concern in this chapter. It is important to appreciate this distinction, lest mistakenly we look for spectacular 'fillings' rather than habitual fulness. Paul is not exhorting his readers to experience great effusions of power or miraculous gifts, but rather to permit the indwelling Spirit to expand within their hearts and fill their lives with fruit.

The results of such fulness are detailed for us here in Ephesians 5. There will be spiritual communion with God within our hearts and spiritual fellowship with other Christians. There will be songs of praise to God in the secrecy of the believing heart and there will be seasons of mutual praise to Him among believers as they share their experience of the love of Christ. Not only will praise dominate the lives and attitudes of those filled with the Spirit, but they will also exhibit the more practical giving of thanks 'for all things' (Eph. 5:20). Other visible fruit will follow. The people of God will be 'subject to one another in the fear of Christ' (v. 21). Wives will be subject to their husbands 'as to the Lord', and husbands will love their wives 'as Christ loved the church' (vv. 22—23). Children will obey their parents 'in the Lord' and fathers will deal gently with their offspring. Servants will be faithful and masters will be honourable (Eph. 6:1—9).

Normally when we read these well-known passages about Christian relationships, we divorce them from the injunction to 'be filled with the Spirit', but this is surely a mistake. For the practical fruit of Christ-honouring relationships must stem from the fulness of the Spirit, as we have already argued. It is the behaviour of the believer towards his fellow men and women that demonstrates the fulness of the Spirit, as well as a heart of praise to God.

How then may we, in practice, obey the apostle's words? How can we 'be filled' in this habitual and fruitful manner? There is a balance in this matter, for both we and God Himself must be involved. Ephesians 5 emphasizes our part, while Ephesians 3, to which we must presently come, emphasizes God's.

The part the believer must play

This is set out in the verses that lead up to the injunction to be filled with the Spirit, namely Ephesians 4:17–5:18. This is an extensive passage full of instruction of a most practical nature. The key, no doubt, lies in the command to 'lay aside the old self' and 'put on the new self, which in the likeness of God has been created in righteousness and holiness' (Eph. 4:22–24). The Christian has been born again, created anew, raised from spiritual death to spiritual life. He has been transferred from the authority of Satan into the kingdom of God's Son. These, and many other pictures, are used in the New Testament to define the new status conferred upon the believer by the work of the Holy Spirit. They delineate the 'new self' created within us in the likeness of God . The 'old self', in contrast, is the sinful human nature with which we were born and which is characterized by the principle of indwelling sin. This principle of sin is not totally expelled when a person becomes a Christian. Indeed, says John, 'If we say that we have no sin, we are deceiving ourselves and the truth is not in us' (1 John 1:8). The sin that dwells within us is located in the mortal body and mind and will remain as long as we are in the flesh. What has happened to the regenerate person is that a new principle or power, namely, 'the law of the Spirit of life in Christ Jesus', has entered our being and 'has set [us] free from the law [or principle] of sin and death' (Rom. 8:2). We are no longer in bondage therefore to the sin that lurks within, but have the means to overcome its every urge.

But to overcome in this manner requires action on our part. 'If by the Spirit you are putting to death the deeds of the body', promises the Scripture, 'you will live' (Rom. 8:13). The 'deeds of the body' are the motions or urges of the sin that dwells within the mortal body. This is not a reference to natural appetites and emotions as such, which are basically God-given. Notice that we have, continuously, to be putting these motions of sin 'to death'. *We cannot do it, of course, except 'by the Spirit'*, for only the new principle within, the indwelling Spirit of God, is strong enough to quell and kill the force of sin. But *we* are to do it!

This is the subject, then, of Ephesians 4:17–5:18.

Christians are to 'walk no longer just as Gentiles'. They are
not to practise sensuality, impurity and greed. They must
'lay aside' falsehood, intemperate anger, theft, unwholesome
speech, bitterness, wrath, clamour, slander and malice. They
are to avoid even the suggestion of immorality, impurity and
greed. They are to 'be careful how (they) walk, not as unwise
men, but wise' (Eph. 5:15).

Fulness, God's gift

There is therefore much for the believer to do in this matter,
in terms of watchfulness, prayerfulness and the quelling of
the sinful tendencies that lurk within his heart and mind.
These things he can perform because he has the power of the
indwelling Spirit to enable him, but he himself must use
it. We must not think, however, that this is all there is to
the fulness of the Spirit. Like all aspects of the Christian
life, we must make room for faith in this matter. This seems
to be the burden of Ephesians 3:16–19, where Paul prays
that the Father 'would grant you, according to the riches of
His glory, to be strengthened with power through His Spirit
in the inner man; so that Christ may dwell in your hearts
through faith; and that you, being rooted and grounded in
love, may be able to comprehend with all the saints what is
the breadth and length and height and depth, and to know
the love of Christ which surpasses knowledge, that you may
be filled up to all the fulness of God'.

Although the fulness of the Spirit is not mentioned explicitly, there can be no doubt that it equates with the terms
used here. It is 'through His Spirit in the inner man' that
Christ is to dwell in their hearts and that they are to be
'filled' with 'the fulness of God'. Indeed, there is no more
comprehensive definition than this in the Scriptures of what
it means to be filled with the Spirit.

Let us notice that Paul's request is for an act of God,
namely that He would *grant* the Ephesians something out of
the glorious storehouse of His riches. Here is grace at work.
This is not an earned reward or entitlement. This is not an
automatic consequence of the believer's diligence in 'putting
off' the old self and 'putting on' the new. That diligence is
a necessary condition for fulness, but not a sufficient one!

There must also be the exercise of faith in God's ability and willingness to bestow the riches of His grace upon His children, who have no resources of their own!

Nor must we be inhibited or limited in our expectations by past experience, for Paul adds that God 'is able to do exceeding abundantly beyond all that we ask or think, according to *the power that works within us*' (Eph. 3:20). We too often refer these words to God's general activity, but it is perfectly clear that their main application is to this very matter of the fulness of the Spirit. To emphasize the point we have italicized the final clause of the verse. It is the Holy Spirit within us who can surprise us by His power to bring the fulness of God into our hearts' experience.

On the other hand we must recognize that there is no 'instant success' in this matter. Paul's prayer suggests that something of a process is involved. He asks first for his readers to be 'strengthened with power' by the inward working of the Holy Spirit. This 'strengthening with all power' (Greek *dunamis*), Paul tells the Colossians, comes through being 'filled with the knowledge of His will in all spiritual wisdom and understanding' (Col. 1:9, 11). We should not therefore expect it to appear in hearts which are ignorant of the Word of God and which neglect to cultivate a knowledge of God's will, namely His purposes for His people. To put it more simply, the Spirit of God must teach us before He can fill us. This is why teaching is the essence of the Christian ministry and why a vigorous Christianity cannot exist in the absence of faithful instruction. Of course, it is the Holy Spirit who fills us with 'the knowledge of His will', but He uses human instruments to do so (see e.g. Eph. 4:11–16).

As we are 'strengthened with might', continues our passage in Ephesians 3, it becomes possible for Christ to dwell in our hearts through faith. This is the second stage of the process. We have already seen that the word translated 'dwell' signifies 'settling down' or 'being at home'. Christ dwells within every believer by the Spirit, but for Him to 'be at home' in our hearts requires us to be filled continually with an understanding of His will and His ways. This is obvious really, since the faith, by which He will occupy our hearts in so secure a manner, must act upon the revealed will of God. Without such knowledge, faith is starved and Christ will live within us obscurely instead of evidently.

But if Christ is at home within us, continues the apostle, love provides a rich soil in which our spiritual lives take firm root. We shall be 'rooted and grounded in love'. And what roots securely below the surface is free to grow and flourish visibly above it. Hence Paul proceeds to ask that the Ephesian Christians, along with 'all the saints', 'may be able to comprehend the breadth and length and height and depth, and to know the love of Christ' (Eph. 3:18).

The enjoyment of God described by these words grows from the seed-bed of Christ's indwelling love. But notice that it does *grow*. It does not appear instantly. It takes time to develop. It is not surprising, therefore, that in the parallel passage of Colossians 1:11 Paul prays for the believers to be 'strengthened with all power, according to His glorious might', that they might attain 'steadfastness and patience with joy'. Patience is needful.

To summarize, then, the first work of the indwelling Spirit is to fill the believer with a knowledge of divine truth. This in turn enables him to be 'strengthened with all power according to His glorious might' (Col. 1:11). As a result of this inward, truth-based dynamic, faith makes Christ 'at home' in the trusting heart and His love fills the soul. This love of Christ is the nursery in which fulness grows, like fruit, in all its richness and perfection.

If this seems complicated, we can only answer that this is what Scripture teaches. There is no short-cut to the fulness of the Spirit. It is something that *grows* in those who are taught of the Spirit, strengthened by the Spirit and rooted by the Spirit in the love of Christ. It is something that develops from a sincere and patient faith, by which Christ becomes the settled resident in the guest-house of our heart and mind. Clearly many things may interrupt this process. We may neglect the task of understanding God's will and purposes. We may lose our relish for the truth of God, starving our faith and grieving the Spirit by our addiction to the ways of the world and our submission to the dictates of sin. But equally, we may ever start again, as children, to discover the wonders of God's purposes. We

can sit once more at His feet and be filled with the knowledge of His will. Our feeble souls will be strengthened with
power by the Spirit who still dwells within, and faith will
revive to welcome Christ afresh to settle in our hearts. And
then, as His love is once more poured out in those hearts,
by the same Holy Spirit, we shall experience fulness upon
fulness; the fulness of His love being the ground in which a
super-added fulness grows, exploring every dimension of that
love until we are filled with 'all the fulness of God'.

The fact that all this is a process does not mean it must be
long postponed. Paul is not trying to defer the hopes of his
readers, but rather to encourage them to press forward into
the experience of the blessedness that he describes. Why
then does he present fulness thus, as the culmination of
many stages? Surely his reason is to emphasize that to be
'filled with all the fulness of God' is not an instant experience like the episodic or occasional fillings discussed earlier.
The habitual and ultimate fulness that he desires for his
readers has a variety of ingredients, all of which have an
abiding character. Firstly, there is the 'knowledge of His
will', something acquired by faithful and earnest hearing
of the Word of God. Secondly, there is the use the Spirit
makes of this knowledge, within the believer, strengthening
the inner man with 'spiritual wisdom and understanding'.
Thirdly, the inward spiritual resources thus created are
deployed by the believer's faith to make Christ at home in
his heart. Consequently the love of Christ fills that heart
and provides the rootage and stability for further spiritual
growth into the limitless sphere of that same love. This is
fulness in its ultimate sense.

Is the fulness of which Ephesians 3 speaks to be experienced emotionally? Yes, without question. How can a
person be so immersed in love and yet not feel it? How can
one who is discovering the immensity of the love of Christ
fail to experience the emotion of love? Surely, also, such
love will overflow to those around in an unmistakable
manner. Of course, fulness of the Spirit and of God must be
felt, experienced, enjoyed to the highest degree. Perhaps
our experience is so limited because our expectations are so
low. We are ignorant of the fact that God wants us to enjoy
Him in this intense degree. Of his persecuted flock Peter

could write, 'You love Him, and though you do not see Him now, but believe in Him, you greatly rejoice with joy inexpressible and full of glory' (1 Peter 1:8). They had learned the secret of fulness of the Spirit. They were rooted and grounded in the love of Christ. They entertained the unseen Christ by belief, by faith, within their hearts. And consequently they experienced a glorious and inexpressible joy.

This discussion of fulness does, of course, raise the problem of the 'deadness' of many undoubted Christians, for whom the language used here by Peter seems extravagant in the extreme. This problem cannot be brushed aside, since it constitutes one of the most powerful arguments in favour of the Pentecostal, Charismatic and Sealer viewpoints. If the love of God has been poured out in the hearts of all believers, how is it that some have so little awareness of this great blessing?

The answer may lie in a distinction between the abundance of God's giving (to every believer) and the measure of our receiving. This is a recurrent theme of the Pauline writings. For example, he prays for the Ephesians, who had unquestionably been sealed with the Holy Spirit of promise (Eph. 1:13), that they might yet 'be strengthened with power through His Holy Spirit in the inner man' (Eph. 3:16). They had clearly known *something* of the Spirit's indwelling power, but Paul prays that they might know more of it. He goes on to pray that they might, in particular, know the vastness of the love of God, namely its 'breadth and length and height and depth' and that they might be 'filled' with 'all the fulness of God' (Eph. 3:18—19). It is clear, then, that God's giving always exceeds our capacity to receive and, whatever we may or may not have experienced of His grace, there is always more to come. Our capacity to receive is limited by many things, such as sin, faithlessness and neglect of the means of grace (such as prayer, meditation on the Scripture, worship, fellowship and the public teaching of God's Word). Scripture abounds with exhortations so to cultivate our spiritual lives that our capacity for God's blessing will increase. We may notice the spiritual condition into which the Corinthians, for example, had sunk. 'I gave you milk to drink', complains Paul, 'not solid food, for you were not yet able to receive it' (1 Cor. 3:2). Their capacity for truth was limited and their growth stunted, on account of their jealousy and strife.

We must draw a distinction, I think, between what is given but not fully received by the believer, and what is withheld by God. This would seem to be the point of difference between the Traditional Reformed viewpoint and the other three. In Traditional Reformed thinking, the baptism and the sealing of the Spirit (see chapters 7—8) have already occurred for every believer, but his *enjoyment* of God's gift of the Spirit, though potentially unlimited, may well be fragmentary on account of his own ignorance, neglect or slothfulness. In Pentecostal and Charismatic thinking, the gift of the Spirit is actually *withheld* from many believers until they fulfil certain conditions. The Reformed Sealers seem to take a middle course, emphasizing the availability of the blessing, but insisting that it must come in a particular, post-conversion experience, or not at all.

These distinctions are subtle but real and to clarify them further I offer the following illustration (well recognizing the danger of basing theology on analogies!).

A man stands beside the dried-up bed of a river. Upstream is situated a dam which holds back a plentiful supply of water. The opening of the floodgates to release the water represents the giving, baptism or sealing of the Spirit, or, in Titus' terms, the rich outpouring of that Spirit through Jesus Christ (Titus 3:6).

To the Pentecostal, Charismatic or Reformed Sealer, the river bed remains dry even after the man's regeneration, and he must fulfil certain conditions and pray that God will open the floodgates at some subsequent time. He thirsts because, for whatever reason, there is still no water in the river, or at best the merest trickle. On the other hand the Traditional Reformed view is that the gates were opened at the man's conversion. The river is filled with water from that moment onwards. All he has to do is 'stoop down and drink and live' in the fulness of what God has provided for him. If he thirsts it is because he neglects to take what has already been given.

The latter picture seems to accord better with what the New Testament teaches on the fulness of the Spirit. The believer may be filled at any time (indeed at all times) from regeneration onwards. There is nothing to wait for, only faith and obedience to exercise.

Let us therefore raise our sights. Let us so learn and meditate upon the revealed will of God, that the Spirit of God will fill us, habitually, with Christ and with His love. Finally, let those of us whose task it is to teach and preach the Word of God within the church and to our fellow believers, recognize that doctrine (that is, 'the knowledge of His will') is not an end in itself. It must always be seen and presented as a means to the experimental knowledge of God Himself. Only then will our teaching and our exhortation, however sound, produce fruit to the glory of God and lead our hearers into the joy of their Lord.

The fruit of the Spirit

What is the connection between the fulness of the Spirit and the fruit of the Spirit? We have already seen that these matters are closely related, since fulness of the Spirit is regularly linked in Scripture with visible evidence in the lives of those who are filled. Wisdom, righteousness, goodness, joy are all recorded as concomitants of the Spirit's fulness.

Fruit is the visible or tangible produce of a living plant and the metaphor is almost always used in Scripture to describe what is evident or external, rather than what is inward, in the heart. The best-known example is found, perhaps, in the sermon on the mount. 'You will know them by their fruits,' explains Jesus. 'Every good tree bears good fruit; but the rotten tree bears bad fruit' (Matt. 7:15—20). Again, in John 15, He describes His purpose in choosing the apostles: 'I chose you', He reminds them, that you should go and bear fruit, and that your fruit should remain' (John 15:16). Obviously, fruit that remains after its producer has passed on must, by definition, be composed of visible or tangible works rather than some private experience of the person concerned. Paul continues the theme in Romans 1:13, desiring to visit the church in that city that he 'might obtain some fruit among [them] also, even as among the rest of the Gentiles'. Once again the fruit in question must be outwardly visible effects rather than inward experiences.

The point is important as we turn to Galatians 5:22, 23,

the classic passage on our subject, which reads as follows: 'The fruit of the Spirit is love, joy, peace, patience, kindness, goodness, faithfulness, gentleness, self-control; against such things there is no law.' Some of the fruit described, admittedly, could be construed in terms of inward experiences. Love, joy and peace, for example, can all refer to emotions felt in the heart and, indeed, these words are normally used in that sense, Since, however, the metaphor of fruit is employed so consistently in the Bible to describe visible actions, it is probable that this usage is also intended here.

The passage in fact contains internal evidence that Paul is speaking of the visible fruit of the Spirit. For one thing, some of the fruit listed must be external. Kindness and gentleness, for example, can only describe actions and attitudes discernible to others. Secondly, the fruit of the Spirit in verses 22 and 23 is contrasted with the 'deeds of the flesh' in verses 19 to 21. The latter fall evidently in the realm of behaviour ('immorality . . . sorcery . . . strife . . . outbursts of anger . . . drunkenness') though some have both an outward and an inward application ('impurity . . . jealousy . . . envyings'). However, it is clear that Paul is thinking about actual behaviour, since he adds that 'Those who practise such things shall not inherit the kingdom of God' (Gal. 5:21). Finally, the passage concludes with the words: 'If we live by the Spirit, let us also walk by the Spirit . . . not becoming boastful, challenging one another, envying one another' (Gal. 5:25, 26). This is the heart of the apostle's argument, namely that behaviour (our 'walk') must match the profession of our relationship to God (we 'live by the Spirit'). It seems abundantly clear, therefore, both from the general usage of Scripture and from the evidence of the passage itself, that the fruit of the Spirit refers chiefly to behaviour, that is, outward actions and attitudes.

This conclusion allows us to propose a clear connection between the fulness and the fruit of the Spirit, namely that the fruit of the Spirit is the product of the habitual fulness of the Spirit. Thus love, viewed as a fruit (see 1 Corinthians 13 for 'love in action'), is the visible counterpart and consequence of the inward experience of the love of God poured out in our hearts by the Holy Spirit (Rom. 5:5). Joy is the visible result of our inward enjoyment of Christ's occupancy of our hearts. Peace, as a fruit, is the attitude observed in those who have the inward peace of God guarding their hearts and minds (Phil. 4:7).

This understanding is in harmony with our original observation that fulness of the Spirit is commonly joined in the New Testament with fulness of some visible quality or behaviour (wisdom, righteousness, goodness, joy). Fulness itself is an inward attribute and, as such, is not observable by others. But true fulness will always produce the visible fruit of Christian behaviour and will be recognized by such fruit.

The apostle James has much to say about this matter. 'What use is it, my brethren,' he asks, 'if a man says he has faith, but he has no works? . . . Faith, if it has no works, is dead' (James 2:14–17). Again, 'One who looks intently at the perfect law . . . of liberty and abides by it, not having become a forgetful hearer but an effectual doer, this man shall be blessed in what he does' (James 1:24, 25). And further, 'This is pure and undefiled religion in the sight of our God and Father, to visit orphans and widows in their distress, and to keep oneself unstained by the world' (James 1:27). The apostle John adds his warning: 'If someone says "I love God", and hates his brother, he is a liar' (1 John 4:20).

Although these verses mention neither the fulness nor the fruit of the Spirit, they emphasize one of the basic rules of Scripture, namely that inward spirituality, if genuine, must issue in appropriate outward behaviour. Indeed, one of the passages that has engaged our attention in this discussion of the fulness of the Spirit makes this very plain. I 'pray for you', declares Paul, 'that you may be filled with the knowledge of His will in all spiritual wisdom and understanding, so that you may walk in a manner worthy of the Lord, to please Him in all respects, *bearing fruit in every good work* and increasing in the knowledge of God' (Col. 1:9, 10). The knowledge of God's will leads not only to spiritual strength in the believer's soul, as we have seen (Col. 1:9, 11), but also and simultaneously to the bearing of fruit in good works. The fruit of the Spirit is therefore a necessary concomitant of the fulness of the Spirit. The fulness produces the fruit, while the fruit bears testimony to the fulness.

Conclusion

The fulness of the Spirit falls into two categories, occasional or episodic fulness, and habitual fulness. The former kind of fulness represents a transient equipment for some special act of service and its donation lies in the sovereignty of the Spirit. Habitual fulness, on the other hand, is both a privilege and a duty for every Christian, but it is clear that all do not enjoy it. Its attainment is a work of the indwelling Holy Spirit, but the believer also has a part in 'putting off' the old self and 'putting on' the new. He must also apply himself to learn and discern the revealed will of God, by which the Spirit of God can strengthen his inward faith for the deeper enjoyment of the love and fulness of God in Christ. Important factors, then, in the experience of the fulness of the Spirit are the avoidance of sin, a knowledge of the revelation of God in Scripture, faith and above all the work of the indwelling Spirit. An awareness of God's desire for us in this matter is vital, for otherwise our expectations will be low.

The fruit of the Spirit is the outward manifestation and evidence of the fulness of the Spirit. But not only this; it is also one of the purposes for which God gives His fulness. For to bear the fruit of the Spirit is, says Colossians 1:10, 'to please Him in all respects', and to represent God truly before men.

Part Four

10. The gifts of the Spirit

In all that has gone before we have been concerned with the gift of the Holy Spirit, that is to say, the gift which is the Spirit Himself. We now turn to a separate though related subject, namely the gifts (or special abilities) imparted to believers *by* the Spirit, enabling them to demonstrate the power of God and to serve and edify the church.

These gifts are referred to in the New Testament by several different Greek terms, but particularly by the word *charisma* (plural, *charismata*) meaning grace, favour or kindness. In other references to these Spirit-given abilities, the Greek words *doma* (a gift), *pneumatikos* (literally an adjective meaning 'spiritual' but rendered 'spiritual gifts' in translation) and *merismos* (something distributed) are employed. Although *charisma* normally refers to a spiritual gift of the kind being discussed here it is also used more generally, to denote for example the gifts of salvation and eternal life in Christ. Similarly, the other Greek words are used in contexts other than that which concerns us here.

The words employed in the original language often help us to understand the things they describe, and the present case is no exception. Even before we consider their context, the Greek words themselves tell us that the 'spiritual gifts' described were of a certain character. *Charisma* speaks of their being unearned and undeserved, the result of a gracious act of God. Those possessing the gifts are said by Peter to be 'stewards of the manifold grace of God' (1 Peter 4:10). *Pneumatikos* emphasizes that they were spiritual as opposed to natural abilities. This is perhaps self-evident in the case of miraculous gifts, but is equally true of certain natural-sounding abilities which could only be exercised properly 'by the strength which God supplies' (1 Peter 4:11). *Merismos*, which occurs only in Hebrews 2:4, tells us that the gifts were distributed to men by the sovereign work of the Holy Spirit acting just as He willed (1 Cor. 12:11). For convenience we shall normally refer to these spiritual gifts by the collective name of 'charismata', using this term to describe not only miraculous abilities but also any ability bestowed upon believers by the work of the Holy Spirit.

This last point is important, as we shall see. Some have confused spiritual gifts with miraculous gifts, thinking that if an ability is not natural but spiritual (that is, imparted to an individual by the Spirit of God) it must therefore, of necessity, be miraculous or incapable of performance by human nature. Some of the New Testament charismata were certainly miraculous and inexplicable in human terms, but other spiritual gifts listed alongside them (e.g. gifts of administration, service and giving) may be considered 'gracious' without being miraculous. In these cases it is the quality of performance of the function that could only be secured by the Holy Spirit's working, rather than the function itself. Thus unbelievers are certainly capable of serving, giving and administering, but only spiritually gifted men and women may do these things in the spiritual manner appropriate to the needs and well-being of the church of Jesus Christ. Thus all the New Testament charismata were spiritual, requiring the work of the Spirit in those who possessed and exercised them; only some of them, however, involved the bestowal of miraculous abilities.

A detailed consideration of the nature of the charismata must be deferred till we have examined the relevant Scriptures, but it will be helpful here simply to list the spiritual gifts to which explicit reference is made in the New Testament. The major passages concerned are four in number, occurring in Romans, 1 Corinthians and Ephesians. The gifts listed in these Scriptures are as follows:

Romans 12:3–8. Prophecy, service (or the office of deacon), teaching, exhortation, giving, mercy.
1 Corinthians 12:8–11. Wisdom, knowledge, faith, healing, miracles, prophecy, discernment of spirits, tongues, interpretation of tongues.

1 Corinthians 12:28—30. Apostolic office, prophetical office, teaching, miracles, healing, helps, administrations, tongues, interpretation of tongues.
Ephesians 4:7—12. Apostolic office, prophetical office, offices of evangelist, pastor and teacher.

It is obvious, firstly, that the lists cover an amazing range of activities, from the exalted office of apostleship to the humblest of 'helps' and, as I have suggested earlier, include explicitly miraculous gifts along with evidently non-miraculous ones. Pentecostals tend to emphasize the 'nine gifts' of the earlier passage in 1 Corinthians 12, even codifying these nine gifts further into groups of three — namely, the 'gifts of revelation' (wisdom, knowledge and discerning of spirits), the 'gifts of power' (faith, miracles and healing) and the 'gifts of utterance' (prophecy, tongues and interpretation). An over-all view of Paul's teaching, however, gives a much less tidy picture, in which the charismata are seen as a wide and diverse range of abilities and functions, both miraculous and otherwise, which defy any neat categorization.

A second general inference from these Scriptures is that the term 'gifts' includes not only certain powers or abilities imparted to believers by the Holy Spirit, but also the people to whom they are imparted. Thus, although the list of spiritual gifts in 1 Corinthians 12:8—11 refers mainly to the powers themselves, their subsequent delineation in verses 28—30 of the same chapter refers to the gifted persons, or offices, in the church. For example, the gift of prophecy in verse 10 is mirrored in verse 28 by the office of prophet, and so on. In Ephesians 4, the gifts of the ascended Christ to His church are specifically listed as the men who perform certain functions and occupy certain offices in that church. Similarly, in Romans 12 the emphasis is not so much upon the gifts themselves, as upon the exercise of those gifts by those who possessed them.

This preliminary point is, I believe, of the utmost importance, for it shows that the New Testament sees the charismata not as disembodied powers, available to believers at their own initiative or whim, but rather as people equipped by the Holy Spirit to exercise varied and complementary ministries in and towards the church. The equivalence of the charismata to ministries in the church is made clear by Paul even in 1 Corinthians 12:4—11 where the gifts are listed as such. 'There are', he asserts, 'varieties of gifts but the same Spirit. And there are varieties of ministries, and the same Lord. And there are varieties of effects, but the same God who works all things in all persons.' This is an obvious case of the repetition of the same idea using different words to drive it home. The gift, the ministry and the effect are all the same thing described by three different words, each word emphasizing a different aspect of the single reality. Thus 'gift' emphasizes the internal work of the Spirit, 'effect' emphasizes the external impressions and occurrences produced and 'ministry' emphasizes the purpose of the gifts, namely to serve, benefit and edify the church. Indeed, even in the list of gifts in 1 Corinthians 12:8—11, the persons entrusted with these gifts are mentioned explicitly, for we read that the Spirit gives 'to one' and 'to another', 'distributing to each one individually'. We conclude, therefore, that the New Testament charismata are not to be viewed simply as powers made generally available to Christians. They should be seen rather in terms of spiritually gifted persons specifically equipped for the benefit of the whole church.

Our next general point is that the charismata were given solely according to the sovereign will of the Holy Spirit who distributes 'to each one individually just as He wills'. The same emphasis is found in Romans 12, where Paul asserts that 'We have gifts that differ according to the *grace* given to us', and also in Ephesians 4, where we read, 'He *gave* some as apostles, some as prophets . . .' and so on. Paul is at great pains to emphasize this teaching, likening the church to one body which nevertheless consists of many parts or 'members', each contributing a different, God-given, role to the integrity, well-being and development of the whole. This illustration is of such importance in Paul's estimation that he expounds it at length both in 1 Corinthians 12 and Ephesians 4. Finally, lest any doubt remain, the apostle tells us in the clearest possible terms that the various gifts of the Spirit are given only to those of His choice: 'All are not apostles, are they? All are not prophets . . .' (1 Cor. 12:29).

This idea, which we might call the 'sovereign donation' of the charismata, is important, for it suggests that the gifts as such should not be sought by believers, as is taught by Pentecostals and Charismatics, except in the general sense that each Christian should desire to be used of God in whatever way He desires. It is probably in this latter sense that Paul tells his Corinthian readers to 'earnestly desire the greater gifts' (1 Cor. 12:31) and to 'desire earnestly spiritual gifts, but especially' the gift of prophecy (1 Cor. 14:1). The words 'desire earnestly' translate the Greek verb *zealoo*, which could also be rendered 'be zealous for' or even 'prize'. There is nothing in the verb employed to indicate whether Paul is addressing individuals at these points (that is, exhorting individual Christians to seek certain spiritual gifts) or whether he is exhorting the church at Corinth generally to desire that the more edifying gifts find greater employment among them. The latter idea, however, is more in keeping with the whole tenor and purpose of these chapters, while the former seems to contradict Paul's very clear teaching on the Spirit's sovereignty in the donation of the charismata.

The question in contention

Although there has been much debate over the precise nature of the charismata, the main point in contention is whether or not certain of the gifts of the Spirit were limited to the apostolic age or should be sought and practised by Christians today. The Pentecostals and Charismatics insist that none of the charismata have ceased or been withdrawn from the church and that their absence throughout much of the Christian era was simply due to lack of faith or spirituality. The Traditional Reformed view, on the other hand, is that the miraculous gifts among the charismata were given to authenticate the apostolic gospel and ceased when the apostles and their immediate successors passed from the scene. The Reformed 'camp' also argues that the completion of the New Testament removed the need for charismata such as prophecy and tongues, since the Scripture constitutes a more secure revelation than any ecstatic utterance. The charismata, they contend, are to be seen as temporary provisions for the emerging church which ceased naturally as the church attained doctrinal maturity.

A further point in contention is the relationship, if any, between the gifts of the Spirit and baptism in the Spirit. Pentecostals and Charismatics see the charismata both as direct evidence of such baptism and as consequences of it. It is true that some Pentecostals differentiate, for example, between the 'sign' of tongues as an indication that a person has received baptism in the Spirit and the 'gift' of tongues as an ongoing exercise in Christian worship. (This enables them to insist upon 'tongues' as proof of baptism for all believers while accepting Paul's teaching that all did not have the gift of tongues — 1 Cor. 12:30.) Nevertheless, the basic Pentecostal and Charismatic position is that the charismata are received as a consequence of baptism in the Spirit.

In the preceding chapters we have concluded that the Pentecostal view of Spirit baptism is not tenable from Scripture. All believers are baptized and sealed by the Spirit at their conversion and He indwells them from that moment onwards, with all His gracious potential. This conclusion, however, does not in any way eliminate the charismatic gifts. If accepted, of course, it means that these gifts cannot be linked with some post-conversion experience called baptism in the Spirit. Pentecostal thinking is wrong at this point. But this does not in any way imply that there are no such gifts as prophecy and tongues to be exercised by believers today. Indeed the views on baptism arrived at in the preceding chapter, if correct, must always have applied, even in the apostolic age. Yet the charismata were most certainly practised during that period. Having accepted the substantial correctness of the Traditional Reformed view on sealing and baptism in the Spirit, we are not automatically committed to this view in respect of the currency or otherwise of spiritual gifts. Thus although the Pentecostal and Charismatic viewpoints link the charismata with the baptism of the Spirit, we need to separate the two topics carefully so that the former may be considered in their own right. It is possible to accept that the baptism of the Spirit occurs at conversion and still to insist that the charismata should be exercised in the contemporary church, and some Reformed believers do indeed adopt this position. The cessation or continuance of the charismata will be considered in detail in chapter 12.

Spiritual gifts: the testimony of the New Testament

We now begin our examination of those passages of Scripture which concern the charismata. At this stage we shall restrict our considerations to the post-Pentecostal era, but in due course we must also see some of these spiritual gifts (notably that of prophecy) exercised in Old Testament and pre-Pentecostal times. This will demonstrate that the charismata cannot be treated solely as the authentication of apostolic authority nor solely as a sequel to the Pentecostal baptism. Some at least of the spiritual gifts are to be found in the pre-Pentecostal dispensation, and we shall examine the implications of this fact later.

The situation in the early church is well summarized in the Epistle to the Hebrews. 'How shall we escape if we neglect so great a salvation?' asks the writer, who continues, 'After it was at the first spoken through the Lord, it was confirmed to us by those who heard, God also bearing witness with them, both by signs and wonders and by various miracles and by gifts (literally, distributions) of the Holy Spirit according to His own will' (Heb. 2:3, 4). This is an important statement, for it makes clear both the nature and primary purpose of the charismata. Concerning their nature, we are told that (a) they constituted a direct witness by God; (b) they authenticated the teaching of those who heard Christ Himself, and (c) they were sovereignly distributed by the Holy Spirit.

Even Christ, whose teaching was so authoritative that thousands waited upon His every word, exercised a miraculous dimension in His ministry with a view to its authentication. 'Believe Me that I am in the Father, and the Father in Me: otherwise believe on account of the works themselves', He said to His disciples (John 14:11). The apostle who recorded this incident uses the same argument towards the end of his Gospel. 'Many other signs therefore Jesus also performed in the presence of the disciples, which are not written in this book; but these have been written that you may believe that Jesus is the Christ, the Son of God; and that believing you may have life in His name' (John 20:30, 31).

If the ministry of the Son of God Himself was confirmed

by miracles, it is not surprising that authenticating signs were also vouchsafed to His disciples. Christ's statement quoted above from John 14 continues, 'Truly, truly, I say to you, he who believes in Me, the works that I do shall he do also; and greater works than these shall he do; because I go to the Father' (John 14:12). The point to notice is that the principle of authentication by God-given signs and wonders is here established not only for the ministry of Christ Himself, but also for the gospel preached by His disciples.

This is exactly what Hebrews 2:14 is saying. The gospel declared by those who heard Christ's teaching was confirmed or authenticated by signs, wonders, miracles and gifts of the Holy Spirit. It is perhaps implied here that only those who heard Christ at the beginning of the gospel era had their ministry thus authenticated and this is essentially the Traditional Reformed position. The verse does not, however, go so far as to state this. It simply says that these 'first generation' disciples did receive such divine confirmation of their gospel. It is only by implication that the writer to the Hebrews, by singling out these disciples for comment, suggests that subsequent generations of evangelists lacked such confirmation. It should, however, be pointed out that the 'first generation' had the special responsibility of writing the New Testament Scriptures and therefore required authentication in a way that their successors did not.

Before examining the testimony of the New Testament generally, we should make reference to the closing verses of Mark's Gospel in which the great commission to 'go into all the world and preach the gospel' is accompanied by the promise that miraculous signs would 'accompany those who have believed' (Mark 16:15—20). These signs are listed as the expulsion of demons, speaking with tongues, immunity from snake bites and poison, and miracles of healing. The claim is further made that such signs actually did occur. 'They went out and preached everywhere, while the Lord worked with them, and confirmed the word by the signs that followed' (Mark 16:20).

The reader will, perhaps, be aware that Mark 16:9—20 is omitted from some older manuscripts and that there is considerable debate regarding its authenticity as Scripture. For our present purposes, however, it really does not affect the issue greatly. No one can dispute (as we have already seen from John 14 and Hebrews 2, and as we shall see further in Acts itself) that the apostolic gospel ministry *was* confirmed by such signs, including tongues and healings, though there is no scriptural record of immunity from poison. As long as this passage is seen to state what actually took place in the early days of the New Testament church, it causes no problem. It is only if the promise of 'signs following' is held to attach to evangelization in every age, that difficulties arise from this passage for some (if not all) of our differing viewpoints.

Spiritual gifts in the Acts

Let us consider the gifts of the Spirit as they are found in the Acts of the Apostles. At this stage we shall not differentiate among 'signs, wonders, various miracles and gifts of the Holy Spirit', regarding them all as attesting signs serving a common purpose, namely the authentication of the gospel preached. A natural distinction must be made, however, between those signs performed by, or mediated through, the disciples themselves and a limited number of manifestations which were quite independent of any action or intent on their part. We are chiefly concerned with the former category of events, since only these fall within the definition of spiritual gifts.

The signs of the Day of Pentecost are well known. They were 'a violent rushing wind' which came 'from heaven', the 'tongues as of fire' which 'rested on each of (the disciples)', and the speaking 'with other tongues' as the Spirit gave them ability so to speak (Acts 2:1–4). The first sign, that of the wind, was independent of the disciples, that is, it was not mediated through them. It came direct from heaven and had the effect of drawing an excited crowd, numbering thousands of men, to the place where the disciples were gathered (Acts 2:6). The function of this sign was obviously to attract an audience for the disciples' polyglot utterances and, later, for Peter's preaching. The second sign, that of flames, was also independent of the disciples and was perhaps more a sign to them than to the curious onlookers. In fact, this is almost certainly the case since they were seated in a house when this phenomenon occurred. It

was, of course, a fulfilment of John's prophecy that Christ
would baptize His disciples 'in the Holy Spirit and fire'
(Luke 3:16).

Our main interest lies in the Spirit-given utterance in
foreign dialects or languages (Acts 2:8). It is obvious from
the context that the tongues being spoken under the influence of the Spirit were known languages. It is equally obvious
that it was not necessary for the sake of comprehension
that the disciples should speak in the native tongues of their
hearers. The entire crowd were able later to understand
Peter's sermon preached in a single language (whether Greek
or Hebrew we do not know; the visitors to Jerusalem would,
arguably, have been fluent in both). Thus the gift of tongues
on the Day of Pentecost was clearly a sign, which impressed
the crowd deeply and obtained an attentive hearing for
Peter's preaching.

Moving on from Acts 2, we next encounter charismatic
powers in the healing of the lame man at the temple gate
(Acts 3:1–10). Significantly, Peter's words to the cripple
include the statement: 'What I do have, I give to you.'
Peter was clearly conscious of possessing the power to
heal the man before he did so, and this is therefore an
example of the gift of healing. Whether or not Peter intended
to create an opportunity for preaching is not stated, but
this was certainly the effect of the miracle. We see again,
therefore, that the spiritual gift was used to create attention
to, and ensure serious consideration of, the gospel. If these
men could perform such a notable miracle of healing, they
must be speaking with divine authority!

We might reflect upon the enormous advantage gained by
a preacher who can work miracles before the eyes of his
congregation. At the very least, he has the undivided attention of his hearers. None will scoff or dismiss his message as
an idle tale. We must also recall that apostolic preaching was
by no means always assisted in this manner. Contrast Paul's
preaching at Lystra (Acts 14:8–18), where a miracle of healing was performed, with his lonely ministry at Athens (Acts
17:16–34) where the majority were clearly unimpressed by
the apostle's reasoned arguments. Again, we see the
sovereignty of the Spirit's working or withholding in the
question of authenticating miracles.

Returning to Acts 4, we next find the disciples praying that their preaching might be accompanied by attesting miracles. 'And now, Lord, take note of their threats, and grant that Thy bond-servants may speak Thy word with all confidence, while Thou dost extend Thy hand to heal, and signs and wonders take place through the name of Thy holy servant Jesus' (Acts 4:30). At this stage of development, the infant church clearly felt the need for divine authentication of the message. After all, they were preaching the resurrection of Jesus from the dead, a miracle if ever there was one! Credibility seemed to demand some demonstration that miracles could and did occur, and appropriate attestations were indeed granted them by God. As Hebrews 2:4 puts it, 'God [was] bearing witness with them both by signs and wonders and by various miracles and by gifts of the Holy Spirit according to His own will.' This state of affairs was perpetuated for some considerable time, at least, for we read further in Acts 5 that 'At the hands of the apostles many signs and wonders were taking place among the people,' who 'held [the apostles] in high esteem'. As a result, 'All the more believers in the Lord, multitudes of men and women, were constantly added to their number.' Such was the power of the Spirit in the apostles that the inhabitants of Jerusalem and the surrounding area 'even carried the sick out into the streets . . . so that when Peter came by, at least his shadow might fall on any one of them . . . people who were sick or afflicted with unclean spirits . . . were all being healed' (Acts 5:12–16).

It is clear from this narrative that the miracles performed made a profound impression on the populace, so much so that Luke attributes to their agency the conversion of 'multitudes of men and women'. It might also be noted that the miracles so won the favour of the people that persecution of the new-born church was significantly muted. 'What shall we do with these men?' complained the Sanhedrin, 'For the fact that a noteworthy miracle has taken place through them is apparent to all who live in Jerusalem, and we cannot deny it' (Acts 4:16). Thus the miraculous dimension of these formative stages of the church both stimulated its growth and inhibited the opposition which might otherwise have overwhelmed it. Stephen likewise exercised a dramatic

ministry, 'full of grace and power', and performed 'great
wonders and signs among the people' (Acts 6:8). The last
phrase, 'among the people', emphasizes the attestatory
character of these miracles. In making his defence before his
persecutors, however, we notice that Stephen makes no use
of miraculous gifts but contents himself with exposition of
Old Testament Scripture (Acts 7:1—53).

We come next to Philip's charismatic ministry in Samaria.
'And the multitudes with one accord were giving attention
to what was said by Philip, as they heard and saw the signs
which he was performing. For in the case of many who had
unclean spirits, they were coming out of them shouting with
a loud voice; and many who had been paralysed and lame
were healed. And there was much rejoicing in that city'
(Acts 8:6—8). Here is an excellent example of miracles of
attestation, since we are specifically told that the people
listened to the gospel message on account of the signs performed. This passage is also of interest because these miracles
(like those of Stephen) were produced at the hands of one
who was not an apostle. This point receives emphasis a few
verses later when two apostles had to be brought from
Jerusalem to lay hands on the Samaritan believers so that
they might receive the Holy Spirit (Acts 8:14—17). Clearly
Philip was able to perform miracles and cast out demons,
but still did not qualify for the office of apostleship.

In Acts 9 we read of two miracles of healing recorded in
juxtaposition. Peter first heals a paralysed man named
Aeneas at Lydda and we are told, 'All who lived at Lydda
and Sharon saw him, and they turned to the Lord' (Acts
9:32—35). Once again a miracle of healing proved to be the
decisive factor in the conversion to Christ of an entire
neighbourhood, a clear case of God authenticating the witness of His servants. This incident is immediately followed
by a further account in which, at first sight, the sole purpose
of the act of healing was compassion. The much-loved
Tabitha had already expired when her distraught friends
sent for Peter at Lydda and begged him to rush to Joppa.
This tragedy within the Christian community was immediately reversed as the apostle raised this outstanding servant
of God from her deathbed. But this was not the end of the
matter for, we read, 'It became known all over Joppa and

many believed in the Lord' (Acts 9:36—42). Thus even an act of compassion, not apparently intended to impress unbelievers, did in fact have this result and did so with saving effect.

Acts 10 records the conversion of the Gentile Cornelius and his household at Caesarea. We have already studied this passage in considering the baptism of the Spirit in chapter 8. We need only notice, therefore, that the charismatic gift of tongues was here vouchsafed to the listeners even while Peter was still explaining the gospel of Christ to them. The major purpose of this gift was clearly to convey to Peter and the Jews who were with him the fact that God had given to Gentiles the selfsame Holy Spirit as they had themselves received at Pentecost (Acts 10:47). Peter argues this at length when challenged by the Jewish believers upon his return to Jerusalem. 'As I began to speak', he explains, 'the Holy Spirit fell upon them, just as He did upon us at the beginning' (Acts 11:15). The explanation satisfied the Jews and they glorified God for granting to the Gentiles also 'the repentance that leads to life' (Acts 11:18).

The first example of New Testament prophecy occurs in Acts 11 when Agabus 'stood up and began to indicate by the Spirit that there would . . . be a great famine all over the world'. Luke adds that this prediction was fulfilled in the reign of Claudius. As a result of this revelation the church at Antioch was able, in advance, to send relief to the more needy brethren living in Judea (Acts 11:27—30). Notice, firstly, that prophecy involved prediction of the future and was clearly miraculous and, secondly, that it served a very practical purpose. This latter point reflects the whole tenor of Acts, namely that the signs, miracles and charismata described in this book are invariably used for clear and practical ends. At no time were they performed or practised simply to satisfy the curiosity of men or by way of spiritual entertainment.

It is not clear whether or not the commissioning of Barnabas and Saul for missionary service (Acts 13:1—4) was the outcome of prophecy. We read that the five brethren named were both 'prophets and teachers' and that as they ministered to the Lord the Holy Spirit said, 'Set apart for Me Barnabas and Saul for the work to which I have called them.' It is quite likely that these words were spoken by one of the prophets in an act of prophecy and accepted by all as the authentic voice of God. This cannot, however, be stated with certainty and it is also possible that the instruction came by way of a mutual inner conviction.

Before passing on from Acts 13, we might notice that the preaching of Paul and Barnabas was attested by a miracle in Paphos (the blinding of Elymas the magician) but that their highly successful ministry in Pisidian Antioch was not. In Antioch, the emphasis is placed upon expository preaching and debate, and no mention is made of miracles.

Attesting miracles reappear during the missionaries' time in Iconium (Acts 14:1–3) where we read, 'They spent a long time there speaking boldly with reliance upon the Lord, who was bearing witness to the word of His grace, granting that signs and wonders be done by their hands.' The emphasis here is interesting. The miracles were attesting signs, God's authenticating witness to the gospel preached by His servants. But the passage also suggests that they were bestowed in a sovereign manner, God *granting* that signs and wonders be done by their hands. The decision as to whether or not miracles would be done seems not to have rested with the preachers, even though they were performed by their hands. The signs were God's gift, given or withheld at God's initiative, and when they were granted they were recognized as such by the apostles (notice that both Paul and Barnabas are so described in Acts 14:4). A further miracle of healing at Lystra excited so much superstitious attention that Paul and Barnabas had to restrain the crowd from offering sacrifice to them (Acts 14:8–18). Paul's amazing recovery from apparent death by stoning also took place in this city (Acts 14:19, 20), but in this case there is no suggestion of the use of a gift of healing by another person.

There is an example of prophetical ministry in Acts 15:32, while in Acts 16:18 Paul casts out an evil spirit. Chapter 19, of course, records the episode in which the disciples of John the Baptist at Ephesus received a baptism in the Spirit, speaking with tongues and prophesying as a result. But also in this chapter we read of the apostle's two-year ministry in the school of Tyrannus during which 'God was performing extraordinary miracles by the hands of Paul, so that handkerchiefs

or aprons were even carried from his body to the sick, and
the diseases left them and the evil spirits went out' (Acts
19:11, 12). The result of these miraculous activities, together
with the experience of the unfortunate Jewish exorcists who
tried to imitate them, was that a remarkable victory was recorded over the 'black arts' of magic and sorcery. 'Many who
practised magic brought their books together and began burn-
ing them in the sight of all: and they counted up the price of
them and found it fifty thousand pieces of silver. So the
word of the Lord was growing mightily and prevailing' (Acts
19:18—20). It is evident that sorcery and witchcraft were
both rife and powerful in Ephesus. Indeed, from the invest-
ment in magical literature noted in these verses, it would
seem that sorcery was a major industry and a pervasive social
force. It is entirely consistent with what we have already seen
in Acts that such entrenched powers of evil should be opposed by a miraculously attested gospel. Luke emphasizes the
extraordinary nature of the miracles performed by Paul in
this situation. It is clear from the narrative that the missionaries faced unusually intense opposition from the magicians
of Ephesus, and we may safely conclude that God gave an
unusual degree of miraculous support to the gospel because
of this. Once again, therefore, we see the level of miraculous
activity is suited to the demands of the situation and mediated by the sovereign wisdom of God. It was the Lord, not
Paul, who performed the miracles, using His servant's 'hands'
as His human instrument (Acts 19:11).

The raising of Eutychus from the dead at Troas (Acts
20:9—12) appears to have been a miracle of pure compassion,
with no evangelistic overtones or consequences. In this respect the incident is exceptional and is probably the only
case of its kind where no effect upon the non-Christian community is recorded.

Further examples of New Testament prophecy are found
in Acts 21:4, 9, 10—12, which relate to a prescience on the
part of many believers, but particularly the prophet Agabus,
that Paul's journey to Jerusalem would result in his captivity.

It is of interest to note that after Paul's imprisonment, his
deliverance from death at the hands of a planned Jewish am-
bush (Acts 23:12—24) was accomplished by providential and
not miraculous means. God used a sharp-eared youth, Paul's

nephew, and a Roman commander's sense of responsibility, to save the apostle from the murderous intentions of the Jews. Nor was Paul accorded any miraculous powers during his long interrogations before Jewish, Roman and civil courts (Acts 23 to 25) even though such manifestations would have vastly strengthened his case. Apart from a possible but somewhat doubtful miraculous element in Paul's escape from snake bite after being shipwrecked on a Maltese beach, there is only one further reference to miracles in the book of Acts.

To summarize, therefore, we see that Acts records a large number of miraculous events in which God bore witness to, or attested, the gospel preached by His servants. In virtually every instance the chronicler makes clear that the effect and intent of miracles was to impress unbelievers or subdue the opposition of those who practised witchcraft and sorcery. We are therefore left in no doubt as to the reason for which these various signs were given, and indeed this reason is plainly stated in Hebrews 2:4. God was bearing His own witness to the truth of the preached gospel. The only general exception to this statement relates to the charismatic gift of prophecy, where the purpose of the gift is equally plain, namely the guidance, comfort and instruction of believers.

It is asserted by some that a gradual withdrawal of attesting miracles is discernible as Acts progresses, and we may test this idea, somewhat crudely perhaps, by noting the number of separate miracles or miraculous episodes recorded in each section of the book, as follows.

Table 2

Chapters	Setting	Number	Average per chapter
1—8	Jerusalem/ Samaria	9	1.12
9—12	Joppa/Caesarea/ Antioch/Jerusalem	5	1.25
13—15	Cyprus/Lystra	3	1.00
16—21	Philippi/Ephesus/ Troas/Caesarea	6	1.00
22—28	Malta	1	0.14

These figures should, of course, be treated with caution, representing as they do a subjective assessment. For example, Paul's two-year ministry at Ephesus is treated as a single episode, as also are the ministries of Stephen (Acts 6:8) and Philip (Acts 8:6), who performed multiple signs and wonders. Nevertheless it is clear that the incidence of recorded miracles, signs and prophetical utterances remains fairly steady up to the time of Paul's imprisonment in Acts 21. If we omit the raising of Eutychus and the prophecy of Agabus, the major miraculous episodes terminate somewhat earlier with Paul's Ephesian ministry in chapter 19. Either way, it cannot be denied that attesting miracles are virtually absent from the last nine chapters of Acts, which thus stand in direct contrast to the first nine chapters of the book. It is true that these closing chapters concentrate upon the imprisonment of one apostle, and that the narrative is consequently of a different kind to that at the beginning of Luke's chronicle. Nevertheless, it is clear that Paul's ministry, at least, became much less charismatic in character after his time at Ephesus.

Spiritual gifts in the Epistle to the Romans

A brief mention of spiritual gifts occurs in Paul's salutation to his Roman readers. 'I long to see you', he writes, 'that I may impart some spiritual gift to you, that you may be established; that is, that I may be encouraged together with you while among you, each of us by the other's faith' (Rom. 1:11, 12). The word used for gift is 'charisma', so that Paul's expression here is identical to that employed in the Corinthian Epistle.

The interest of this statement lies in the apostle's claim to be able to impart spiritual gifts to believers. There is an analogous reference in 1 Timothy 4:14 where Paul exhorts his younger friend, 'Do not neglect the spiritual gift within you, which was bestowed upon you through prophetic utterance with the laying on of hands by the presbytery.' The translators have here supplied the adjective 'spiritual' but are probably correct to do so. This was obviously no natural ability but one specifically imparted to Timothy by the Spirit of God using external means (prophecy and the laying-on of hands) as a vehicle. Thirdly, of course, we may cite the

Samaritan episode, where the reception of the Holy Spirit
Himself was mediated through the actions of Peter and John,
and the parallel occurrence at Ephesus, where Paul was the
apostle involved. Notice that in Timothy's case the human
agents were apparently not apostles, but prophets and elders,
though it is certainly possible that Paul was also present on
that occasion.

It is clear, therefore, that spiritual gifts, although deriving
from the Spirit's sovereign donation, were sometimes imparted to individuals by the deliberate actions of others, for
example, by the laying-on of hands. Apostles, prophets and
elders all seem to have been involved in such events. There
is no reason to suppose, however, that spiritual gifts were
always imparted by means of human agency. The gifts of
tongues and prophecy vouchsafed to Cornelius and his
household, though occurring in Peter's presence, were certainly not given at his instigation. Indeed he was as surprised
as his companions at their manifestation.

We must conclude that the charismata were sometimes
imparted directly to individuals by the Spirit and sometimes by means of human vehicles or agencies. It would appear that the choice between these two methods lay entirely
in the sovereign will of the Holy Spirit Himself.

As we come to Romans 12 we find the first New Testament representation of the church as a body. The importance
of this illustration for our present enquiry cannot be over-
stressed, for it occurs as a central theme in each of the three
major Pauline passages on the charismata. Indeed it would
probably be no exaggeration to suggest that Paul always
thought of the charismata in these terms.

The argument is perfectly straightforward. 'Just as we
have many members in one body and all the members do not
have the same function, so we, who are many, are one body
in Christ, and individually members one of another.' Accordingly argues Paul, 'we have gifts (charismata) that differ
according to the grace given to us' (Rom. 12:4—6). Recognizing this, no Christian will 'think more highly of himself
than he ought to think', seeing that it is God who has 'allotted to each' that measure of faith that enables the believer
to exercise his gift and function within the church (Rom.
12:3).

There is here a strong suggestion that every believer has
received some gift from the Lord to exercise in the context
of the church. Paul addresses 'every man among you' and
asserts that 'God has allotted to each a measure of faith.' He
surely includes all believers when he says, 'We, who are many,
are one body in Christ.' It would hardly be natural if, in the
following sentence ('We have gifts . . .') the apostle was
referring only to certain Christians among the many. We shall
see that this impression concerning the generality of the
charismata is strengthened by other New Testament passages
and, if correct, is a most important point. Without the illustration of the body and the church, we might naturally suppose that the charismata were a limited range of abilities imparted by the Spirit to a limited number of individuals. The
inseparable link that Paul establishes between this illustration
and the charismata, not only here in Romans but also in 1
Corinthians and Ephesians, suggests instead that every member of the body of Christ receives some spiritual gift for the
benefit and edification of the whole. Every Christian is,
without question, a member of the body. And no part of a
body is devoid of function. It follows that every believer has
a function, a Spirit-given gift, by which he or she contributes
to the well-being of the whole. The charismata, it would
seem, are altogether general, though any given function or
charisma is granted to a limited number of people, as the
Spirit of God wills.

The verses that follow in Romans 12 are interesting in that
they begin with specific, identifiable gifts but move almost
imperceptibly to those general qualities of life that ought to
characterize all Christians. Prophecy, service, teaching, exhortation, giving, leadership and the ministry of mercy are
spoken of in terms of particular functions within the church.
This is not to say, of course, that all believers should not, for
example, give or exercise mercy. It is simply that some have a
particular ministry in this direction and an unusual degree of
ability to function in these ways. With hardly pause for
breath, however, Paul continues, 'Let love be without hypo-
crisy . . . Be devoted to one another in brotherly love . . . fervent in spirit, serving the Lord, rejoicing in hope . . . devoted
to prayer, contributing to the needs of saints, practising hos-
pitality.'

Here, at least, the apostle does not differentiate sharply between the gifts of the Spirit and His fruit in the lives of believers. This is particularly interesting since all viewpoints, from Pentecostal to Traditional Reformed, tend to distinguish the gifts from the fruit of the Spirit, mainly on the basis of 1 Corinthians where they are, indeed, set in contrast, as we shall see. However, it must be remembered that there were particular problems at Corinth so that the situation pictured in the twelfth chapter of Romans may well be more representative of normality.

Spiritual gifts in 1 Corinthians

We come now to the best known of the several passages dealing with the charismata, namely the three chapters embedded in the heart of Paul's first letter to Corinth. Unless the reader is already thoroughly acquainted with these chapters it is suggested that he or she reads again 1 Corinthians 12 to 14 before continuing with this chapter. It is important to grasp the broad sweep of Paul's argument in this section of the Epistle before considering detailed questions on individual texts.

It would appear that Paul's dissertation on spiritual gifts arose from a question that the Corinthians had themselves asked. Chapter 7 of this Epistle begins, 'Now concerning the things about which you wrote . . .', and Paul then proceeds to give his advice and counsel on a number of matters including marriage (7:1–16, 25–40), slavery (7:17–24), food sacrificed to idols (8:1–13) and certain aspects of public worship (11:1–34). The words 'Now concerning . . .' run as a refrain through this section of the Epistle (7:1; 7:25; 8:1) and also serve to introduce the subject of the charismata. 'Now concerning spiritual gifts, brethren, I do not want you to be unaware' (1 Cor. 12:1). Since the apostle refers in chapter 7 to the things (plural) about which they had written to him, it is natural to suppose that each time he uses the words, 'Now concerning . . .,' Paul is introducing a further answer to their questions.

If this is the case, it means that the Corinthians were having certain problems with the charismata. Indeed, Paul's injunction not to forbid speaking in tongues (1 Cor 14:39) suggests that some at Corinth were contemplating just such a ban upon the practice. The precise nature of their questions to Paul cannot, of course, be ascertained, but it will help our understanding of these important chapters if we remember that the apostle is responding to points that had been raised with him.

There is one other major piece of 'background' that we need to mention before looking at chapters 12 to 14 in detail. The Corinthian church was highly gifted and precocious, but, at the same time, immature and unspiritual. 'In everything you were enriched in Him', Paul acknowledges, 'in all speech and all knowledge, even as the testimony concerning Christ was confirmed in you, so that you are not lacking in any gift . . .' (1 Cor. 1:5—7). In spite of this, however, the apostle has to remonstrate with them concerning divisions and party spirit (1:10—17), immaturity (3:1, 2), spiritual ignorance (3:16), a critical spirit (4:3—6), arrogance (4:6—18), gross immorality (5:1, 2), boastfulness (5:6), misuse of legal processes (6:1—11), further immoralities (6:16—20), complacency (10:12), misbehaviour at the Lord's table (11:20—22) and other matters. It is surely for this reason that Paul emphasizes so strongly in chapter 13 the need to cultivate Christian character and the fruit of the Spirit, namely love. The gifts of the Spirit were greatly in evidence, but the sanctifying work of the same Spirit was sadly lacking. Bearing this in mind, we realize that Corinth was hardly a typical New Testament church and we should be cautious in generalizing too widely either its practices or the advice Paul proffers to its members.

In the opening verses of chapter 12, the apostle refers to their pagan background, reminding them that they were 'led astray' by the idolatrous worship of the society in which they lived. This worship may have involved magic and sorcery (compare the situation at nearby Ephesus, Acts 19:18, 19) and might well have featured ecstatic utterances by the officiating priests. Paul seems to be anxious that similar influences should not gain a foothold in the church through satanic imitation of the charismata. There must be an ability to distinguish between the activities of spirits and the Spirit of God (see verse 10, where the distinguishing of spirits is listed as one of the gifts of the Spirit and also 1 John 4:1—3).

It would appear that the Corinthians had been disturbed and puzzled by certain miraculous utterances in their meetings in which Jesus had been pronounced 'accursed'. Whether this had occurred in prophecy or tongues is not clear, but that it had happened is almost certain for Paul would hardly have referred to such a bizarre event if his correspondents had not raised it with him. It probably happened during speaking with tongues, since a believer would be more likely to be deceived into blasphemy when speaking words unknown to himself than when conscious of what he was saying. Either way, however, the Corinthians had been faced with a serious dilemma. Here was a miraculous or ecstatic utterance, and therefore to all appearances the work of the Holy Spirit. But Christ was being blasphemed! Paul has to instruct them that even well-meaning Christians may be wrought upon by evil spirits imitating the genuine work of the Holy Spirit. He warns his readers not 'to be unaware' of this possibility and to remember how they were once led astray by such influences during their unconverted days. He then lays down what might to us seem an obvious test, namely that a man speaking ecstatically under the influence of the Spirit of God can only honour and glorify Jesus, not blaspheme Him. The fact that Paul had to make such an obvious point shows that the Corinthians were gullible and easily led, thinking that any miraculous phenomenon must, by definition, be the work of God. Not so, say both Paul and John. 'Beloved, do not believe every spirit, but test the spirits to see whether they are from God; because many false prophets have gone out into the world' (1 John 4:1).

This counsel is as important today as it was then. We must not suppose that ecstatic utterances, whether prophecy, tongues or of some other kind, are necessarily from God. Even the prophets at Corinth were required by Paul to subject their words to the judgement of their peers (1 Cor. 14:29). The danger of satanic deception is specially present if believers abandon their minds to possession by external powers and speak ecstatically with no knowledge of what they are saying. The genuine charismata at Corinth specifically excluded such a 'handing over' of control by the speaker. Of prophecy we read, 'The spirits of prophets are subject to prophets,' so that a prophet might choose to speak up, or to cease speaking, whichever was required by sound judgement, good order and even courtesy to others (1 Cor. 14:29—33). Likewise, the genuine tongues-speaker was enjoined to remain silent if there was no one present to interpret (1 Cor. 14:28), implying once again that the person concerned had complete control over the gift. Those Charismatics today who advocate mind-emptying techniques and who abandon the powers of judgement and self-control in an attempt to obtain charismatic gifts, are treading on extremely dangerous ground. This is, of course, recognized by some Pentecostals and Charismatics who take pains to avoid excesses, but there are others who no doubt need to heed Paul's warning at the beginning of 1 Corinthians 12 that the charismata are susceptible to satanic imitation.

Having dealt with the more obvious dangers associated with miraculous gifts, the apostle next addresses himself to a more subtle problem, namely that of arrogance and disunity. In verses 4—11 he enumerates the nine famous gifts of the Spirit (the word of wisdom, the word of knowledge, faith, healing, miracles, prophecy, the distinguishing of spirits, tongues, interpretation of tongues). But it is certainly not Paul's purpose here simply to catalogue the charismata, as some writers appear to think. Indeed the individual gifts themselves are incidental to the main argument, which is that all such gifts, whatever their nature, are the work of the same Holy Spirit. The expressions 'the same Spirit' or 'one Spirit' occur five times in the space of eight verses, and the nub of the argument is set out at the commencement of this passage. 'There are varieties of gifts', explains Paul, 'but the same Spirit. And there are varieties of ministries, and the same Lord. And there are varieties of effects, but the same God who works all things in all persons' (1 Cor. 12:4—6).

The first conclusion, then, is that the gifts mentioned here are merely illustrative of the whole range of charismata and in no way a definitive list. Whatever the gift, argues Paul, the important thing to grasp is that there is only one Holy Spirit involved, dispensing His gifts in a sovereign manner, 'to each one individually just as He wills' (1 Cor. 12:11). And why does God act thus? The apostle answers this obvious question by expounding at length his favourite illustration of the church as a body. We have already noticed when commenting on Romans 12 that Paul nowhere discusses the gifts of the Spirit without alluding to this picture. The visible, local church is an organic whole. Like the physical body, it cannot function except in unity. It cannot prosper, grow or develop unless every diverse component makes its contribution to the well-being of the whole. Every such component must supply some function, whether major or minor, obvious or concealed, splendid or mundane. No part is dispensable and no part is independent of the remainder. And 'God has placed the members [of His church], each one of them, in the body just as He desired' (1 Cor. 12:18), so that no one member can vaunt his gift above another. None can despise another's contribution or claim that he can dispense with it. Division in the physical body is logically inadmissible, and so it should be in the church (1 Cor. 12:25). Finally, Paul returns to the charismata (verses 28–31) giving a different list, which confirms the idea that the earlier catalogue was illustrative rather than definitive. Moreover, here the gifts are listed as offices and functions rather than mere abilities, emphasizing the role of gifted persons within the church. The particular point being made is that different people have different roles or functions. 'All are not apostles, are they? All are not prophets . . . All are not teachers . . . All do not speak with tongues, do they?' (1 Cor. 12:29–30).

The main thrust of chapter 12 (after Paul's initial warning against satanic mimicry of the charismata) therefore concerns the manner in which the church should function and grow by the exercise of divine gifts within it. In His tender care for the church, God has determined what gifts and abilities are needed for her development and has sovereignly entrusted those gifts to individual members. The Corinthians must understand what God is about, they must grasp His design for church life and growth. Such comprehension of God's plan would neutralize the self aggrandizement and divisiveness that so bedevilled the Corinthian fellowship, and they would learn to respect and value the contributions made by all, whether great or small in man's estimation.

The twelfth chapter of the Epistle closes with the following words: 'But earnestly desire the greater gifts. And I show you a still more excellent way' (1 Cor. 12:31). These words serve to introduce Paul's classic discourse on love, which occupies the thirteenth chapter and, at the same time, to link the twelfth and thirteenth chapters together.

The injunction to 'desire earnestly' the greater gifts has been the subject of much debate. Pentecostals and Charismatics maintain that this clause, together with a similar word in 14:1, provide scriptural warrant for individual believers to seek the bestowal of specific charismata such as the gift of tongues. Although such a conclusion is reasonable at first sight, there are several reasons for doubting that this is Paul's meaning. Firstly, of course, he has already indicated that the charismata were sovereignly distributed by the Holy Spirit (12:11) and that only God has the right to determine what role in the body is to be played by each member. It cannot be Paul's intention, therefore, to teach that each Christian should decide what gifts he would like and earnestly seek them. That would be a contradiction of the concept of sovereign donation and would also make nonsense of the lengthy argument concerning the body and its members. Secondly, such an interpretation of Paul's injunction to 'desire earnestly' the gifts of the Spirit would contradict the apostle's plain statement that all do not exercise the same gift (1 Cor. 12:29, 30). When in chapter 14 he says, 'I wish that you all spoke in tongues, but even more that you would prophesy' (v. 5), it is clear that he is employing the literary device of hyperbole. He cannot really be proposing that everyone should either speak in tongues or prophesy. He has already denied such a possibility in the most categorical terms at the end of chapter 12. Here, then, we have a clear case of hyperbole, or deliberate exaggeration for effect. It is a common device, and one which interestingly enough was used by Moses in the context of prophecy. The Spirit of God had come upon the seventy elders to equip them to administer the nation, and as a sign of His supervention the elders prophesied. Joshua protested that two of them were prophesying in the camp and asked Moses to forbid them. Moses replied, 'Are you jealous for my sake? Would that all the Lord's people were prophets, that the Lord would put His Spirit upon them!' (Num. 11:26–29.) Obviously Moses did not expect every Israelite to prophesy, so why did he express a wish that they should do so? The answer is clear. He was using hyperbole to emphasize that what Joshua was seeing was the direct work of God and that they should desire to see more, not less, of His power in their midst.

Similarly, Paul is emphasizing to the Corinthians that they should desire to see the working and power of God's Spirit in their midst. It is in this general and collective sense that he urges them to desire spiritual gifts. He is not, however, recommending individual Christians to seek specific gifts, as if choosing them from a supermarket shelf! It is the church collectively that is to desire spiritual gifts and they are to do so in the sense that these gifts are evidence of God's working among them. Only such an interpretation is consistent with the remainder of chapter 12 and, especially, with the idea of God's sovereignty in the donation of the gifts.

Furthermore, when Paul's words are studied more closely we see that he never says simply, 'Desire spiritual gifts,' but that this injunction is always qualified. In chapter 12:30 he says, 'Earnestly desire the greater gifts', while in chapter 14:1 he adds, 'Desire earnestly spiritual gifts, but especially that you may prophesy.' In both cases the apostle makes a distinction between greater and lesser charismata and urges the church to have the maturity to prize the superior gifts.

The thrust of Paul's words, therefore, is not that the Corinthians should seek gifts, but rather that they should learn to discern and value those gifts that would most benefit their church in its particular needs. This line of reasoning is particularly evident in chapter 14, where the gift of tongues is compared unfavourably with that of prophecy.

The Greek verb translated 'desire earnestly' does not have the primary sense of 'desire' and is nowhere used in Scripture to signify 'seek'. Its basic meaning is to be 'jealous over' or 'zealous for'. Paul uses it in 2 Corinthians 11:2 to denote his deep concern for those to whom he has preached the gospel. 'I am jealous for you with a godly jealousy', he protests, 'for I betrothed you to one husband, that to Christ I might present you as a pure virgin. But I am afraid lest . . . your minds should be led astray from the simplicity and purity of devotion to Christ.'

Paul does not seek their espousal to the Lord, for that has already been accomplished. The essence of his concern is that, being committed to Christ, his readers might nevertheless be led away again and lost to the gospel cause. To put it simply, people are jealous over what they possess and fear to lose, not over what they do not yet have.

If we now apply this idea to the charismata at Corinth, we see Paul's injunction, to 'desire earnestly' the best gifts, in a fresh light. He is not telling them to seek gifts they do not possess, but rather to guard jealously what they already have. There is a danger that the superior gifts might be withdrawn by the sovereign Spirit, to their great loss. How might this come about? By their abusing, rather than using the Spirit's gifts. What abuses has Paul in mind? Many, including the toleration of satanic imitation (1 Cor. 12:1–3), failure to recognize the true source of the gifts (12:4–13), making the gifts an occasion for arrogance and factional divisions (12:4–13), exercise of the gifts without love (that is, without corresponding Christian virtues, 13:1–13), failure to recognize the proper use and purpose of certain gifts (14:1–25) and, finally, disorderly conduct in the use of gifts (14:26–40). In the face of these dangers they are to be 'jealous over' what the Holy Spirit has, in His sovereign will, entrusted to them (12:11, 18), lest the charismata be withdrawn by an equally sovereign action. A central aspect of their 'earnest desire' or jealousy over what God has given them should, counsels the apostle, be a prizing of the 'greater gifts' (12:31), especially the greater gift of prophecy (14:1, 12). It is not for the individual to seek certain charismata, not even that of prophecy, since who receives what gift is a matter for God to decide (12:11, 18), not man. It is, however, for the church to guard jealously what the Spirit has given and especially to cultivate those gifts that serve to edify its members.

We have spent a considerable time on this matter because it is central to a proper understanding of Paul's teaching here in First Corinthians. Beginning with the fact that the Spirit had richly endued the Corinthian church with charismata (1 Cor. 1:7), the apostle responds to questions raised by that church in a letter (1 Cor. 7:1), by exhorting them to cherish and guard jealously these gifts lest they become forfeit through misuse. He details the possible abuses that had arisen (or might arise) and gives advice on their correction. In the course of his argument he makes it clear that the distribution of the charismata is the sovereign prerogative of the Spirit of God and provides no grounds for arrogance,

boastfulness or factional attitudes. The primary purpose of
the charismata is the building up or edification of the church,
the chief exception being the gift of tongues. This gift has the
primary role of a sign to unbelievers, and should be used
sparingly within the church.

The thirteenth chapter of First Corinthians is, of course, a
classic. But the very familiarity of Paul's discourse on love
often obscures the fact that it is an integral part of his teaching on spiritual gifts and must not be wrested from its context. The apostle's thesis is that the charismata are useless
unless employed and exercised in Christian love. Why? Because the whole purpose of the Spirit's gifts to the church is
the blessing and edification of that church. 'To each one is
given the manifestation of the Spirit for the common good'
(1 Cor. 12:7). But love is an essential ingredient in the
relationship of believer to believer. Hence the whole purpose
of the charismata is frustrated if love is absent.

This understanding of Paul's argument is supported by
Ephesians 4, where the gifts of the risen Lord to His church
are also under discussion and the illustration of the church
as a body is again employed. From Christ, the apostle explains, 'The whole body, being fitted and held together by
that which every joint supplies, according to the proper
working of each individual part, causes the growth of the
body for the building up of itself in love' (Eph. 4:16). The
emphasis to notice comes in the final clause. The body (that
is, the church) is built up by the exercise of individual gifts
in love. The deployment of gifts alone is not sufficient, for
it lacks the vehicle of love by which the gifts are made effective. The prophet cannot edify his brethren unless he speaks in
love, nor can his words benefit those who do not hold him in
esteem. Similarly, the other charismata are profitless and ineffective unless exercised in love. Only love can properly
direct the gifts and abilities imparted by the Spirit. Only love
can make their ministries acceptable to their fellow belivers.
Only love can provide a climate for spiritual growth. Without
it, the most amazing miracles, the most powerful ministry,
the most self-sacrificing actions, are ineffectual in producing
spiritual prosperity within the church.

Some interpret Paul's words differently. They point to the
closing statement of the twelfth chapter ('I show you a still

more excellent way') and argue that the apostle is here offering love as an alternative to spiritual gifts. The Corinthians,
they say, had to make a choice between the charismata and
love, the latter being the better of the two.

It is very difficult to sustain this view, based as it is upon a
narrow interpretation of the phrase 'a more excellent way'.
The Greek here is not strictly comparative, as if Paul is offering love as the better of two options, but refers rather to a
'way' which is 'beyond measure'. We might thus paraphrase
verse 31 as follows: 'Guard jealously the greater gifts, but do
not be satisfied even with these. Gifts may be measured,
some being judged lesser and some greater. But I will show
you something that is beyond measure, a way of life that cannot be assessed or measured! That way of life is the way of
love, and without it the gifts become useless for their God-
intended function.' Paul is not saying, 'Set the gifts aside in
favour of love,' otherwise he could not logically return to the
subject in chapter 14 with the words: 'Be jealous over spiritual gifts.' On the contrary, he is telling his readers that the
gifts must be valued and safeguarded and that without love
they will atrophy and die. Love is the *sine qua non* of Christian fellowship and mutual edification, and without it the gifts
are frustrated and useless. The church can only edify itself 'in
love' (Eph. 4:16).

In the latter part of 1 Corinthians 13, it is true, Paul opens
up a distinction between the charismata and love. He is not,
however, saying that the two are mutually exclusive but
rather that love outlasts the gifts. Prophecy, tongues and gifts
of knowledge, argues the apostle, are all partial and temporary. In contrast, love will never fail or cease. Indeed, the
fruit of the Spirit — namely faith, hope and love — all 'abide'
(13:13) in contrast to the charismata which will be done away
(13:10), but love is the greatest of these, being of the essence
of the nature of God Himself. As John proclaims, 'God is
love' (1 John 4:8).

The question of the cessation of the charismata is obviously
a major one, sharply dividing the Pentecostal and Charismatic
viewpoints from the Traditional Reformed position. The last
six verses of 1 Corinthians 13 constitute the only passage of
Scripture bearing directly on this matter and we shall consider these verses at length in the next chapter.

We have already had occasion to refer to parts of 1 Corinthians 14, but let us now look at this chapter as a whole. In contrast to chapters 12 and 13, the only charismata mentioned in this discussion are prophecy, tongues and the interpretation of tongues. Having indicated at the end of chapter 12 that some spiritual gifts are 'greater' and some lesser, Paul now illustrates this distinction powerfully by a direct comparison between prophecy and tongues. His message is straightforward enough. Speaking in tongues, whatever it may do for the person exercising the gift, does nothing for the assembled believers because they do not understand what is being said. Unless, therefore, the tongues are interpreted into the familiar language of those present, they are not to be used in the church. 'If there is no interpreter, let [the tongues speaker] keep silent in the church; and let him speak to himself and to God' (1 Cor. 14:28). Furthermore, tongues were given primarily as a sign to unbelievers (14:22), and their employment in the worship of the church fails even to serve this purpose (14:23) because it is essentially a misuse of the gift.

Having proved the superiority of prophecy as a means of edifying the believers, and having prohibited the public use of uninterpreted tongues, Paul nevertheless adopts an attitude of tolerance towards interpreted tongues, allowing them a limited and carefully regulated employment in the worship of the church. 'If anyone speaks in a tongue, it should be by two or at the most three, and each in turn, and let one interpret' (14:27). Although he expressly excludes a prohibition on tongues (14:39), the apostle makes his own preference abundantly clear: 'I speak in tongues more than you all; however, in the church I desire to speak five words with my mind, that I may instruct others also, rather than ten thousand words in a tongue' (14:18, 19).

Finally, Paul returns to his plea for order and decorum in the worship of God. He has already stated that any tongues-speaking must be done in turn and not simultaneously, and that every such utterance should be interpreted plainly. He has further required that even prophecy should be limited to two or three speakers and subjected to the judgement of those who sit by. Further, the prophets are to give way courteously to one another as occasion demands. 'If a revelation

is made to another who is seated, let the first keep silent'
(14:30), instructs the apostle. For what reason? Because
babble and confusion in the church are a denial of the nature
of God and cannot constitute true worship. 'God is not a
God of confusion, but of peace' (14:33), and clearly those
who worship Him must do so in a manner that reveals and
exalts this particular aspect of the divine character. Therefore, concludes Paul, 'Let all things be done properly and in
an orderly manner' (14:40).

Here we conclude our survey of the Corinthian dissertation
on spiritual gifts. We shall, however, return to this passage of
Scripture in our subsequent discussions on the nature of individual charismata and the question of their cessation.

Spiritual gifts in Ephesians

We come now to the third major New Testament passage on
the charismata, namely Ephesians chapter 4. Once again, the
reader is urged to refresh his or her memory by turning to
that chapter and reading verses 1 to 16. Much of what Paul
has to say here is reminiscent of Romans 12 and 1 Corinthians 12—14, though there are, of course, particular aspects
appropriate to the Ephesian believers.

The Epistle to the Ephesians is outstanding in its double
emphasis upon God's ultimate purpose for the church and
His gracious provision for it. Both aspects are highlighted in
the opening verses of the letter. 'He chose us in [Christ],'
declares the apostle, 'before the foundation of the world,
that we should be holy and blameless before Him. In love He
predestined us to adoption as sons through Jesus Christ to
Himself' (Eph. 1:4, 5). Christ gave Himself for the church, he
adds, 'that He might present [her] to Himself in all her glory,
having no spot or wrinkle or any such thing' (Eph. 5:27).

Concerning His provision for the church, we read that God
'has blessed us with every spiritual blessing in the heavenly
places in Christ' and 'lavished upon us' the 'riches of His
grace' (Eph. 1:3, 7, 8). Not only did Christ die for His people
(5:25), but in rising again and ascending to the right hand
of God (1:20—23) He has given His Spirit both to indwell
the church and to bring her to her final glorious state (2:21,
22; 4:30). In particular, the ascended Christ 'gave gifts to

men . . . for the equipping of the saints for the work of service, to the building up of the body of Christ'. This work of
building would go on 'until we all attain to the unity of the
faith and of the knowledge of the Son of God, to a mature
man, to the measure of the stature of the fulness of Christ'
(Eph. 4:8–13, mg.). Paul's prose may be involved, but his
message is clear. The gifts of the ascended Christ had the
ultimate purpose of bringing the church to full maturity.
Even in its infancy, the church was the body of Christ. But
like any infant, it had to grow to maturity, to manhood. One
day it would achieve such a stature that it would express
visibly its true nature as the 'fulness' of Christ. This maturity
would be characterized by love, unity of faith and an intimate knowledge of the Son of God. The process of maturation was already under way in Paul's day, promoted by the
mutual love and service of every member of the body, each
exercising his or her proper role and function and doing so
in love (Eph. 4:16). The apostle therefore urges his readers
to further this growth by cultivating Christian character,
avoiding sin and obeying God (Eph. 4:17–6:20).

The conjunction of the two ideas (of the church as a body
and of its growing to maturity) is not unique to Ephesians.
We also meet it in 1 Corinthians where the illustration of the
body is developed in chapter 12 and the idea of growth to
maturity in chapter 13. 'When I was a child, I used to speak
as a child, think as a child, reason as a child; when I became
a man, I did away with childish things' (1 Cor. 13:11). The
Lord's gifts to His people, then, have the purpose of bringing
the visible church to a maturity commensurate with its
hidden status as the body of Christ, 'the fulness of Him who
fills all in all' (Eph. 1:23). We shall need to enquire later, just
when this final maturity was to be attained, whether at some
point in human history or only at the return of Jesus Christ.
Whatever our answer, however, there can be no question
that Paul looked for a process of maturation, which would
be visible and evident even in his day.

Having emphasized the purpose of the gifts, we may now
look at the gifts themselves as enumerated in verse 11 of
Ephesians chapter 4. They are the gifts of apostleship, and
the offices of prophet, evangelist, pastor and teacher. We
notice that the emphasis here, as in 1 Corinthians 12:28–30,

is upon the gifted persons rather than the gifts themselves. We also notice that the more miraculous charismata (tongues, healing and miracles, for example) are absent from the Ephesian catalogue and that the emphasis is rather upon teaching or ministerial activities.

Some may argue that we should distinguish between the gifts (*charismata*) of the Spirit as listed in First Corinthians and the gifts (*domates*) of the risen Christ detailed here, especially since different Greek words are employed. This, however, is difficult to sustain. Apostleship and the prophetical office are not only mentioned but given deliberate precedence in 1 Corinthians 12:28, and this corresponds exactly with the order expressed here ('He gave some as apostles and some as prophets . . .' Eph. 4:11). This overlap and identical ranking of the gifts enumerated in the two Epistles demonstrate that in Paul's mind the gifts of the Spirit and the gifts of the risen Christ are the same. The reason why he here omits certain of the charismata listed in Corinthians is a matter for speculation. It could be that these omitted gifts were not practised in the Ephesian church, but we cannot be sure. Certainly we can say on the authority of 1 Corinthians 14 that Paul regarded as superior those gifts that instruct and edify, and these are the very charismata detailed here in Ephesians.

Other New Testament references to spiritual gifts

Two interesting references to spiritual gifts are found in Paul's letters to Timothy. 'Until I come', urges the apostle, 'give attention to the public reading of Scripture, to exhortation and teaching. Do not neglect the spiritual gift (*charisma*) within you, which was bestowed upon you through prophetic utterance with the laying on of hands by the presbytery' (1 Tim. 4:14). Paul returns to the matter at the very outset of his second letter, as if it is the subject uppermost in his mind as he remembers Timothy 'constantly' in his prayers 'night and day' (2 Tim. 1:3). 'I remind you', says Paul earnestly, 'to kindle afresh the gift (*charisma*) of God which is in you through the laying on of my hands. For God has not given us a spirit of timidity, but of power and love and discipline. Therefore do not be ashamed of the testimony of our Lord . . .' (2 Tim. 1:6—8).

It is likely that the gift referred to in these two passages
is one and the same, even though the circumstances surrounding its acquisition are somewhat differently described in the
two places. In the first reference, the gift was imparted by
prophecy and laying-on of hands by a group of elders among
whom Paul himself was probably numbered. We are not told
that Paul was present, but the detail given suggests strongly
that he was an eyewitness of the event, and may even have
been the prophet involved (compare Acts 13:1). In the
second reference Paul speaks only of himself laying hands
on Timothy, but this may be only because the apostle is
here writing in the context of his personal relationship with
the younger man. In verse 2 he calls him 'my beloved son',
in verse 4 he expresses a longing to see him and recalls his
tears, in verse 5 he refers to Timothy's mother and grand-
mother and in verse 8 he pleads that Timothy should not
be ashamed of 'me His prisoner'. The passage is thus
intensely personal in nature and it is not surprising that Paul
emphasizes his own role in the events recounted.

The likelihood that both passages refer to the same gift
is enhanced when we consider what the gift in question was.
It was almost certainly a pastoral or teaching gift. In
1 Timothy the reference is embedded in an entire section
concerned with Timothy's work and responsibility as a
teacher of the Word of God. 'Prescribe and teach these
things,' says Paul. 'Let no one look down on your youth-
fulness . . . give attention to . . . reading . . . exhortation and
teaching . . . do not neglect the spiritual gift . . . pay close
attention to yourself and to your teaching . . . ensure salvation for those who hear you' (1 Tim. 4:11–16).

Similarly, in 2 Timothy, the apostle urges Timothy to
rekindle the gift, explaining that timidity, or the fear of men,
is inconsistent and that his young friend must 'not be
ashamed of the testimony' of Christ. Clearly Timothy was
faced with just such temptations as might well assail one who
publicly ministers the gospel in the face of opposition.

Apart from noticing that the teaching ministry is plainly
delineated here as one of the charismata, the most interesting
aspect of these references is that Timothy received the gift
by the laying-on of hands. The question arises as to whether
such human agency was always involved when men were

endued with spiritual gifts or whether the gifts were sometimes imparted directly by the Spirit of God without any
such means. The fact is that we cannot tell from Scripture
which answer is correct. The laying-on of apostolic hands
was certainly involved in some instances (compare Acts
8.17, 19:6 and possibly 13:3), but the major passages on the
charismata in Romans, 1 Corinthians and Ephesians are
silent as to the means, if any, employed in imparting the
gifts of the Spirit. In the few cases where we are told how
people were endowed with gifts, as in these passages in the
Pastoral Epistles, the laying-on of hands by an apostle
(accompanied by other elders) is the only means specified.

An important reference to the charismata occurs in
Hebrews 2 and we have already cited it several times. The
verse, however, deserves examination in its own right. 'We
must' declares the writers, 'pay much closer attention to
what we have heard [i.e. the gospel], lest we drift away
from it. For if the word spoken through angels [i.e. Moses
law] proved unalterable . . . how shall we escape if we
neglect so great a salvation?' (Heb. 2:1—3.) What was this
salvation? Nothing other than the gospel which was 'first
spoken through the Lord . . . was confirmed to us by those
who heard [Him]' and divinely attested, 'God bearing witness with them, both by signs and wonders and by various
miracles and by gifts [distributions] of the Holy Spirit
according to His own will' (Heb. 2:3—4).

Spiritual gifts are here represented as one means by
which God authenticated the gospel preached by the apostles
('those who heard' Christ). There were, additionally, signs
and wonders which were independent acts of God not mediated through His servants. But the special powers or gifts,
exercised by the apostles, and by such men as Stephen and
Philip, rank alongside such miracles, as attesting signs given
in a sovereign manner 'according to His own will'.

In what way did God employ the charismata to authenticate the heavenly nature of the gospel? Firstly, by empowering the apostles and certain of their brethren to perform
miraculous acts (tongues at Pentecost, miracles of healing
and so on), and secondly by enabling the apostles to impart
such gifts to others (usually by the laying-on of hands; see
our earlier discussion). Why did the apostles and their

colleagues need such special attestation? Because they were
not only preachers of the gospel but also those who laid the
foundation of the church. 'You . . . are of God's household',
Paul tells the Ephesians, 'having been built upon the foundation of the apostles and prophets, Christ Jesus Himself being
the corner-stone' (Eph. 2:19, 20).

We noticed in our survey of Acts that the preaching of
the gospel by the apostles was not always accompanied by
miracles. We cannot therefore say that signs and wonders
must necessarily be performed if the gospel is to be received.
That was not the case even in apostolic times. Why did God
sometimes give miraculous attestation and sometimes not? It
would seem that He gave sufficient miraculous evidence to
convince people that what these men preached was indeed of
divine origin. Every act of evangelism was not confirmed by
signs. It was the men, the apostles and their fellow pioneers
in the gospel, who were being authenticated by such signs,
rather than their every utterance. Hebrews 2:4, then, suggests
that God bore witness to these pioneers in a manner that
would not necessarily apply to their successors. Ephesians
emphasizes their special role as 'foundation layers' of the
church. In what respect were they foundation layers? Ephesians 3:5 explains. The gospel secret, writes Paul, 'which in
other generations was not made known to the sons of
men . . . has now been revealed to His holy apostles and
prophets by the Spirit'. It was to *these* men, both apostles
and prophets, that God entrusted the gospel revelation which
is now enshrined in New Testament Scripture. These men,
therefore, needed God's miraculous authentication in a way
that no one has since required it. It is not needed for the
preaching of the gospel, for we have seen that even the
apostles on occasions preached effectively without performing signs and wonders. It was needed by those who claimed
to be the agents of God's revelation concerning Christ. This
emphasis is evident in Hebrews 2, for there we read that God
bore special witness to those who confirmed the gospel of
salvation to 'us', that is to the church at large.

These considerations lead to the conclusion that the
charismata, together with other signs and wonders, were
given to the apostles and certain of their companions to
authenticate their role as the human originators of New

Testament revelation. This was done not only by their own possession of the gifts, but also by their ability to impart the charismata to others. Remember how Paul longed to visit Rome that he might impart some spiritual gift to them, that they might be 'established' (Rom. 1:11).

This latter quotation also clarifies a further point that has emerged progressively from our review of the charismata in the New Testament. It has become clear that spiritual gifts fulfilled two distinct purposes. For the apostles and their fellow labourers, like Stephen and Philip, the charismata were attesting or authenticating signs. On the other hand, for those to whom they imparted the gifts, like Timothy for example, or the church at Rome, the charismata served a different purpose, namely that of establishing or edifying the church until such time as it attained maturity. These will be important distinctions when we turn later to the question of the cessation or continuation of the charismata. As miracles attesting those who laid the foundation of the church, it seems clear that they must have ceased with the completion of New Testament Scripture. As means of edifying the church, their continuance beyond the apostolic era is both logical and plausible (though we do not say proved!).

Our final reference to spiritual gifts is found in 1 Peter 4:7—11. 'The end of all things is at hand,' warns Peter. 'Therefore be of sound judgement . . . keep fervent in your love for one another . . . be hospitable to one another without complaint.' He then continues with the following reference to spiritual gifts: 'As each one has received a gift (*charisma*), employ it in serving one another, as good stewards of the manifold grace of God. Whoever speaks, let him speak, as it were, the utterances of God; whoever serves, let him do so as by the strength which God supplies; so that in all things God may be glorified through Jesus Christ' (1 Peter 4:10, 11).

Though brief, this passage is full of illumination concerning our subject. For one thing, it is good to have a non-Pauline comment on the charismata, which nevertheless expresses identical sentiments to those of Paul himself. Secondly, Peter tells us plainly what Paul continually implied but never states in so many words, namely that 'each one has received a gift'. No member of the body of Christ was

without a charismatic gift, from the greatest to the least!
And Peter seems quite deliberately to use as his two examples
one miraculous gift, namely speaking the 'utterances of God'
(presumably prophecy) and one non-miraculous gift, namely
that of service. The activity of serving, though non-
miraculous, is nevertheless a genuine gift of the Spirit, for
it can be done only 'by the strength which God supplies'.

Peter emphasizes two further points. Firstly, the charismata have their source in the 'grace of God', that is they
are undeserved and sovereignly donated as their very name
implies. Secondly, this grace of God is 'manifold', that is,
many-sided. Thus a great diversity of gifts are possible, and
none without usefulness or meaning. Indeed, not only are
they possible, but the very nature of the grace of God
requires that an abundance of spiritual gifts be poured out
upon the church. We are blessed with 'all spiritual blessings'
because the grace of God is so wide and so abundant in both
its essence and its expression. But, warns Peter, these gifts
are entrusted to us and we have a practical responsibility to
use them aright. Above all, they are to be employed 'in
serving one another' with the love that Peter has already
underlined as an essential aspect of Christian inter-
relationships.

Summary

We have reviewed at length the New Testament testimony
concerning spiritual gifts. It still remains for us to examine
some of the charismata in detail and to consider the all-
important question of their cessation or continuance. But
what have we learned so far?
1. We have seen that the term 'spiritual gift' or charisma is
used in the New Testament to describe any ability imparted
to a believer by the Holy Spirit, whether miraculous or non-
miraculous. The charismata were not limited to the 'nine
gifts' listed in the first half of 1 Corinthians 12 but appear
to constitute an open-ended catalogue of Spirit-given roles
or abilities ranging from apostleship to humble service.
2. We have seen that the gifts were not given as disembodied
powers to be selected and acquired by believers at their own
whim or fancy. Rather they were given in the form of gifted

men and women, people chosen and equipped by the Spirit with diverse abilities for the common good.

3. We have identified the doctrine of sovereign donation, namely that the distribution of the charismata was made according to the sovereign will of God the Spirit and not at man's insistence or request. In this context we saw that Paul's injunction to 'desire earnestly' spiritual gifts is accurately and more consistently rendered 'be jealous over' them. The idea is not that individual Christians should seek what they had not received but rather that they should collectively and zealously guard what they already possessed lest, through misuse, the gifts be taken from the church.

4. We have found that every believer had received some spiritual gift. This is clearly stated by Peter and strongly implied by Paul's illustration of the church as a body ('the body . . . held together by that which every joint supplies . . . the proper working of each individual part . . .' Eph. 4:16).

5. We have recognized that the purpose of the charismata was twofold. Firstly, they served to attest and authenticate the apostolic gospel. Together with other signs and wonders, they constituted God's witness to the heavenly source of the message preached by the apostles and their associates. These men stood in particular need of such divine confirmation because, on the human level, they formulated the body of Christian doctrine. Some of them wrote it down in what we now know as the New Testament. These 'apostles and prophets' thus constituted the 'foundation' on which the church has been built. By definition, therefore, no subsequent generation of Christian leaders required the same kind of heavenly attestation.

6. The charismata, secondly, served to establish, strengthen and build up (edify) the church. They were to be used in harmony and love for the benefit of the whole body, which would grow thereby. To this end, the ascended Christ gave to His church men gifted by the Holy Spirit in many diverse ways. Peter refers to this giving as 'the manifold grace of God' towards His people. The presence of the Spirit in the church, distributing His gifts sovereignly for the comfort and edification of the whole, we will call the 'charismatic principle' of the church. There is no suggestion in the New Testament that this charismatic principle would cease to

apply at some point in history. The needs of the church, however, would certainly vary from age to age, as indeed they varied in New Testament times even from one local church to another. The precise manner in which the charismatic principle operates might therefore be expected to change according to those needs. For example, the needs of the church before and after the completion of New Testament Scripture would certainly differ. This matter will be considered further in the next chapter.

7. The charismata were susceptible to neglect (as in the case of Timothy), misunderstanding, misuse and satanic imitation (all as at Corinth). The answer to these problems lay largely in the cultivation of Christian character, maturity and love without which the gifts of the Spirit were ineffective in achieving their desired ends.

11. The individual charismata

In the previous chapter we considered the charismata as a whole, distinguishing between them only in the sense that some were classed as 'miraculous' and others as 'gracious' or non-miraculous. We now wish to look more closely at some of the individual gifts of the Spirit. This is important because there is a great deal of interest in, and confusion over, certain of the charismata, particularly prophecy, tongues and healing. Pentecostals and Charismatics claim to practise these gifts today, while Sealers and Traditional Reformed adherents assert that they ceased after the apostolic period and that contemporary manifestations are not genuine.

We need therefore to examine the nature and purpose of these particular charismata as revealed in Scripture to see whether we can differentiate between the conflicting claims. At the same time we shall look at the gift or charisma of apostleship, since this has a particular bearing on the permanence or otherwise of spiritual gifts. Only after we have done this will we be in a position to decide on the question of cessation or continuance of the charismata.

The Gift of Apostleship

Apostleship is ranked among the gifts of the Spirit and of the risen Christ in 1 Corinthians 12:28 and Ephesians 4:11, and in both cases it is accorded precedence over all other gifts. Who, then, were the apostles, and what was special about them?

The word 'apostle' is taken directly from the Greek verb *apostello*, to send. The apostles were therefore persons sent forth among their fellow men to carry to them the message of Christ. The basic meaning of the word is virtually identical to our modern word 'missionary', which is in fact the Latin-based equivalent of 'apostle'. It is in this sense that Paul and Barnabas are called apostles in Acts 14:4, 14 in spite of the fact that they were not among the twelve apostles chosen by Christ. (Paul is a special case, as we shall see presently.) In the very next chapter of Acts, however, we read that Paul and Barnabas went up to Jerusalem to see the apostles and elders (Acts 15:2, 4) and it is obvious that the term is used here in a rather different way. The Jerusalem apostles were not missionaries in the sense that Paul and Barnabas were, having never left their homeland. These apostles were the twelve (less the traitor Judas) who had been chosen originally by Jesus and sent out 'to proclaim the kingdom of God and to perform healing' (Luke 9:1—6). These were, therefore, Christ's personal missionaries, whereas Barnabas, for example, was a missionary of the church at Antioch (Acts 13:1—4). In making this distinction we do not overlook the fact that the missionaries from Antioch were 'sent out by the Holy Spirit', not just by the church. Nevertheless, it is clear that the 'eleven' had a distinctive office, and exercised a distinctive ministry, which Barnabas did not share. In a similar way, Andronicus and Junias whom Paul describes as 'outstanding among the apostles', were probably apostles in the sense of missionaries (Rom. 16:7).

This is not to say that the office of missionary in our modern sense cannot be ranked among the charismata. Indeed, it is surely embraced in the term 'evangelist' listed in Ephesians as one of the gifts of the ascended Christ. Nevertheless, the apostleship to which Paul accords priority among the charismata is almost certainly the office occupied uniquely by 'the eleven', Matthias (Acts 1:26), and by Paul himself. This can be stated with some assurance, firstly because every New Testament reference apart from those already cited concerns this select group of men and, secondly, because the very priority accorded to the office in the charismatic catalogue itself implies a unique role. Further evidence in support of this contention is found in the book of Revelation where we are told, 'The wall of the city had twelve foundation stones, and on them were the names of the twelve apostles of the Lamb' (Rev. 21:14). Leaving aside the question of whether Paul, rather than Matthias, was the correct replacement for Judas, this verse tells us that the apostles were a fixed number of men appointed once for all in the history of the church, and not an unlimited order.

What then were their special functions? For conciseness we shall list the relevant points made in the New Testament concerning this question.

1. The twelve were specially chosen from among a larger body of disciples (Mark 3:13, 14; Luke 6:13).

2. Their immediate role was spelled out by Mark. 'He appointed twelve', states the evangelist, 'that they might be with Him, and that He might send them out to preach, and to have authority to cast out the demons' (Mark 3:14, 15). As we have seen, Luke adds that Christ 'sent them out to proclaim the kingdom of God and to perform healing' (Luke 9:2) and Matthew that He 'gave them authority over unclean spirits . . . and to heal every kind of disease and . . . sickness' (Matt. 10:1). Being 'with Him' obviously meant more than just keeping company with Him. Peter speaks of the many men 'who have accompanied us all the time that the Lord Jesus went in and out among us, beginning with the baptism of John, until the day that He was taken up from us' (Acts 1:21, 22). One of these, claimed Peter, should be chosen to replace Judas. The point is that many disciples were with Christ in a general sense throughout His earthly ministry, but only the twelve shared His more intimate counsels. In particular, He entrusted to them both His teaching, that they might proclaim the kingdom of God, and His power, that they might heal and cast out demons. Concerning Christ's teaching, Peter refers to 'the commandment of the Lord and Saviour spoken by your apostles' (2 Peter 3:2), emphasizing the particular authority with which the apostles taught on His behalf. Similarly, Paul stresses that as an apostle he had been specially entrusted with the gospel (1 Thess. 2:4-6). One particular aspect of this entrustment was, of course, the origination of New Testament Scripture. This is almost certainly what Paul is referring to when he states that the church is 'built upon the foundation of the apostles and prophets' (Eph. 2:20). It is to these people that the mystery of Christ had been revealed following Pentecost, and it was their task both to declare it and to record it for the benefit of others (Eph. 3:2-10).

3. The twelve were accorded special gifts of healing and exorcism (Matt. 10:1). Before Pentecost these abilities were restricted to the apostles but they were later practised by a small number of other disciples, notably Philip (Acts 8:7). It cannot be said, therefore, that these powers were limited to the apostles, but it is nevertheless a fact that such gifts were among the 'signs of a true apostle', as Paul explains to the Corinthians (2 Cor. 12:12).

4. The last point will stand repetition. It is implicit in Paul's statement in 2 Corinthians 12:11, 12 that it was possible to establish whether or not a man's claim to apostleship was genuine. 'In no respect', protests Paul, 'was I inferior to the most eminent apostles . . . The signs of a true apostle were performed among you with all perseverance, by signs and wonders and miracles.' The apostles were therefore distinguished from their fellow believers by special miraculous powers. Although a few others, such as Philip, were enabled to perform similar feats in certain circumstances, it was arguably only the apostles who exhibited 'perseverance' or continuance in the exercise of these gifts. The church at Ephesus was commended for having 'put to the test those who call themselves apostles, and they are not' (Rev. 2:2).

5. The apostles were further distinguished in being witnesses of, or to, the resurrection of Christ. In seeking a replacement for the traitor Judas, Peter declared, 'It is necessary that of the men who have accompanied us . . . one . . . should become a witness with us of His resurrection' (Acts 1:22). Notice that the new recruit to the apostolic band was to 'become' a witness of the resurrection, even though he must have been among the crowd of more than five hundred disciples who had seen the risen Christ before His ascension (1 Cor. 15:6). Being an apostolic witness to the resurrection was not, therefore, simply a matter of having witnessed the fact, otherwise all five hundred would have been apostles! It signified rather that the apostles had special authority and special responsibility in this matter. Equally important, however, is the point that no one could become an apostle who was not a direct eyewitness to the fact that Christ had risen from the dead. On this score alone, the apostolic order was necessarily limited to a single generation of believers.

6. We come now to the testimony of Paul to the nature of

the apostolic ministry. Paul was not among the original twelve chosen by Christ, nor was he among the five hundred who saw the Saviour before He ascended to heaven. He claims, however, to qualify as an eyewitness of the resurrection by virtue of the Lord's appearance to him on the Damascus Road. 'He was raised on the third day,' writes Paul, 'He appeared to Cephas, then to the twelve. After that He appeared to more than five hundred brethren at one time . . . then . . . to James, then to all the apostles; and last of all, as it were to one untimely born, He appeared to me also. For I am the least of the apostles . . .' (1 Cor. 15:4—9). Elsewhere in the same Epistle Paul protests his fitness for apostolic office with the words: 'Have I not seen Jesus our Lord?' (1 Cor. 9:1.) Paul plainly regards his own vision of Christ as fully equivalent to the physical observation vouchsafed to the others listed here. Admittedly, the appearance was delayed, as a baby may exceed the normal period of gestation and be late to see the light of day. Nonetheless, the man from Tarsus sets himself firmly among the witnesses of the resurrection and thus establishes his eligibility for apostolic office. 'I am', he says, 'the least of the apostles.' But apostle he was, nonetheless.

Notice also that he claims to be the final witness of the resurrection, the 'last of all' to see the risen Christ. This signifies that none who followed would be allowed, as Paul was, to enter belatedly into that select band of eyewitnesses. His experience, he claims, was unique and no one subsequently would qualify for apostleship by such a route. We must conclude that the order of apostles was not perpetuated and that it passed for ever with the deaths of the twelve and of Paul himself.

There is much else that Paul tells us in his letters concerning the role of an apostle in the early church, but we will conclude on the note that he himself loved to emphasize. This is the fact that he had been specifically called and separated by God to fulfil this ministry. I am, he declared, 'a bond-servant of Christ Jesus, called as an apostle, set apart for the gospel of God'. Through Christ, he continues, 'We have received grace and apostleship to bring about the obedience of faith among all the Gentiles, for His name's sake' (Rom. 1:1, 5). Not only does Paul show here that all are not apostles, and that the charisma of apostleship lay in the gift of the Holy Spirit's sovereign will; he shows us also why this particular ministry ranked first among the charismata. To the apostles, as to no other person, the essential message of salvation through Christ was entrusted. They alone were 'set apart for the gospel of God' in a unique and unrepeatable manner.

The Gift of Prophecy

Prophecy in the Old Testament

Before we consider the role and purpose of prophecy in the early church, it is necessary to understand the function of the Old Testament prophets. We cannot do more than sketch this subject in outline, since a thorough treatment would take us too far from our main concern. The degree of continuity between the two Testaments is such, however, that we shall not understand the teaching of the New unless we grasp the import of the Old.

Prophecy is one of the pivotal concepts of the Old Testament. Indeed, the New Testament states clearly that all Old Testament Scripture was prophetical in nature. These writings were often summarized by the term 'the Law and the Prophets', but even the Law was prophetical! 'All the prophets and the Law prophesied until John [the Baptist]', Christ told His disciples (Matt. 11:13). Peter tells us that 'no prophecy of Scripture . . . was ever made by an act of human will, but men moved by the Holy Spirit spoke from God' (2 Peter 1:21). Although there were many prophets in Old Testament times whose utterances are not preserved as Scripture, it seems clear from Peter's statement that all Scripture can be regarded as the result of prophetical activity.

What bearing does this conclusion have upon our subject? Very simply, it helps to define the essential nature of prophecy. For if, as we believe, these Old Testament writings were inspired by God and were not the result of human art or logic, and if they were prophetical in character, we arrive at the conclusion that prophecy itself must involve some level of inspiration. It is not merely an act of public speaking.

The verb 'prophesy' in the Hebrew means 'to flow forth', while one noun translated 'prophecy' denotes a 'burden' or load that must be picked up. These words convey the idea that in prophetic utterance the message of God was laid upon the heart of the prophet and flowed forth from his lips or from his pen. We have already identified the ancient Scriptures as examples of the prophetic ministry, and embedded in those writings are further, and even more explicit references to this kind of activity. Innumerable examples could be given from the Old Testament where the prophet directly ascribes his words to the Lord. 'The word of the Lord came by the prophet Haggai . . .', writes Haggai himself, 'saying, "Thus says the Lord of hosts . . ."' (Hag. 1:1, 3). Note that it was God's word, not that of the prophet himself, and that Haggai was merely the vehicle through whom the message was interpreted to human ears. God is actually the speaker, though the voice is Haggai's. Even when dealing with the problem of false prophets, the Old Testament makes the nature of true prophecy quite plain. 'I did not send these prophets, but they ran. I did not speak to them, but they prophesied. But if they had stood in My council, then they would have announced My words to My people' (Jer. 23: 21, 22). The true prophet, therefore, was one sent by God to announce the words of God that He had first spoken to him.

Thus whether we use the word 'prophecy' to describe the Old Testament writings in their entirety, or to signify the specific utterances of individual prophets, we are led to the conclusion that the act involved far more than public speaking or human authorship. The prophet was God's mouthpiece, conveying God's message and not his own thoughts about God. The prophet's watchword was 'Thus says the Lord of hosts, the God of Israel' (Jer. 35:13), not 'This is what I think about God.' Prophecy was therefore an inspired utterance, not a normal act of human communication.

This Old Testament concept of prophecy is supported by the Gospel writers. The various predictions made by the prophets concerning Christ were, we are told, fulfilled.

(See for example Matt. 1:22; 2:15, 17 and so on.) This tells us that the Old Testament prophets accurately foretold the future, something quite impossible without inspiration. Indeed Peter asserts that the authors of the Old Testament did not understand the full import of their own writings, it being revealed to them that they prophesied for the benefit of a future generation rather than their own (1 Peter 1: 10–12). Inspired or 'ecstatic' utterance is also implied in the earliest examples of New Testament prophecy. Elizabeth 'was filled with the Holy Spirit' and 'cried out with a loud voice', both of which statements imply something abnormal in what she was about to say. Similarly, her husband 'was filled with the Holy Spirit, and prophesied' (Luke 1:41, 42, 67). It is clear that the Old Testament view of the nature of prophecy is maintained in the New. In fact most references to the subject in the New Testament concern the Old Testament prophets, who are freely quoted throughout the Gospels and Epistles. An obvious example of this is Joel's Pentecostal prophecy in which we are told that the coming of the Spirit would be accompanied by unusual and remarkable signs. One of these signs was to be that 'your sons and your daughters shall prophesy', an occurrence that would hardly have been significant if prophecy were merely an act of human religious address.

Although, therefore, the Greek word translated 'prophesy' means simply a 'speaking out' or public utterance, it is clear that the Old Testament concept of 'speaking from God' is fully preserved in the New. When we come to consider the role and nature of the New Testament prophets we must obviously bear this in mind. Prophecy was not the same thing as preaching or teaching, for which in any case quite different Greek words are used in the New Testament writings.

New Testament prophecy

The gift or charisma of prophecy is referred to in Romans 12:6, Ephesians 4:11 and 1 Thessalonians 5:20, as well as in 1 Corinthians where, of course, it is discussed in great detail. We notice from these references that the office of prophet ranks high in Paul's estimation, deferring only to apostleship in its importance. We shall see presently that this is no mere preference on the part of the apostle but has an important theological significance. The Thessalonian reference is interesting, for there Paul advises his readers not to 'despise prophetic utterances'. Since we cannot imagine Paul asking believers not to despise preaching, this certainly suggests that a clear difference should be drawn between the two. This is also implied by the fact that prophecy and teaching are represented as two distinct charismata. It is easy to demonstrate that preaching is a form of teaching and may also take the form of evangelism. (See for example 2 Tim. 4:2—5 and compare with 1 Tim. 4:11—13.) But both teachers and evangelists are clearly differentiated from prophets in Ephesians 4:11. Another pointer to the same fact is that both men and women were numbered among the New Testament prophets, as stated in 1 Corinthians 11:5 and Acts 21:9. Yet Paul would 'not allow a woman to teach or exercise authority over a man', requiring that women should 'remain quiet' in this matter. We must conclude that the prophetic and teaching ministries were totally distinct and this would follow naturally if prophecy were of an ecstatic character.

This view of prophecy is supported by the various examples of the phenomenon recorded in the Gospels, the Acts and the Epistles, which we will now briefly review. We have already referred to the cases of Elizabeth and Zacharias in Luke, and the only other instance we need to cite from the Gospels concerns the high priest at the trial of Jesus (John 11:51). Without realizing the fact, Caiaphas 'prophesied that Jesus was going to die for the nation; and not for the nation only . . .' Nothing was further from the mind of the high priest than to exalt the saving work that Christ was about to accomplish, but under the influence of the Spirit of God he did exactly this, enemy of the gospel though he was. The ecstatic or miraculous dimension of prophecy is thus well illustrated by this incident.

Most examples of New Testament prophecy occur in Acts, and we have already referred to them in chapter 10. We need only notice, therefore, what they show us concerning the essential nature of the prophetic gift. We find Agabus predicting 'by the Spirit' that a world-wide famine would

take place, and later foretelling Paul's imprisonment (Acts
11:27, 28; 21:11). Judas and Silas, 'being prophets . . .
strengthened the brethren with a lengthy message' (Acts
15:32). The Ephesians upon whom Paul laid his hands
spoke with tongues and prophesied (Acts 19:6). In most of
these references it is plain that the prophets spoke under the
constraint or inspiration of the Holy Spirit and not by way
of normal human communication. The one exception is the
case of Judas and Silas, where ecstatic utterance, though not
ruled out, is not explicitly indicated.

An example of prophecy is also found in 1 Timothy where
Paul refers to the 'prophecies made concerning' his younger
friend, and reminds him that he should 'not neglect the
spiritual gift . . . bestowed . . . through prophetic utterance
with the laying on of hands' (1 Tim. 1:18; 4:14). Once again
it is clear that prophecy was something more than a normal
act of communication.

The role of prophecy in the New Testament

Having identified prophecy as ecstatic in nature, we now
come to the most important question. What was the role and
purpose of this gift in New Testament times? Here we must
turn to a key verse in Ephesians. 'You are', Paul tells these
Gentile believers, 'fellow citizens with the saints, and are of
God's household, having been built upon the foundation of
the apostles and prophets, Christ Jesus Himself being the
corner-stone . . .' (Eph. 2:20). In this well-known reference
to the church of Jesus Christ, Paul tells us that the prophets,
along with the apostles, constituted the foundation of that
church. This is an important and definitive statement and we
must examine it in some detail.

Firstly, of course, we need to be clear that the apostle is
speaking of the New Testament prophets and not their Old
Testament forerunners. This is apparent from the order
employed. If Paul had been thinking of the Old Testament
prophets he would more naturally have employed the
chronological order 'prophets and apostles'. Instead he
follows his normal practice of placing these two charismata
in order of precedence, as he does in other places where
there is no doubt that New Testament prophecy is in view

(Eph. 3:5; 4:11; 1 Cor. 12:28). The clearest proof, however, is found in Ephesians 3:5 where we are told that things concealed from former generations were 'now . . . revealed to His holy apostles and prophets in the Spirit'. The prophets here can only be New Testament figures, and Paul's earlier use of the expression 'apostles and prophets' must therefore be taken in the same sense.

In what way, then, were the prophets part of the foundation of the church? We turn again to Ephesians 3:5, which verse actually constitutes a commentary on Ephesians 2:20. We are told that the apostles and prophets were the recipients of the essential Christian revelation, no less. It was to these two classes of people, apostles and prophets, that the previously unrevealed truth concerning Christ and His gospel was made known by the Holy Spirit. The gospel was not self-apparent. It was foreshadowed by the Old Testament Scriptures, but not fully revealed therein. It was therefore necessary to unveil that which remained to be declared concerning God's eternal counsels. And this God chose to do through the agency of selected men. Notice that the 'mystery of Christ' was revealed to the apostles and prophets, not to believers in general. The message only became common property as these chosen messengers themselves declared it.

It is evident, therefore, that New Testament revelation was, on a human level, the work of the apostles and prophets, and our written New Testament Scriptures are a result of this work. This fact harmonizes with our earlier conclusion that the Old Testament canon could also be described as prophecy in its entirety. Prophecy is revelation, inspired by the Holy Spirit. But the production of the written New Testament was not the only function of the prophets, since there were obviously many prophets who had no part in penning those writings. (The prophets at Corinth are an example.) What role did those prophets play who were not authors of Scripture? Here we must exercise a certain amount of caution. It would be easy to conclude that there were two levels of prophetic utterance, namely a higher level that became Scripture and a lower level that, under Scripture, served to encourage and strengthen believers. There is not the slightest support in the Bible, however, for such a two-level interpretation of prophecy. It is true that Judas and

Silas 'encouraged and strengthened the brethren' by their prophecy, but this only tells us that prophetical ministry was edifying to the church, which was surely always true. It does not imply that their prophecy on that occasion served only this purpose to the exclusion of the higher purpose defined in Ephesians 3:5. How then may we properly understand the role of those prophets who were not involved in the origination of written Scripture?

Negatively, we must not lower our view of prophecy. The New Testament defines the function of prophecy as the revelation of the essential Christian message under the inspiration of the Spirit of God. This was the foundation the prophets helped to lay, and their ministry was thus unique by definition. As foundation-layers they shared with the apostles, and indeed with Christ Himself, the privilege of providing the doctrinal rock on which the church was built. The Lord Jesus, the corner-stone of that edifice, left us no written Scripture from His own hand, yet provided (in both His teaching and His person) part of the same foundation. For by Him, God spoke to mankind (Heb. 1:2).

The question is not difficult to resolve. Although the New Testament prophets, generally, did not write Scripture, their prophecies consisted of the very same truths that have been preserved for us in the New Testament. Their work was not to originate Scripture, for that task devolved mainly upon the apostles themselves. But neither was their role to minister under Scripture, for that activity is fully embraced in the terms preaching, teaching and evangelism. Their function was surely to provide a verbal parallel to the origination of Scripture during a period when that Word was either still unwritten or else not widely available to the early church.

This explanation of the purpose of New Testament prophecy has much to commend it. Firstly, it allows the prophetic ministry its full stature as defined in Ephesians 2:20 and 3:5. It was in no way inferior to the process of revelation that gave us the New Testament. It afforded a wholly equivalent but unwritten revelation of foundational truth which served the scattered church until the written Scriptures became widely available. Secondly, this immediately explains why prophecy was an ecstatic or inspired utterance. Had it been merely the repetition of apostolic teaching, with no revelatory content, it would have constituted teaching, not the distinct charisma that it was. Thirdly, this understanding of prophecy explains why Paul ranks it second only to apostleship among the charismata (1 Cor. 12:28). It was the revelatory content of prophecy that alone could give it a higher standing than the teaching and preaching of the Word of God. Fourthly, our explanation avoids any implication that there was, or still is, a process of revelation distinct from, or additional to that of Scripture. This suggestion is forced upon those who maintain that there were two different kinds of prophecy in New Testament times, namely scriptural prophecy and 'normal' prophecy. Once one admits that the latter was in some way different in kind or content from the revelation of Scripture (even if it is held to be subservient to Scripture), one is faced with the dilemma of accepting a process of revelation that is separate from Holy Writ. To accept this is to undermine the sole authority of the Scriptures in matters of faith and practice. This subversion of the doctrine of the sole sufficiency of Scripture is, we repeat, implied even when 'normal' prophecy is said to defer to the biblical revelation. The very notion that prophecy may be different in content or purpose from Scripture is enough to create the problem.

Against this view, Reformed Sealers and others sometimes advance the argument that preaching today contains a revelatory element. A preacher may utter words that apply to his hearers so directly that they must have been 'given' by revelation, even though he himself may be unaware of the fact. But such utterance is, they argue, typical of prophecy as described in 1 Corinthians 14:24, 25. 'If all prophesy, and an unbeliever or an ungifted man enters, he is convicted by all, he is called to account by all; the secrets of his heart are disclosed; and so he will fall on his face and worship God.' If this is so, it can be maintained that the act of prophecy remains even though the office of prophet may have been transitional, as we have proposed above.

In one sense, this is a question of the use of words. There is no doubt that preaching does exceptionally involve the revelation of specific detail known only to the hearer, and this occurs as the Holy Spirit leads the speaker in his choice of utterance. If we choose to label this aspect of preaching as 'prophecy', we may, of course, do so. This is not, however, New Testament usage and thus confuses rather than illuminates the issue. It leads to an illogical and forced distinction between the act of prophecy and the office of prophet, and introduces the wholly unnecessary idea of two levels of prophecy, as discussed earlier. In New Testament usage, the act and the office are not separated. (See, for example, 1 Cor. 12:10, 28; 14:24, 31, 32.) Although both prophecy and preaching may sometimes have the same effect upon an unbeliever, so that the 'secrets of his heart are disclosed', we must not conclude that the two can be equated. Indeed, in this same passage, Paul makes it clear that the effect referred to was incidental to the prophetic ministry, for 'prophecy is . . . not to unbelievers, but to those who believe' (1 Cor. 14:22). In contrast, preaching has the conviction of the unbeliever as one of its foremost purposes, as in Acts 2:37, where Peter's hearers were 'pierced to the heart'.

While not denying, therefore, that preaching occasionally contains a 'revelatory' dimension, it seems unwise to call this 'prophecy', merely on the basis of a similarity of effect, especially since the effect in question is incidental to prophecy but central to evangelism. The evangelist is clearly distinguished from the prophet in Ephesians 4:11.

The Gift of Healing

The healing ministry of Christ

The gifts of healing are among the charismata listed in 1 Corinthians 12 where they are mentioned in verses 9, 28 and 30, and we also see these powers exercised in remarkable degree throughout the Acts of the Apostles. Before we consider the healing gifts bestowed upon the members of the early church, however, it will be of value to consider the way in which the Lord Jesus Christ exercised this capacity during His three-year public ministry.

The Gospels abound with examples of healing performed by the Lord Jesus. The 'recovery of sight to the blind' was to be one of the signs of the Messiah (Luke 4:18), and when John the Baptist needed reassurance concerning the authenticity of Jesus' mission, he was told that 'The blind receive sight, the lame walk, the lepers are cleansed and the deaf hear' (Luke 7:22). The obvious implication was that such miracles constituted the clearest proof possible that Jesus was indeed the awaited Christ.

Healing so characterized the ministry of the Lord Jesus that we are told He 'was going about in all Galilee, teaching in their synagogues, and proclaiming the gospel of the kingdom, and healing every kind of disease and every kind of sickness among the people' (Matt. 4:23). The evangelist thus ranks Jesus' healing ministry alongside His teaching of Scripture and His proclamation of the gospel as a key aspect of His work here upon earth.

The reason for this is not difficult to see. Matthew tells us that this healing ministry was a fulfilment of Old Testament prophecy. 'He cast out the spirits with a word, and healed all who were ill, in order that what was spoken through Isaiah the prophet might be fulfilled, saying, "He Himself took our infirmities and carried away our diseases"' (Matt. 8:17). The Gospel writer is telling us that Christ's healing powers were evidence that He was the suffering Servant, the Messiah of Old Testament prophecy.

There can be no doubt, then, that Christ's work of healing was part of the external evidence by which His messianic office was declared and authenticated. Indeed, claimed Jesus, it was the demonstration of His unique relationship with God the Father. 'The Father loves the Son, and shows Him all things that He Himself is doing; and greater works than these will He show Him, that you may marvel' (John 5:20).

The importance of this brief discussion of healing in the ministry of Christ is simply that it establishes, in His case at least, an indisputable reason for miracles of this nature. Naturally, all Christ's acts of healing were deeds of compassion. They were all deeds of power and of grace. But above all they were demonstrations of the reality of His claim to be the unique Son of God, the promised Messiah. Their chief function, therefore, was to authenticate Him and the teaching that He brought from the Father.

The ministry of healing in Acts

Accepting that healing characterized the ministry of Christ, and that its purpose was to demonstrate His messiahship, how did similar powers come to reside in His disciples? Well, of course, Jesus promised that this would happen as a result of the coming of the *Paracletos*. It was to be an integral part of the Holy Spirit's work in them that they would perform miracles similar to Jesus' own signs and wonders. 'He who believes in Me', explained the Saviour, 'the works that I do shall he do also; and greater works than these shall he do, because I go to the Father' (John 14:12). Indeed, the twelve apostles had already been favoured with a foretaste of this power, for Jesus had previously given them 'authority . . . to heal every kind of disease' (Matt. 10:1).

It is clear from these references that the followers of Christ were enabled by the Spirit to effect miracles that could only be wrought by the power of God. But what was the purpose of this divine enabling? The answer is surprisingly simple. The purpose of these miraculous deeds was exactly the same as it had been throughout Christ's public ministry – namely, to authenticate Jesus as the Christ of God! This is the clear implication of the accounts of healing recorded in Acts. Consider, for example, Peter's words to the lame man at the temple gate: 'In the name of Jesus Christ the Nazarene, walk!' (Acts 3:6.) Notice that Peter does not merely exercise the gift of healing, but specifically attributes the miracle to the power of Jesus' name and identifies Him both as the Christ and as the Nazarene. It was Christ's miraculous deed, performed as it were by proxy, through the agency of His servant. As Peter explains the incident later to his accusers, he emphasizes the point that he had been acting, not on his own account, but in the name (that is, on behalf) of the Man of Nazareth. 'Let it be known to all of you', he said, 'that by the name of Jesus Christ the Nazarene, whom you crucified, whom God raised from the dead – by this name this man stands here before you in good health' (Acts 4:10). Nor was this emphasis limited to the first apostolic miracle in Acts, for when the church at prayer requested God's miraculous authentication of their own preaching, they recognized that 'signs and wonders' could only take place 'through the name of . . . Jesus' (Acts 4:30).

We see, then, that the healing miracles of the apostles and their associates were in a very real sense a continuation of the ministry of Christ. He had gone away, but yet He remained among them in the person of His Holy Spirit, continuing to produce the messianic signs. These signs, accordingly, continued to authenticate Jesus as the Christ. But in addition they served to authenticate the apostles and others as the true followers of the Christ; as we have seen already, God was bearing them witness by 'signs and wonders and by various miracles' (Heb. 2:4). In either case, however, the purpose of the miracles was to authenticate. They were God's own mark of approval upon those who performed them. Although most would agree that the ministry of healing in Acts did carry this significance of authentication, it might be argued that the gift of healing was also an ability imparted to some individuals without regard to such a purpose. If this were the case, we would expect these gifted persons to be able to exercise their charisma at will. It is clear, however, that the power to heal was not always available, even to the apostles themselves. There are several instances where Paul was unable to deal with cases of illness, as when he left Trophimus sick at Miletus (2 Tim. 4:20) and when Epaphroditus nearly died (Phil. 2:27). Other examples of an inability to heal miraculously are found in Paul's own affliction, where he 'entreated the Lord three times' to remove his 'thorn in the flesh', and in Timothy's 'frequent ailments' for which Paul prescribes, not miracles, but wine! (2 Cor. 12:8; 1 Tim. 5:23.) Obviously the Spirit of God retained the right of decision as to whether healing would or would not take place in a given instance, and it follows that there was always a specific purpose in the mind of God for each act of healing. This purpose could not have been that of compassion, for this was no less needed in cases where healing was not granted. The only discernible purpose for miracles of healing in the New Testament therefore remains that of authentication.

The next question to be considered is whether this divine authentication was limited in some manner to the early church, or whether it was intended to be valid for all time.

When we examine the book of Acts we find that by far the greater number of healing miracles were performed by the apostles themselves. The only exceptions to this arise in Philip's ministry in Samaria and Stephen's in Jerusalem (Acts 8:7; 6:8). In Stephen's case we are not actually told that he healed the sick, but simply that he performed 'great wonders and signs among the people', but it is a reasonable assumption that these acts included healing. However, a single exception is sufficient to establish the fact that the ministry of healing was not an exclusive mark of apostleship.

Alternatively, we might suggest that healing was a power possessed by all those who preached the gospel in those days and that it served the purpose of authenticating the gospel itself. We saw in the previous chapter that the miracles performed in Acts did indeed draw attentive audiences for the preaching that invariably followed. But was this their primary purpose? The difficulty with this idea is that miracles of healing did not, in fact, always accompany the evangelistic activities recorded in Acts, an obvious example being Paul's visit to Athens recorded in Acts 17. Once again we see the sovereignty of the Holy Spirit displayed in the granting or withholding of miraculous signs. They were not a necessary accompaniment of the gospel. Salvation through Christ could be, and frequently was preached without their aid, even in the times of the Acts when miracles were so frequent.

The clue to this whole question seems to lie back where we began this discussion of healing, namely in the ministry of Jesus Christ Himself. His miracles were predominantly miracles of healing, though not exclusively so, of course. The New Testament makes it plain that the purpose of His miracles was to vindicate and demonstrate His claims to be the long-awaited Messiah. By attributing their own healing powers to the 'name' of Jesus of Nazareth, the apostles declared the same truth. And whenever such powers were subsequently employed, they served exactly the same purpose.

Who, then, were given these powers? Surely only those who had known Jesus during His earthly ministry. They alone were 'eyewitnesses of His majesty' (2 Peter 1:16), though we must also include Paul who saw Christ, after His ascension, on the Damascus road. This privileged number included many disciples besides the apostles themselves, and it is highly likely that Stephen and Philip were among those who followed Christ during His days on earth. They were certainly men of established standing in the church by the time they were chosen as deacons.

The major point here is that miracles of healing were employed by the Holy Spirit to support the testimony of those who witnessed to the messiahship of Jesus from their own personal experience. It was their eyewitness testimony that received divine vindication by the granting of miracles, for only they could identify the Nazarene as the Christ.

Some will no doubt disagree with this suggestion that the gift of healing in Acts was limited to those who had known Christ personally before His ascension. But the idea gains credence from the verse in Hebrews to which we have referred several times previously. God, we are told, was 'bearing witness with them, both by signs and wonders and by various miracles and by gifts of the Holy Spirit according to His own will' (Heb. 2:4). Notice that witness was borne with them, not just to them or for them. This implies that the Holy Spirit's concern was to reinforce and substantiate what they were saying about Jesus of Nazareth. And who were these people so favoured with the witness of God? Those who had 'heard' the gospel 'spoken through the Lord', that is from the lips of Christ Himself (Heb. 2:3). It was to these individuals that miraculous authentication was given, for only they were able to speak as true witnesses of Christ's incarnate glory. 'The Word became flesh, and dwelt among us,' declares John, emphasizing the incarnation, 'and we beheld His glory, glory as of the only begotten of the Father' (John 1:14). Only one who had walked with Christ on earth could speak in these terms, and it was this kind of eyewitness testimony that the miracles of healing in Acts seemed calculated to support.

Healing in the Epistles

There are very few references to healing in the Epistles. Indeed, with the exception of 1 Corinthians 12 and James 5, the Epistles contain no examples of the subject at all. Rather do we find several instances of non-healing, as has already been pointed out. These negative cases are instructive, and we will briefly re-examine them.

We have already referred to Paul's inability to heal himself of the 'thorn in the flesh' described in 2 Corinthians 12:7–10. This passage is even more remarkable because it immediately precedes Paul's protestation that he performed the signs of a true apostle, including 'wonders and miracles', when he ministered at Corinth. The apostle's ill health was permitted by God to teach him that divine strength is made perfect in human weakness. Plainly, sickness is sometimes part of the positive will of God, and He could not permit the exercise of gifts of healing to frustrate that purpose. It follows, then, that healing was not at the discretion of man but was mediated by the sovereign Spirit according to the will of God (Heb. 2:4).

The second instance concerns Paul's 'brother and fellow worker' Epaphroditus, whom the apostle describes as being 'sick to the point of death' (Phil. 2:27). It is clear that Paul, although present throughout this harrowing illness, was unable to heal his companion. This failure of the gift of healing is the more remarkable when Paul's healing ministry recorded in Acts is brought to mind. Nor was this a case where the apostle deliberately refrained from employing his powers because he knew God wished to take His servant to Himself. Epaphroditus' survival was clearly important both to Paul himself and to the Philippian church (see Phil. 2:27–30). Indeed, Paul actually attributes the illness to the demands of 'the work of Christ', giving the best of reasons for the exercise of healing powers. Yet the gift which Paul undoubtedly possessed was not employed on this occasion, and healing came by natural process under, of course, the sovereign will of God.

The lesson to be learned, surely, is that miracles of healing were only performed by God's servants at the specific instigation of the Spirit and did not constitute an ability that they could use at their own discretion. This ensured that the primary purpose of such miracles could never be forgotten or superseded.

The use of medicinal means rather than miraculous gifts is advocated by Paul as he writes to Timothy concerning the latter's frequent indisposition (1 Tim. 5:23). In this case, of course, Paul was not physically present to exercise his gift of healing, but neither did he recommend Timothy to seek out someone locally who possessed similar gifts. The implication is either that the gift of healing was not commonly found in the churches of that day, or that it was not normal for believers to have recourse to miraculous means when they became sick. Both of these situations may have applied, but either of them militates against the idea that miraculous gifts of healing should be practised regularly by certain persons in every church.

The last mention of non-healing in Paul's letters is a cryptic reference in 2 Timothy 4:20: 'Trophimus I left sick at Miletus.' It was clearly not part of Paul's plans that his travelling companion should remain in Miletus, but it was impossible for Trophimus to continue his journey with the apostle. Again it would have seemed an obvious thing for Paul to exercise his healing power so that the missionary work might proceed unhindered. But God's purposes were otherwise and the apostle was not permitted to heal his friend, in spite of the many good reasons for doing so. The gift of healing was once again withheld by the sovereign design of God. Paul was not free to use it as he willed.

These Scriptures taken together indicate that the gift of healing was an occasional gift, given to certain of God's servants from time to time and for definite purposes in the plan of God. It was not a power bestowed on an individual for him to use at will, and whenever the outcome seemed to serve the interests of the gospel. Healing in the New Testament always represents a sovereign act of God, having the function of a witness to the power of Christ. That such acts of healing were mediated through men, and can thus be described as charismata or 'gifts', is always secondary.

The gift of healing at Corinth

We must now return to the mention made of the gift of healing in 1 Corinthians 12, where it is listed among the charismata in verses 9 and 28. We are told in verse 30 that all do not possess healing powers, but otherwise the chapter throws no light on the church's usage of the gift. The question arises whether the gift of healing was actually possessed or practised

in the Corinthian church at all. In listing the charismata
here, Paul is obviously speaking of the church at large. This
is clear from the fact that he puts apostleship at the head of
the charismatic catalogue in verse 28. The Corinthian church
did not have its own apostles, and the gift of apostleship was
not therefore exercised in that particular local assembly. In
contrast, we know from chapter 14 that the gifts of tongues,
interpretation and prophecy were practised there. Paul himself, of course, had demonstrated 'signs and wonders' and all
the powers of a true apostle in their midst, as he reminds
them in 2 Corinthians 12, so that they were no doubt familiar with the gift of healing. But this does not mean that it
was practised by anyone else in Corinth. It would be entirely
consistent with all we have said about the gift of healing in
the Acts and the Epistles, if Paul were referring in 1 Corinthians 12 to the apostolic healing gifts and not to phenomena
current in the Corinthian church itself.

It is, in fact, clear that no such gifts were in use at Corinth
at the time Paul wrote. This may be deduced from the previous chapter of the Epistle in which the apostle refers to the
state of health of many of the Corinthian believers. 'Many
among you', he points out, 'are weak and sick, and a number
sleep' (that is, have died) (1 Cor. 11:30). The context makes
it plain that God was judging the church there with physical
illness on account of their wanton disrespect for the Lord's
table. Obviously the Spirit's healing was not being afforded
to the considerable number involved.

If, in spite of these arguments, we still wish to ascribe
healing powers to some of the congregation at Corinth, it
raises a very real problem of interpretation. If our conclusions are correct, that the gifts of healing in Acts were vouchsafed to the physical witnesses of Christ's earthly ministry,
the gift of healing at Corinth must have been a different
phenomenon altogether, and one concerning which the
Scripture is elsewhere completely silent. The most consistent
interpretation, therefore, is that when Paul lists the charismata in 1 Corinthians he is referring to the church generally
and not solely to the local assembly. This immediately explains his reference to apostleship and very naturally identifies the gifts of healing with those practised by the apostles
and their companions in Acts and, of course, with Paul's

own demonstration of such powers at Corinth itself. Had the 'signs, wonders and miracles' which marked his ministry among them been commonly practised at Corinth, Paul could hardly have used them as evidence of his apostleship as he does in the second Epistle.

Healing in James 5

Our final reference to healing occurs in James' Epistle, as he exhorts his readers to patient continuance in the face of suffering and provocation. He cites the patience of Job as an example to be followed, pointing out that in the end God vindicated His servant of old. As he writes in this vein, James asks, 'Is anyone among you sick? Let him call for the elders of the church, and let them pray over him, anointing him with oil in the name of the Lord; and the prayer offered in faith will restore the one who is sick, and the Lord will raise him up, and if he has committed sins, they will be forgiven him. Therefore, confess your sins to one another, and pray for one another, so that you may be healed. The effective prayer of a righteous man can accomplish much' (James 5:14—16).

It is evident that James is not here discussing the gift of healing in the sense that it is used elsewhere in the New Testament. In this case it is not the power vested in some apostle or specially gifted person that effects the healing, but rather prayer. It is not the elders' presence, nor the anointing with oil, but the prayer of faith that raises up the sick. The elders do no more than represent the church fellowship in this situation, for James exhorts Christians generally to 'pray one for another, so that you may be healed'. It is implicit, of course, that any healing must be subject to the overriding will of God. No one would suggest that Paul lacked the faith to pray effectively for the healing of Epaphroditus and Trophimus. But within the limits imposed by the purposes of God, James tells us here that the prayer of the church, offered in faith, will be honoured by the Lord in the healing of the sick, and the forgiveness of sin, if this is a contributing factor.

The great importance of this passage in James is that it offers an alternative approach to the whole question of divine healing. The apostle does not tell his sick readers to call for those who possess the gift of healing, and the clear implication is that such gifts were not available to the church in general. Rather he points to faith in prayer, by the whole local assembly, as the God-appointed means of aiding the sick. This does not contradict the New Testament references to the gifts of healing if we identify those gifts as the special and occasional powers granted to the apostles and others who knew Christ in the flesh. These gifts fulfilled the criteria laid down in 1 Corinthians for the charismata, since they contributed in a notable manner to the establishment and building up of the church of Christ in its formative years. Their contribution stemmed not so much from their miraculous character, as from the fact that they served to authenticate the claims of Christ and of those who proclaimed Him as Saviour and Lord.

The Gift of Tongues

Tongues in the Acts of the Apostles

The gift or sign of tongues on the Day of Pentecost was given so that the cosmopolitan crowd that had gathered (as a result of the sound of a violent wind), should hear in their own languages 'the mighty deeds of God'. We have already noticed that this was not necessary for the purpose of communication. All these men, Parthians, Medes, Elamites and so on, could understand whatever common language Peter used when he preached his sermon later that day. The first reason for the Pentecostal glossolalia, therefore, was to create amazement and attention. The strange and wholly unexpected phenomenon of Galilean peasants speaking fluently in foreign languages, seized the attention of the multitude. 'What does this mean?' they cried (Acts 2:12). Clearly, the Pentecostal tongues were a miraculous sign to an initially unbelieving audience, designed to capture their attention and make them receptive to the message that Peter was about to preach. As always, there were sceptics, who attributed what they heard to drunkenness. This was a spurious explanation, of course, for inebriation impairs, rather than imparts, linguistic ability! But, for some, any explanation was preferable to the admission that a miracle was taking place before their eyes. For the majority, however, the result of this phenomenon was to create perplexity, wonder and attention to what ensued.

There was a second purpose in the glossolalia of the Day of Pentecost. They provided a miraculous dimension that went far to substantiating Peter's claim that this was the fulfilment of Joel's ancient prophecy. It was not only appropriate, but necessary, that the arrival of the promised Spirit should be marked by miraculous signs. Otherwise no one could have been sure that the promise had in fact been fulfilled.

Having defined these two reasons for the Pentecostal glossolalia, we may now ask whether they have any bearing on subsequent occurrences of tongues. The second purpose we discerned (that the tongues were an inaugural sign) obviously cannot apply to the phenomenon in general, though it can be argued that it was so in Samaria (if, indeed, tongues were spoken there) and at Caesarea, since on these occasions new representative groups were being baptized into the church. The first reason we identified for the gift of tongues, however, clearly can apply generally, for it is always desirable to win attention for gospel preaching. Even here we must be careful, since the Pentecostal sign only had the desired effect on those who recognized that their mother tongues were being spoken. It was this that excited their interest, not that the disciples were speaking gibberish! In fact it seems that some among the crowd, hearing only unintelligible speech, came to the conclusion that the speakers were simply drunk. This reflects Paul's concern expressed to the Corinthians that the ignorant or unbelieving visitor to their assembly might consider them mad if he heard them speak in tongues unknown to them (1 Cor. 14:23). The generally positive reaction from the Pentecostal audience arose because they understood what was being said, not because they witnessed a bizarre occurrence.

For tongues to play a part in the process of evangelization, as happened at Pentecost, it was therefore necessary for certain conditions to apply. In particular it was essential that the hearers should understand what was being spoken and that

The Spirit has come

they should also recognize the miraculous nature of the events they witnessed. It is possible that these conditions were met at Corinth because, being a busy seaport, the city had a large cosmopolitan population. This might account for the currency of the gift of tongues among the Corinthian believers, though we are admittedly speculating at this point. It would, however, explain why the gift of tongues is not mentioned in any other Epistle and harmonizes with what we are told in the New Testament about the purpose of tongues as a sign to unbelievers.

Returning to Acts, we next note that speaking with tongues is not recorded during the effusions of the Spirit in chapters 4:31 and 8:17. In the Samaritan episode, admittedly, there was some visible manifestation of the Holy Spirit's outpouring, since we read, 'When Simon saw that the Spirit was bestowed through the laying on of the apostles' hands, he offered them money' (Acts 8:18). It is sometimes maintained that the visible sign in question must have been glossolalia, but this must remain a speculation. If tongues were spoken on that occasion it would establish a closer similarity with Pentecost and Caesarea, and this would not in any way contradict the idea presented in chapter 8 that these three effusions were closely related in their historical uniqueness.

Nevertheless, the second clear reference to tongues in Acts is not found until we reach chapter 10 and the account of the conversion of Cornelius and his household. The purpose of tongues on this occasion is perfectly plain, for it was this that persuaded Peter and his doubtful Jewish companions that the Gentiles had indeed been granted the Holy Spirit. Not only had they received a gift of the Spirit, but the self-same gift that had been vouchsafed to the Jews at Pentecost. Notice how Luke emphasizes this point. 'All the believers from among the circumcision who had come with Peter were amazed, because the gift of the Holy Spirit had been poured out upon the Gentiles also. For they were hearing them speak in tongues and exalting God. Then Peter answered, "Surely no one can refuse the water for these to be baptized who have received the Holy Spirit just as we did" ' (Acts 10:45—47 mg.). Again, as Peter recounts the events to the Jewish believers at Jerusalem, he argues, 'The Holy Spirit fell upon them, just as He did upon us at the beginning . . . If God therefore gave to them the same gift as He gave to us also . . . who was I that I could stand in God's way?' (Acts 11:15−17). What was it that convinced Peter that the Gentiles had received 'the same gift', if not the glossolalia that accompanied the Spirit's outpouring? This was the only miraculous element in the events at Cornelius' home, and the only obvious link with Pentecost itself.

As the purpose of tongues at Caesarea is plain, so the reason for their manifestation at Ephesus is obscure (Acts 19:6). Pentecostals and Charismatics would maintain that tongues-speaking is a normal, or even necessary, consequence of an effusion or baptism of the Spirit. Against this it can be argued that the phenomenon is not reported in Acts 4:31 or 8:17, that the Pentecostal visitation of Acts 2 was a historically unique occasion which cannot be generalized, and that the occurrence in Acts 10:46 was necessary to demonstrate that the Gentiles had received the authentic gift of the Spirit. It cannot be said, therefore, that there is any clear pattern of tongues-speaking in Acts, and the incident at Ephesus remains unexplained. The only clue to this matter is that Paul's whole ministry in this city was characterized by an extraordinary measure of miraculous power, no doubt on account of the equally entrenched power of the black arts. The incident may then be viewed as a special vindication of the apostle's authority in the eyes of the first Ephesian believers. In much the same way, the Jerusalem apostles were accorded authority in the estimation of the first Samaritan Christians through their ability to impart the Holy Spirit by the laying-on of hands.

Tongues at Corinth

We return, then, to the only remaining passage in the New Testament that refers to the glossolalia, namely the twelfth to fourteenth chapters of the First Corinthians. What do these chapters tell us concerning the purpose of the gift of tongues? The key passage is 1 Corinthians 14:20−25, where Paul actually defines the purpose of tongues very plainly. His statement is complicated, however, by an apparent contradiction between verses 20−22 and verses 23−25, and the

exegetical problems of this passage have exercised many commentators and confused even more! J.B. Phillips in his paraphrase of the New Testament Epistles ('Letters to Young
Churches') actually reverses Paul's words in verse 22 in an
attempt to 'correct' what the apostle is saying and reconcile
that verse with those that follow. Phillips frankly admits
that this is the only solution he could find to the dilemma.
But this 'solution' fails completely to solve the problem,
as we shall see more clearly by quoting the passage at length.
For ease of reference we include the verse numbers in
brackets. '(20) Brethren, do not be children in your thinking;
yet in evil be babes, but in your thinking be mature. (21) In
the Law it is written, "By men of strange tongues and by the
lips of strangers I will speak to this people, and even so they
will not listen to me", says the Lord. (22) So then tongues
are for a sign, not to those who believe, but to unbelievers:
but prophecy not to unbelievers, but to those who believe .
(23) If therefore the whole church should assemble together
and all speak in tongues, and ungifted men or unbelievers
enter, will they not say you are mad? (24) But if all prophesy, and an unbeliever or an ungifted man enters, he is
convicted by all . . . (25) the secrets of his heart are disclosed: and so he will fall on his face and worship God,
declaring that God is certainly among you.'

Now it is clear that Paul's exegesis of the quotation from
Isaiah 28:11 *et seq*. is correct, namely that the 'strange
tongues' were to be addressed to an unbelieving audience. By
reversing the meaning of verse 22, therefore, and stating that
tongues are a sign to believers, Phillips reconciles that verse
with verses 23–25, but introduces a new contradiction between the quotation from Isaiah and Paul's interpretation of
it! The problem is merely shifted, not removed.

The correct procedure is to recognize that verses 20–22
represent a clear and definitive statement as to the purpose of
tongues and then to attempt to understand the later verses
in the light of this. We shall follow this procedure, looking
first at verses 20–22.

The passage begins with an appeal to the Corinthians to
be mature in their understanding of the matter under debate
in this chapter, namely the relative merits of tongues and
prophecy. Throughout the chapter Paul emphasizes the

shortcomings of the glossolalia, and this demonstrates that the Corinthians were displaying immaturity in giving undue prominence to this gift. This lack of spiritual maturity was characteristic of the church there, as evidenced elsewhere in the Epistle (1:10—13; 3:1—4; 5:1—8; 6:1—9; 11:18—22 and so on). It was time for them to grow up, declares Paul robustly, concerning the matter of tongues-speaking. How were they to do so? By taking notice of the Scriptures. Had not Isaiah spoken of the gift of tongues, asks the apostle? And was it not obvious from that reference that tongues were intended as a sign to unbelievers? What, then, were the Corinthians doing, using this gift in public worship? Was this not an act of immaturity, a misuse of the charisma? No wonder that tongues were unsuitable for the edification of the church, as Paul argues throughout this chapter, seeing that the gift was never intended to be employed in this manner! This is the obvious burden of these verses, and it is difficult to construe them in any other way.

This scriptural explanation of the purpose of tongues as a sign to unbelievers is wholly consistent with their use in Acts 2. There the phenomenon was instrumental in securing the attention of the crowd for the preaching of the gospel. In the case of Cornelius in Acts 10, there were probably no unbelieving onlookers and the glossolalia were given for the unique purpose of convincing the Jews that the Gentiles had received the Spirit. In one sense, then, the tongues of Acts 10 were a sign to believers, but this case was so obviously special that it could be considered the exception that proves the rule. Caesarea was an echo of Pentecost, and similar manifestations were therefore necessary. In Acts 19 we do not know whether there were unbelievers present or not, but nothing is said there to contradict Paul's claim that the primary purpose of the gift of tongues was to affect the unconverted. In any case, the apostle's statement to this effect is so categorical that it really requires no circumstantial evidence to support it.

What, then, are we to make of verses 23 to 25? Here Paul sketches a scenario in which the entire church at worship is engaged in tongues-speaking and an untaught or unbelieving visitor appears on the scene. The effect on such a person, says Paul, would be entirely negative. Instead of drawing him to the gospel, the experience would convince him that the Christians were mad. How, then, in these circumstances could it be claimed that tongues were acting as a sign to the unbeliever? The simple answer is that under the circumstances envisaged they would not constitute such a sign because they were being misused! The sign of tongues did not consist of an indiscriminate use of foreign languages, but in the unbeliever hearing himself addressed in an unexpected tongue which the speaker had acquired by miraculous means. This is the unmistakable import of the Day of Pentecost. Paul makes it clear in verses 20—22 that the situation pictured in verse 23 would represent an abuse of the glossolalia. Here was the church 'assembled together' for worship. The unbeliever enters, unexpectedly. The tongues-speaking is not addressed to him at all, for he is a mere onlooker. The languages employed are not suited to his ears. He observes only the misuse of the glossolalia and can make neither head nor tail of them. He concludes, not unreasonably, that the Christians are out of their minds.

So then, tongues properly given by the Spirit in appropriate evangelistic circumstances were an authentic and powerful sign to unbelievers that they were in the presence of God. But tongues being misused in a church as a result of immaturity were good for nothing, neither edifying the church nor challenging the unbeliever. This seems to be the burden of Paul's teaching here, and if this is so, it is clear that no contradiction arises between verses 22 and 23.

The other alleged contradiction concerns prophecy and it will be convenient to deal with it here since it occurs in the passage we have been considering. In verse 22 we are told that prophecy was for believers, not unbelievers, and this is obviously true, in that prophecy served chiefly to edify the church. This does not mean, however, that the evident wisdom and spiritual power of the prophetic gift would not impress and convict an unbeliever who witnessed it. The prophecy would not have been addressed to the person in question. (Remember, Paul is discussing an unexpected visitor who appears suddenly upon the scene.) But prophecy has an impact upon the onlooker that unintelligible tongues could never produce. Prophecy, therefore, could serve the secondary function of an evangelistic means, though it is clear from the New Testament that preaching, not prophecy, was the chosen means of saving sinners, as this same Epistle testifies in chapter 1:21.

In favour of tongues

Throughout 1 Corinthians 14 the gift of tongues suffers severely at Paul's hands, as he compares it unfavourably with prophecy. The great problem with tongues, argues the apostle, is that they do not edify the church. Since to do so is the whole purpose of the charismata (1 Cor. 12:7), this represents a fundamental failure of the gift. Once one sets aside their primary function of awakening the unsaved (or, for that matter, judging them for their unbelief), the best that can be said about tongues is that the one who uses them 'edifies himself' (14:4).

In spite of all these contra-indications, however, there remain some statements in this fourteenth chapter that set the gift of tongues in a more favourable light. In verse 5 Paul says, 'I wish you all spoke in tongues, but even more that you would prophesy.' Although the gift of prophecy is obviously rated more highly, that of tongues is nevertheless commended. Again, in verse 13, the problem of the unintelligibility of the glossolalia is offset by the gift of interpretation. This gift is mentioned explicitly in chapter 12:10 and would hardly have been given by the Holy Spirit if the gift of tongues was not intended to be used in the church. Next we read Paul's own testimony in the matter when he states, 'I thank God, I speak in tongues more than you all' (14:18). Then we find specific instructions given as to the regulation of tongues in worship, rules which would not have been needed if they were to be avoided completely (14:27, 28). Finally, Paul specifically instructs that the glossolalia were not to be forbidden (14:39). There is an implication here that some members of the church at Corinth had suggested they be banned.

What may we conclude from these various references in favour of tongues? Firstly, it is clear that Paul does not disapprove of the gift of tongues as such, since he himself used it in private devotions. This is implied, at least, in verses 4, 18 and 28. What he does condemn is an unregulated employment of the gift in the church, publicly. Its public use was intended as a sign to the unconverted, and only immaturity led the Corinthians to exercise it otherwise. However, if accompanied by interpretation, even this objection could be set aside, and the gift be used in the worship of the church. We must conclude that the problem at Corinth lay not in their possession of the gift of tongues, but in its misuse and particularly in an unhealthy preoccupation with this charisma to the exclusion of the more edifying prophetic ministry.

Having said this, we must recognize that Paul is obviously wary of the glossolalia. While not forbidding their use, he clearly seeks to direct the zeal of the Corinthians elsewhere (see 14:12, for example). There are particular pitfalls, he seems to indicate, associated with this particular charisma. Possibly this was because the gift had a specially strong effect upon the emotions. This possibility can be inferred from the fact that the gift of tongues is always associated with the praise and glorification of God and not with the exercise of the critical faculties. It therefore constitutes dangerous ground for the immature and unwary (1 Cor. 12:1–3).

There is no necessary contradiction between our earlier conclusion, that tongues were first and foremost a sign to the unconverted, and the idea that they could legitimately be used in private devotions and even in the church if limited and subject to interpretation. We have to recognize that there were both primary and secondary uses for some of the charismata and that the Spirit's sovereignty was at work in either case. Although Paul clearly tolerated the use of tongues in the church if properly interpreted and regulated, the tone of these chapters is unmistakable. The secondary use of the gift should preferably be limited to the private realm (14:18, 19), and the spiritually immature should beware the special pitfalls associated with such a powerfully emotive experience.

We need only add that what we have described concerns the situation at Corinth at the time of Paul's letter to them. The implications for today must be considered in our final chapter rather than here.

12. The cessation or continuance of the charismata

In our final chapter we come to the subject that possibly causes more division than any of the other controversial matters we have discussed so far. Pentecostals and Charismatics not only believe that the charismata were intended to endure throughout the age of the church and until Christ's return, but actually claim to practise and experience these spiritual gifts today. Their opponents maintain that the charismata were limited to the apostolic age and, specifically, ceased when the New Testament Scriptures became generally available. The miraculous gifts were intended to serve a transitional purpose while the early church, under the guidance of the Spirit, formulated its doctrine and practice. Such manifestations as are current today, says the Traditional Reformed position, are the product of psychological manipulation or even satanic deception. It is plain that the two sides are very far apart.

Once again we must repeat that our main objective is not to reconcile opposing views but rather to see what Scripture really does teach concerning these things. The answer to our divisions must lie in a humble submission to the Word of God rather than any formula for compromise. Nevertheless we should remember that such submission requires of us all a spirit of humility and love towards our fellow believers even where we are unable to agree. It is with this attitude, then, that we seek to draw our conclusions. The reader may feel that the previous chapter, by arguing against the continuance of certain of the charismata, committed itself to the Traditional Reformed position on this subject and that little more remains to be said. This is not the case, however. It is still necessary to ask the important question whether the charismata as a whole have ceased or whether only certain of them have been withdrawn, having fulfilled their purpose in the plan of God. It also remains for us to discuss the closing verses of 1 Corinthians 13 which bear directly upon the issue of cessation or continuance. The matters considered in this chapter are therefore far from being redundant. Indeed it could be argued that our most important positive conclusion has yet to be drawn.

The interpretation of 1 Corinthians 13

This chapter of 1 Corinthians is best known for its description and elevation of Christian love. It also contains, however, the most direct teaching to be found in Scripture on the subject before us. Unfortunately, Paul's comments on the matter can be interpreted in various ways and both sides in the argument claim that these verses support their position! We must therefore examine what they say in some detail. The passage will be quoted here in full (verse numbers are given in brackets).

'(8) Love never fails; but if there are gifts of prophecy, they will be done away; if there are tongues they will cease; if there is knowledge, it will be done away. (9) For we know in part, and we prophesy in part; (10) but when the perfect comes, the partial will be done away. (11) When I was a child, I used to speak as a child, think as a child, reason as a child; when I became a man, I did away with childish things. (12) For now we see in a mirror dimly, but then face to face; now I know in part, but then I shall know fully just as I also have been fully known. (13) But now abide faith, hope, love, these three; but the greatest of these is love.'

There can be no question that this passage teaches that some, if not all, of the charismata were or are temporary in character. Those particularly mentioned are prophecy, tongues and the gift of knowledge (1 Cor. 12:8. This is unlikely to be a reference to knowledge as such in the light of verse 12). The problem is to decide just how temporary the gifts were intended to be. Pentecostals and Charismatics maintain that the cessation that Paul anticipates in these verses will only occur when Christ returns. The Traditional Reformed view is that cessation was linked with the maturation of the church at a very early stage in its history.

The debate turns upon the interpretation of two things in the passage. Firstly, what does Paul mean by 'the perfect' (or 'that which is perfect') in verse 10? Secondly, what era is indicated by the word 'then' in verse 12? On one view, that which is perfect refers to the state of the church after the return of the Lord Jesus. On the other, it refers to the complete or 'perfect' revelation constituted by the New Testament Scriptures. Similarly, the two opposing interpretations differ as to the significance of the word 'then'. For the Pentecostal, the era in question is that of Christ's return and the rapture of the church. For the Reformed party, it was the time when the knowledge of God became complete as a result of the publication of New Testament Scripture. Let us consider the arguments in favour of these alternatives.

The main argument for the Pentecostal interpretation is found in verse 12, where the cessation of the charismata seems to be assigned to a time when believers will enjoy a direct and immediate knowledge of God. This knowledge is described in terms that suggest far more than an inferential understanding derived from the study of the New Testament, or even the experimental knowledge of God through the Spirit that we have discussed earlier in this book. At that time, the apostle seems to say, we shall see God 'face to face' and know Him fully, just as He now knows us. This degree of knowing God cannot, by any stretch of the imagination, be attributed to believers in the present age. Our present situation is well described, they argue, by verse 12: we see dimly and we know in part. It is possible to find similar descriptions of our current state of knowledge in 1 Peter 1:8 and 1 John 3:2. 'Though you do not see [Christ] now, but believe in Him', states Peter, 'you greatly rejoice with joy inexpressible and full of glory.' Even the extreme joy and spiritual exultation described here fall short of the complete knowledge of God that is their inheritance and waits 'to be revealed in the last time' (1 Peter 1:4). John is even more explicit concerning the incompleteness of the believer's knowledge of God during the present age, Scripture notwithstanding. 'Beloved, now we are children of God, and it has not appeared as yet what we shall be. We know that, when He appears, we shall be like Him, because we shall see Him just as He is.' Thus John links our

final transformation to Christ's appearance and our seeing
Him 'as He is', that is, in the fulness of His glory. This, claims
the Pentecostal argument, is just what Paul means by seeing
Christ 'face to face' and such direct knowledge must await
His second coming. Until then, the charismata are provided
as an admittedly imperfect and partial means of knowing
and enjoying God.

The Traditional Reformed position argues differently.
The Greek word translated 'perfect' in verse 10 is *teleios*,
which means simply 'finished' or 'complete'. It does not
necessarily convey the idea of absolute perfection, but
rather of wholeness or maturity. In this sense it is used to
describe the condition of certain believers when Paul tells
the Corinthians, 'We do speak wisdom among those who
are mature (*teleios*)' (1 Cor. 2:6), and a similar usage is
found in Philippians 3:15, Colossians 4:12, and James 3:2.
Although the word does sometimes refer to the perfection
of God, the basic meaning is always 'whole' or 'complete'.
It is also obvious from the passage itself that Paul must be
using the word in this sense, for that which is 'perfect' is
explicitly contrasted with that which is partial or incomplete (verse 9). It is not necessary, therefore, to project the
arrival of 'the perfect' forward to the time when Christ
restores all things. The New Testament Scriptures are perfect
in the sense that they are both inspired of God and complete.
Their finished revelation has replaced the partial knowledge
afforded by the ecstatic charismata (gifts of knowledge,
wisdom, prophecy and tongues, for example) so that the
latter are no longer required by the church.

The Traditional Reformed case continues by reference to
verse 11, where Paul illustrates his argument from the growth
to maturity of a child. The charismata are represented by the
'childish things' which are left behind in the process of
maturation. But how long does this process continue? Since
Paul constantly urges the Corinthians to be mature (see, for
example, 1 Cor. 3:1 and 14:20), we must accept that
maturity is achievable in the present age and does not have
to await the return of Christ. It follows that the age of the
charismata was intended to be brief, and that their prominence at Corinth was a result of that church's immaturity.

The argument also questions the idea that 'face to face'

necessarily refers to our view of God in glory. The expression could just signify an open view in contrast to the dim reflection afforded by the mirrors of Paul's day. The object seen in a mirror is, of course, one's own face. Before the completion of Scripture, therefore, Christians saw themselves only imperfectly. But in the light of a completed revelation they would soon be able to see themselves (as the objects of God's great salvation) as clearly as if they were looking directly at another person, that is, face to face. They would then know themselves (not God) as they were already known by God.

Against this it can be argued that Paul's other use of the illustration of a mirror, in 2 Corinthians 3:18, states clearly that the object reflected therein is 'the glory of the Lord'. Admittedly a different Greek word is employed for 'mirror' in that reference, but it means the same as the word in our verse and cannot constitute a significant difference. Why, in any case, does Paul use the allusion at all in 2 Corinthians, if it is not to signify an imperfect or incomplete view of the glory of God? If this is so, the parallel between the two passages is very close and suggests that 1 Corinthians 13 does refer, after all, to the believer's dim apprehensions of the Lord's glory, and not of his own nature.

The final argument for the Traditional Reformed position arises from verse 13. Here Paul asserts that there 'now abide faith, hope, love, these three'. The word translated 'abide' means to remain or continue. The continuance of these fruits of the Spirit is thus deliberately contrasted with the impermanence of prophecy and tongues. But of these three, neither faith nor hope will remain once Christ has returned! We walk by faith only until faith is superseded by sight (2 Cor. 5:7), and hope will similarly become redundant at His appearing (Rom. 8:24). Thus these things that now remain will themselves be done away at the return of Christ. Since the charismata are less permanent than faith and hope, being subject to cessation (v. 8) while the latter still 'abide', it follows that the gifts of the Spirit were intended to disappear during the gospel era rather than at its end.

It is clear that both viewpoints have powerful arguments on their sides, and we must therefore consider the possibility that neither have it quite right! It is unlikely that Paul intended to teach two opposing doctrines in the same passage. Is there, then, a way of understanding the passage that does justice to all it contains? I believe there is.

To begin with, we are compelled to accept the force of the Pentecostal argument that verse 12 appears to describe the situation after the return of Christ. It is extremely difficult to ascribe to the present era such a degree of direct knowledge as is delineated there. Even though we possess the Scriptures in their entirety, we are still 'beholding as in a mirror the glory of the Lord' (2 Cor. 3:18). If Paul is at all consistent in his use of the 'mirror' illustration, 1 Corinthians 13:12 must refer to a future time when such an indirect means of beholding Christ will no longer be necessary. Does this then mean that the specified charismata will continue right up to the time of the Lord's return? Not necessarily. All it means is that Paul is considering in this passage the whole sweep of human history, from his own day to that future age when our knowledge of Christ will be complete and we shall know Him as He knows us. This is typically Pauline. Again and again he spreads before his readers, often in only a few words, the whole historical and post-historical panorama of God's purposes for His church. (Other examples can be found in Romans 8, 2 Corinthians 3:18 and 4:16—18). During this comprehensive period, Paul tells us in these verses, certain events would take place, with particular implications in the realm of knowledge.

Our present situation is in some respects the same as Paul's. Although he wrote at a time when the New Testament documents were not complete, he could still speak of the essential Christian revelation as already accomplished (Eph. 3:5; Gal. 2:2). For the apostles themselves, at least, the completion of the written revelation would have had no special significance. Yet Paul does not say, '*You* see in a mirror, dimly', but '*we*', indicating a situation common to all believers. Thus we conclude that our present knowledge of God is indeed deficient in relation to that knowledge we shall possess when we see Him 'face to face'. On the other hand, we are not in a stationary condition as regards the knowledge of God. The Scripture exhorts us to be 'bearing fruit in every good work and increasing in the knowledge of

God' (Col. 1:10). In Ephesians 4, as Paul expounds the illustration of the church as a body, he says we 'are to grow up in all aspects into Him, who is the head, even Christ'. He tells us that this process of growing up, or maturation, must continue 'until we all attain unto the unity of the faith, and of the knowledge of the Son of God, to a mature man, to the measure of the stature which belongs to the fulness of Christ' (Eph. 4:13, 14). The ministerial gifts of the Spirit listed in verse 11 of Ephesians 4 were provided to this very end, namely for the building up of the body of Christ until its full maturity is reached.

Does this then mean that the gifts of apostleship and prophecy, which head the list, are to remain in force until the church is complete in all respects? Not necessarily. If we accept the conclusions reached in the previous chapter, the ministry of revelation, exercised by the apostles and prophets, is complete. But the Scripture which embodies that revelation remains the most potent agent for the edification of the church today. 'They, being dead, yet speak.' Their work endures and continues to contribute mightily to the ongoing process of the maturation of the body of Christ. Thus it is wholly consistent to say that the process of growth described in Ephesians 4:13 is still in progress and yet to maintain that some of the offices defined in verse 11 have run their course and been terminated. The offices of apostle and prophet may thus have ceased, without their ministry having been set aside. If we have correctly interpreted the nature of that ministry in chapter 11, it is one which still exerts a primary influence on the growth and development of the church today.

We therefore see that the continuing process of maturation, which will go on until Christ returns, is still served by the charismatic gifts. But this principle does not imply that all those gifts are still current today. Some of the charismata have fulfilled their purpose, though the foundational nature of the work they accomplished ensures for them an abiding value, even though the gifts themselves have ceased. The transmission of the Christian revelation by the apostles and prophets is the most obvious example. But the miracles and acts of healing that authenticated the messiahship of Christ also illustrate our point, for they still serve this same purpose today and make their contribution as recorded history, though not as current phenomena. The position of tongues is less clear, but we have seen that they were given primarily as a means of evangelism and that their use in the church was tolerated rather than encouraged by Paul. He does certainly seem to recommend their use in private devotions, but this may well have been a privilege accorded to those who possessed the gift for its primary purpose. This is one area where it is not possible to be dogmatic.

This way of looking at the closing verses of 1 Corinthians 13 also allows full weight to the comparison Paul makes between the abiding fruit of the Spirit and the temporary nature of prophecy and tongues. The latter would cease when they had served their purpose in the strategy of God for the building of the church. The work of the Spirit would, however, continue unabated and especially in His ministry of making believers fruitful. The illustration of the child and the man also fits well into this scenario. Children do not suddenly become adults, but grow into that mature state over the course of time. Maturation is a process in which 'childish things' are left behind progressively. I do not think that Paul was deriding the charismata when he calls them 'childish'. The word in Greek does not hold the pejorative meaning of its English equivalent. It simply means 'things pertaining to childhood'. Thus the charismata in question belonged to the childhood of the church, and properly so. To despise them would be to set at nought the very foundation on which we, as Christians, are built. That foundation was given us by those who exercised the charismatic ministries. As the church grew, however, and as the various ministries fulfilled their foundational purpose, so they were progressively put away, as a child, little by little, lays aside its early attitudes and ways.

This illustration of the maturing child is followed in 1 Corinthians 13 by the reference to the time yet to come when we shall see Christ face to face. This will be the culmination of the growth process, the day when faith will be replaced by sight, and hope by fulfilment. Even these 'abiding' qualities will then have served their purpose and will vanish away, as the more temporary provisions had already done. The partial nature of prophecy and tongues rendered them unnecessary once the full revelation of New Testament Scripture became widely available. But even Scripture is partial, as it itself testifies, and will be replaced in that great day by a knowledge that is as yet beyond our comprehension (1 John 3:2). In that day, of all the apprehensions of God vouchsafed to us in this life, only love will retain its currency. That is why it is greater than all other fruits of the Spirit. It is of the essence of the nature of God, for God is love, and it will never be redundant.

This thought brings us back to where we began this review of 1 Corinthians 13. The message of the whole chapter is that all edification, all growth in the spiritual realm, must be a growth in love. For that is the destination towards which we progress. The charismata could only serve their appointed purpose if they produced such growth. 'The proper working of each individual part', explains Paul, 'causes the growth of the body for the building up of itself *in love*' (Eph. 4:16). Apart from this, prophecy, knowledge and tongues were of not the slightest value or interest to the church.

The charismatic principle

Most of this chapter, and the previous one also, will appear somewhat negative, for we have spent our time showing that certain of the gifts of the Spirit have been withdrawn, having served their intended purpose. It is important therefore to consider the positive aspect of all this. This positive element we shall term 'the charismatic principle', and it is best expressed in terms of the 'body' illustration so beloved of Paul. Briefly, the principle states that the Spirit of God continues to this day to distribute His gifts 'to each one individually just as He wills' (1 Cor. 12:11). The church is still properly and accurately described as an organic unity, a body, in which each part contributes to the growth and welfare of the whole. The members' ability to make such contributions still depends upon the enabling of the Holy Spirit, just as it did in Paul's day. The church is therefore still 'charismatic' in this most profound of senses.

The point to be emphasized here is that the cessation of certain of the charismata does not mean the cessation of them all, nor does it mean that the Spirit of God is any less present or any less powerful in the church today than He was in New Testament times. The cessation of the miraculous charismata, we have suggested, was part of God's programme for the church and should be viewed in terms of progress rather than loss or deprivation. Peter tells us that God's written revelation is to be preferred above the most wonderful of ecstatic visions. Referring to the transfiguration of Christ, he says, 'We ourselves heard this utterance made from heaven when we were with Him on the holy mountain. And we have the even surer prophetic word . . .' (2 Peter 1:18, 19, mg. The NASV text inserts words quite unjustifiably to change the meaning and the marginal rendering is what the original actually says.) The passing of the apostolic and prophetic ministries marked the rise of a Christianity based upon the complete written revelation of the New Testament. We have only to recall the power with which the early church used the Old Testament Scriptures to understand what the arrival of the New must have meant to them. Perhaps today we have lost our view of the power and immediacy of the Word of God, and mistakenly hanker after a return to the prophetical epoch. Similarly, the loss of the gift of tongues, with all its capacity for emotional satisfaction, would have seemed no deprivation to those who had really learned to pray 'with the spirit and the mind also'. For, as Paul explains, 'If I pray in a tongue, my spirit prays, but my mind is unfruitful. What is the outcome then? I shall pray with the spirit and I shall pray with the mind also; I shall sing with the spirit and I shall sing with the mind also' (1 Cor. 14:14, 15).

The miraculous charismata were not only transitional. Their role was much too positive to be dismissed in such terms. They were, rather, foundational, and their foundation remains to this day. Their passing signalled the completion of the groundwork and the commencement of a new phase in the building of Christ's church. That work of building continues and is being accomplished by the very same means that Paul describes by his oft-used illustration of the body. In this respect nothing has changed.

The charismata that remain are not only sufficient to accomplish the task, but are the gifts most appropriate to that task. Thus the offices of evangelist, pastor and teacher are still the gifts of the risen Christ 'for the equipping of the saints for the work of service, to the building up of the body of Christ' (Eph. 4:11, 12). The 'gifts that differ according to the grace given to us' still include today such New Testament functions as 'service . . . teaching . . . exhortation . . . giving . . . leadership . . . mercy' (Rom. 12:6–8). Every function within the church, when properly understood, is charismatic in nature. Along with apostleship and prophecy, Paul lists such humble roles as helping and administering, and says that 'God has appointed' them in the church (1 Cor. 12:28). Such divine appointments were no less important in God's sight than the ability to perform miracles or speak in foreign tongues. Indeed, their very 'ordinariness' secures for them a more lasting validity. What we must not forget is that these humble roles are only effective in so far as they *are* charismatic. If we attempt to perform them in the strength of the flesh, or with dependence upon human wisdom, we shall destroy the church, not build it. It is essential that believers be empowered by the Spirit of God in their serving, helping and administering. Only then will these things be done in love and with that spiritual wisdom and effectiveness that come only from above.

We need therefore to rediscover the charismatic principle in all aspects of the church and Christian life. Believers are indwelt by the Spirit of God. 'Each one has received a special gift' and all are 'stewards of the manifold grace of God' (1 Peter 4:10). Our gifts may not have been bestowed upon us through prophecy, as was Timothy's, but we have the same responsibility as he to 'kindle afresh the gift of God which is in [us]' (2 Tim. 1:6). Only then will our churches and Christian assemblies begin to function as living bodies, growing and building themselves up together in love (Eph. 4:16). Only then will Christ's headship be apparent, and His fulness attained.

Conclusion

In the previous chapter we reached the tentative conclusion that certain of the charismata were intended to be of a temporary or foundational nature. This conclusion was reached on the basis of an examination of their role in

Scripture and not upon any extra-biblical or historical reasoning. The present chapter has considered the direct scriptural evidence for cessation or continuance, seeking the most consistent interpretation. This appears to lie in one positive and one negative proposition. Positively, we find that the charismatic principle, by which the Spirit of God equips His people to serve the church, and by which that church still reaches forward towards full maturity, is still in force today, in all its glorious potential for believers individually and corporately. Negatively, we have confirmed that the foundational charismata, having served their purpose in God's grand strategy, have ceased, having left behind, however, a rich heritage of which the written Scriptures are the chief example.

What, then are we to make of those manifestations displayed today among our Pentecostal and Charismatic brethren, as well as among many groups whose Christianity is not biblical in its doctrine (Catholics and Unitarians, for example)? In one sense our self-imposed remit forbids us to speculate. We set ourselves the task of discovering what Scripture has to say on these matters, not of judging our neighbours. Scripture does, however, contain certain warnings to the effect that ecstatic and seemingly miraculous phenomena can be produced by satanic imitation (1 Cor. 12:1–3; 1 John 4:1–3). These warnings are given in Scripture to believers, indicating the possibility that sincere Christians may be deceived and misled into accepting these things as genuinely spiritual. 'Test the spirits to see whether they are from God', advises the disciple whom Jesus loved, 'because many false prophets have gone out into the world' (1 John 4:1). We would humbly suggest that for us today the means of testing the spirits lie in the whole testimony of the Word of God concerning these matters. We must try the spirits by searching the Scriptures, to see whether these things are so. That is what we have attempted to do in this volume.

It is, of course, possible to suggest that certain phenomena such as tongues and incidents of healing may be produced by psychological means, and that they are mistakenly attributed to the work of the Holy Spirit but are not otherwise harmful. That may be so, but the devil can use our mistakes to create both division and diversion; division between brethren who see these matters differently, and diversion from the task of preaching the authentic gospel of Jesus Christ to a lost world. It is not therefore possible to ignore the activity of Satan even when his involvement is indirect rather than direct.

Having said this, we do not condemn others. In one matter, that of private tongues-speaking, we have not in fact been able to come to any clear view as to their cessation. 1 Corinthians 13 suggests that tongues and prophecy shared the same temporary character, and the strong internal evidence concerning prophecy therefore implies that the authentic glossolalia were also limited to the apostolic era. But this is an implication rather than a direct proof. In the final analysis, it is for each of us to satisfy ourselves that our beliefs and practices conform to the Word of God, and that we are not simply projecting on to Scripture our own personal prejudices. If this book has helped the reader to submit his or her views to the scrutiny of God's Word, it will have served its purpose. If it has enabled any of us to grasp with new understanding the extent of God's provision for us in the Spirit, it will have more than fulfilled its task.

Bibliography

1. General books on the Holy Spirit

Pink, A. W., *The Holy Spirit*, Baker Book House, 1970.
Smeaton, G., *The Holy Spirit*, Banner of Truth Trust, 1958.
Wood, L., *The Holy Spirit in the Old Testament*, Zondervan, 1976.

2. Books written from the Pentecostal and Charismatic viewpoint

Gee, D., *The Pentecostal Movement*, Assemblies of God Publishing House, 1941.
Gee, D., *Concerning Spiritual Gifts*, Gospel Publishing House, 1972.
Watson, D. C. K., *One in the Spirit*, Hodder and Stoughton, 1975.
Harper, M., *This is the Day*, Hodder and Stoughton, 1979.
Harper, M., *Power for the Body of Christ*, Fountain Trust, 1964.
Horton, H., *The Gifts of the Spirit*, Assemblies of God Publishing House, 1976.
Ranaghan, K. and D., *Catholic Pentecostals*, Paulist Press, Deus Books, 1969.
Smail, T. A., *Reflected Glory*, Hodder and Stoughton, 1975.

3. Book presenting the Reformed Sealers' position

Lloyd-Jones, D. M., *God's Ultimate Purpose*, Banner of Truth Trust, 1979 (with special reference to chapters 21–26).

4. Books presenting the Traditional Reformed viewpoint

Warfield, B. B., *Miracles: Yesterday and Today*, Eerdmans, 1965 (first published 1918 as *'Counterfeit Miracles'*).
Gromacki, R. G., *The Modern Tongues Movement*, Presbyterian and Reformed Publishing Co., 1972 (revised).
Stibbs, A. M. and Packer, J. I., *The Spirit Within You*, Pickering and Inglis, 1967.
Stott, J. R. W., *Baptism and Fulness*, Inter Varsity Press, 1975.
Gaffin, R. B., *Perspectives on Pentecost*, Presbyterian and Reformed Publishing Co., 1979.
Judisch, D., *An Evaluation of Claims to the Charismatic Gifts*, Baker Book House, 1978.

Scripture References